The Immigrants' Son,
An American Story

A Memoir

George Trebat

AuthorHouse™
1663 Liberty Drive
Bloomington, IN 47403
www.authorhouse.com
Phone: 1-800-839-8640

© 2012 George Trebat. All rights reserved.

No part of this book may be reproduced, stored in a retrieval system, or transmitted by any means without the written permission of the author.

Published by AuthorHouse 11/9/2012

ISBN: 978-1-4772-8005-8 (e)
ISBN: 978-1-4772-8006-5 (sc)

Library of Congress Control Number: 2012919187

Any people depicted in stock imagery provided by Thinkstock are models, and such images are being used for illustrative purposes only. Certain stock imagery © Thinkstock.

This book is printed on acid-free paper.

Because of the dynamic nature of the Internet, any web addresses or links contained in this book may have changed since publication and may no longer be valid. The views expressed in this work are solely those of the author and do not necessarily reflect the views of the publisher, and the publisher hereby disclaims any responsibility for them.

This book is dedicated to my wife Doris;
my children Betsy, Alan and Julie;
and my grandchildren
as well as those unimagined future generations
who may carry my seed into eternity.

I don't know who most of my ancestors were.
I won't know who most of my descendants will be;
but I want them to know me.

Table of Contents

Dedication	v
Yorkville	1
Preface	1
Background – How the Czech Nation Emerged	3
My Czech Uncles and Cousins	7
Relatives in the U.S.	10
Aunt Barbara	10
Uncle Joe	12
Aunt Stella	13
My Father	13
My Mother	19
(*Anthony Trebat Pictures*)	25
(*Pictures from 1930 and Earlier*)	26
Growing Up	27
The Early Years	27
Memories of a Funeral Experience and what I was told about Grandparents' Dying	29
Real Life	30
Face Times with Tony	32
A Happy Coincidence	33
Olga's Book	35
Kick the Can and Other Stories	38
Sundays in Pelham Bay Park	42
Some Random Thoughts	42

The Adolescent Years	47
Playing Ball	50
High School Years	54

The 1940s   63

Tensions in Yorkville – War Clouds in Europe	63
Getting Into College	66
My Time at Hamilton	67
The Events That Probably Saved My Life	71
Truman	72
Initial Basic Training	73
Second Training Group	75
Some Historical Perspective	76
Occupation Duty in Germany	78
Six Weeks Furlough	79
A Short-lived Freedom	82
'BLACK HUMOR'	83
College Graduation	85
Good Advice and Legal Details	88
The Crash	90
Reflections on the Crash	93

Early Career   103

Some Historical Perspective	104
McCloy's Tip	106
Retrospective – G. Champion	108
Size Matters	110
Early Investment Success	113
Starting in the Loan Department	113
Access to the Chairman	115
The 20-30 Club	116
A Special Girl	118
Doris' Notes	119
Doris at Six	120
No Television	121

Visiting My Grandparents	122
Finishing College	123
Marriage	125
Getting the First House	127
Expanding the Family – Betsy Arrives	129
My Job at the Meadow Brook National Bank	130
At Home on Long Island – Alan Arrives	131
Leaving Meadowbrook	132
Going to California – Julie Arrives	133
A California Curveball	135
A Finale in the Silverlake District	137

Life in New Jersey — 141

The Highland Park Years	141
Working with Roosevelt	142
An Entrepreneur Arises	143
Life in Highland Park	145
A Bank President	146
More Historical Perspective – The Prague Spring	148
An Emotional Trip	150
The Two Sides of Prague	154
Returning a Favor	158
A Friendship Renewed	159
Covering My Bases	163
A Full Time Legal Struggle	166
(**1978** *Christmas News Letter*)	171
Details and a Reprise of Retribution Monday	172
Investment Management	176
1980 – A Year of Celebration	178

Final Directions — 181

Cleaning up the Carteret Bank	181
Sending Christmas Letters	182
(**1981** *Christmas News Letter*)	183
A Smaller House	184

Notes from 1982 and 1983 Christmas Letters	186
Expanding Commercial Lending	187
1986 – Year of the Tiger	188
(**1986** *Christmas News Letter*)	189
The Folly of a Verbal Contract	190
My Final Bank	191
More Historical Perspective	192
The Final Word on 1988	194
Another Day, my Final Merger	195

The Stage Changes — 199
Shakespeare quote — 199
Years of Abundant Changes — 199
The Velvet Revolution — 200
The 'Cousins' Visit — 201
(**1992** *Christmas News Letter*) – 2 pages — 203
The Velvet Divorce — 204
Consulting Jobs — 205
Enjoying Great Britain — 208
My Philosophy – The Fiddler Poem — 208
1994 was a "Mix" — 209
(**1995** *Christmas News Letter*) — 211
One of Many French Trips – August 1995 — 212
Some Family Visits — 215
(**1998** *Christmas News Letter*) — 217
(**1999** *Christmas News Letter*) – 2 pages — 218

In the Czech Republic — 221
My Czech Connection — 221
Visiting Jiři in Plzeň — 225
The Forester's Cottage — 227
The Baron's Tenants — 228
The Chateau at Lnáře — 230
A Walk in the Woods — 232
Some Czech Geography — 235

The Millennium and Beyond	239
Entering the Millennium	239
Our Neighborhood Changed	241
(**2006** *Christmas News Letter*)	243
Doris' Accomplishments	243
My Medical Adventures	252
Genetic Inheritances	252
The Memo	252
Alzheimer's disease	254
More Recollections	256
1998 Bypass Surgery	257
Unexpected Surgery – 2005	259
Seneca – A Serious Comment	262
Retirement and Recollections	263
The Futurist - A Meditation – "Looking at 2100"	268
Acknowledgment	273

Handwritten note:

Erratum
Typo Pg 19 – Vaňová
Other typos have minor impact
Too much repetition in early sections. Needed better editing.

[signed]

Yorkville

Preface

My name is George Trebat. Welcome to my book of hits and misses ... and maybe a home run or two.

I hope you enjoy perusing these pages about my adventures and misadventures; a collection of memories, recollections and reflections on a life spent well. Every once in a while you'll see a few paradoxes of life that added spice to my existence.

I think it might be appropriate to start this section about Yorkville with some background and explain why I have been more concerned about my origins in comparison with people who were brought up in relative middle class luxury.

Yorkville[1] was a distinct part of Manhattan. For much of the nineteenth and twentieth centuries its streets and tenements were occupied mostly by people of Albanian, Czech, German, Hungarian, Irish, Jewish, Polish, and Slovak descent. In our ethnic neighborhood there were about 10,000 Czechs: they had their own newspaper and social institutions.

My parents didn't come to the US for religious or cultural reasons but came to escape the grinding poverty of

---

[1] Within the borough of Manhattan the historic neighborhood called "Yorkville" extended south from 96th Street to either 59th Street, or at least to 72nd Street; was bounded by the East River on the east and by Third Avenue on the west.

rural peasant life. Very briefly, my grandfather, Jan Vane, and his wife Marie had 13 children, 7 of whom survived to adulthood. The two oldest boys, Jan, Jr. and Anton stayed behind. My mother's sisters Marie, Barbara and Anastasia and their brother Joseph were already in America when my mother arrived.

My mother and four of her siblings were more or less "sent" to America in the hope that they would enjoy a better quality of life. She had a sixth grade education and when, in 1922, she arrived in New York at her older sister's apartment, she was immediately put to work as a servant. No English classes.

My father came from an even poorer family of migrant farm laborers, in 1906 at the age of 17. He had no education or skills and his crude relatives in Bridgeport, Connecticut "celebrated" his arrival by all getting drunk. That's the kind of family he found in the Promised Land. They got him a job in a salt factory shoveling salt into a truck. By the time I came along in 1927 he worked at the Nathan Manufacturing Company on 105th Street in NY.

Not long after I was born the Great Depression came and my father was out of work. I had no siblings because my parents could not afford more than the one child. We lived in a small walk-up three room apartment on 75th Street with the toilet in the hall and the bathtub in the kitchen. There was no unemployment insurance. My mother refused to file for welfare and continued her job.

In various ways it came to my attention that we were POOR, but so was everyone we knew. I studied Czech after regular school and acted in Czech plays. As I grew up Central Park was my playground and Manhattan could be explored for a nickel. My friends and I hitched rides on trucks as transportation; exploring the museums for free.

As you read further than these brief highlights, you

will readily be able to see why money and security became important in my life.

Background – How the Czech Nation Emerged

The Czechs, living as they do in the center of central Europe, have been battered from pillar to post by their larger neighbors in their 1000 and some odd years of their history.

The first ethnically identifiable inhabitants of the area, a Celtic people, lived there from the fourth century B.C.E. until about the second century C.E. They were followed by a Germanic people who left during the so-called migration of nations in the fifth century.

My family's ethnic background was established when my ancestors came to Europe by way of the Caucasian Mountains and Asia a mere 800 or 1200 years ago. Slavic tribes from the Vistula basin settled in the region of Bohemia, Moravia, and Silesia no later than the sixth century. Among them were the Czechs in central Bohemia and the Moravians along the Morava and Dyje rivers to the east.

"Czech lands" describe the combination of Bohemia, Moravia and Czech Silesia (the present Czech Republic). These lands had been settled by the Celts and then later by various Germanic tribes until the beginning of 7th century and then by Slavic people. German colonists settled the area on the basis of the Bohemian kings' invitation during the second part of 13th century (they already lived in Prague from the early 12th century) and lived alongside the Slavs.

I can trace my ancestors back only to about 1850. That's not very far as ancestors go. On both sides of my family tree my forebears were peasants in central Europe. In 1995, when Doris and I were in Slovakia, we met a Slovak tour guide/teacher who asked me the origin of the Trebat name. My father was originally named Trebaticky (or Trebatieki – according to the immigration records) and that it was changed to Trebat when he came to the United States in 1906. The tour guide looked it up somewhere and told me that it is an ancient name meaning "a clearing in the woods". I carried this information around with me for a number of years until our son, Alan, discovered that the name Trebat is quite unique. There is evidence that it may have popped up thousands of years ago in a slightly different form.

Venture with me now to the days of republican Rome, especially to the Roman philosopher, statesman, orator and lawyer Cicero, who lived in the final century before the Common Era. In his Horace Satires, Book II, Cicero included a character named Trebatius. This character was based on his protégé, Gaius Trebatius Testa who was a renowned jurist of ancient Rome. The name Trebatius has obviously, well maybe, been shortened over the centuries and through various permutations to Trebat.

Cicero sent a timely message to the protégé while the latter was serving in Gaul in the winter of 54 BC. "'Too late they learn wisdom.' You, however, old man, were wise in time. ... Not here and there, but everywhere, be wise and ware: No sharper steel can warrior bear." In these pages I have sometimes skipped by that advice in favor of being foolhardy and venturesome.

Incidentally, one of Cicero's famous quotes illustrates my philosophy on knowledge and expanding my horizons. "Not to know what happened before you were born is to be a child forever. For what is the time of a man, except it be interwoven with that memory of ancient things of a superior age?"

It would not be unreasonable, however, to assume that this Trebatius came to the Slovakia area when it was on the outskirts of the Roman Empire and liberally spread around his name and seed. There is a town named Trebatice in the area from which my father came and there are many towns in both Slovakia and the Czech Republic that have the "Treb-" prefix. I have no trouble believing that the name comes from G. Trebatius Testa (the middle name was the family name) or some other Roman Trebatius, but, as to how it came to be our name is a deep mystery to me. Although it is romantic to think that there might be an undiscovered family tree reaching back to antiquity, it is more likely that the Slovak peasants living around a town using the "Treb-" prefix simply took on that name when the Slovak tribe arrived in central Europe sometime around 700 AD. You can take your choice, but, I'll opt for the antiquity connection. It's better than anything else I can conjure up.

My Czech mother's family name can also bear some investigation and the making of some romantic assumptions. My mother started life as Albina Vanova, her father was Jan Vane. Vane is not a typical Czech name, in fact, the London phone book lists several Vanes and there are more of them spread all over England. It is well documented that a certain Sir Henry Vane (1613-62), a British statesman and author was involved in the religious wars between Catholics and Protestants. Neither Sir Harry, nor his fellow Catholic, the Scarlet Pimpernel, were successful in making England the Pope's religious domain.

Harry, as he was known, having incurred the ire of the English King, was exiled. He took his entourage to Bohemia in central Europe, set up housekeeping in a manor house, or castle, in that Catholic country, and presumably, lived happily ever after. If he did, indeed, live happily ever after, he no doubt spread his seed far and wide just as Trebatius may have done. Since my Czech relatives, named Vane, have never shown any interest in tracing their family name, this leaves the field open to me to conjure up my own version of how my mother got to be named Vane.

As a child I heard a lot of anecdotal family history by listening to my parents and their friends talk about the "old country". I'll try to tie my recollections in with some actual history and my scant knowledge of the life and times of my parents and grandparents. First I'll discuss my mother's family, of whom I know a lot more, and then I'll put down such details as I know of my father's background.

In 1858 my mother's father Jan Vane was born in Tisov in southern Bohemia. All I know about Jan Vane's family is that they were Catholic, and poor. My grandfather probably had a number of siblings but they were apparently dispersed. The only Vane family, not in my immediate family, was a family in New York in the 1930s, described to me as distant relatives. Family legend has it that my grandfather was a journeyman bricklayer taking jobs within walking distance of his home village.

Sometime around 1880 my grandfather was reportedly working on a job building a brick wall around the manor house in Lnáře (a nearby town) for an Austrian member of the ruling gentry. The baron, or whatever he was, lived in Vienna during the fall and winter social season and came to his house in Bohemia in the spring and summer to tend to his fishery business, and to supervise the cutting of lumber in the surrounding forest. Years before, when the Hapsburg kings acquired the Czech lands, they gave large tracts of land and villages to their faithful retainers whose job it then was to make the land productive and put the local peasants to work. In the process, these retainers would build a manor house, palace, or more, according to their means. Southern Bohemia was a pleasant forested land and the overlords built many hunting lodges where they entertained during the hunting season. This area was particularly desirable because it was only a day's ride, by horse and coach, from Vienna.

At the time my grandfather came to work on the manor house at Lnáře, he was twenty-some years old. According to my mother, Jan came to the favorable notice of the land owner who hired him to be his forester and keeper of the artificial ponds and lakes which became the locus of a profitable fish breeding industry. Being settled in a regular job, and with a small cottage at his disposal, Jan apparently found some spare time from his tending of the ponds and forests to look for a wife.

He married Marie Klima, a local girl from Kladrubce, two years his senior and they promptly got busy producing the first of their thirteen children. As was not uncommon in the 1880s, only seven of the thirteen made it to adulthood. My grandparents were observant Catholics and they took the deaths of six of their children in infancy and childhood as "God's Will." My mother, their thirteenth child, was born in 1902 when her mother was 49. She told me that her parents often explained the poverty and tragedies of their lives with the phrase: "God gives and God takes away." The only way for a family, in those days, to limit the size of their family was by abstinence and, clearly, abstinence was not the path taken by Jan and Marie Vane.

My Czech Uncles and Cousins

My grandparents' first child was a son, aptly named Jan, Jr., and he eventually inherited his father's job as forester and fish ponds keeper. We met for the second time (the first was as a three year old in 1930) when I was an American soldier. As of 1999 the "old forester's cottage" still stands, but now it is empty.

My uncle Jan, was the father of my cousin, Miroslav, who became an Ob-Gyn physician, and father of my "nephews," Martin and Tomas.

Martin became a project manager for a large Catholic charity and, at last sighting was on assignment in Malaysia.

Tomas became a neurologist and took over his mother's practice in Pisek, marrying a Slovak doctor, Monika, in 2007, the year their son Simon was born. A daughter Madelaine was born in 2011.

Uncle Jan became an employee of the new Czechoslovak government in 1918 when the Austro-Hungarian Empire was dissolved and the "stolen" properties returned to the Czech people. He and another uncle, named Anton, were the only two of the seven siblings to remain in the old country. Anton, the second oldest, served a five year apprenticeship to a tailor in Vienna around 1915 and then came home to set up a tailor shop, and raise a family, in Hvožďany.

I wish I could include in this memoir some detailed information about my paternal grandparents and their final years in Slovakia, but my father, born in 1889 and 38 by the time I was born, never spoke much of them. My paternal grandparents were migrant farm laborers who lived in western Slovakia and went south into Hungary every summer and worked their way north to their home village tilling the soil and gathering the wheat, and other products, for farmers who employed them on a day work basis. My father came to the United States in 1906 when he was seventeen, and, as far as I can determine, he never looked back.

The Immigrants' Son, An American Story

George's Genealogical Chart

Jan Vane (b. 1855)
(m. 1883)
Marie (b. 1853)

[my grandparents]

(13 Children)

Jan Jr. (forester)	Anton (tailor)	Marie b. 1884 (Aunt Klima)	Barbara b. 1886 (Aunt Levak)	Joseph b. 1890 (Uncle Joe)	Anastasia b. 1895 (Stella)	Albina Vanova b. 1902 d. 1968
→ Miroslav, Martin, Tomas	→ Jiří (not Trebat)	(m) Josef Klima	(m) Mike Levak → Georgianna 3 stepsons	(m) ? Joseph, Jr.	(m) Javoslav Zoudlik	(m. 1926) Antony Trebat b. 1889 d. 1945
						(m. 1953) Charlie Holub b. 1884 d. 1972
						George Trebat b. 1927
						(m. 1953) Doris Jones b. 1923
						Betsy T. Waller b. 1955 Alan Trebat b. 1956 Julie Trebat b. 1960 → Various

Relatives in the U.S.

In the years prior to the First World War, many Czechs and Slovaks joined the mass migration of Europeans, especially eastern Europeans, to the United States. They referred to it as "going to America".

I think Marie was the first of the five children to come to the United States. In New York, she married her first cousin, Josef Klima, a baker, and they raised five children, all born before the World War One. She must have immigrated around 1905 since my mother, who came to New York in 1922, had never even met her eighteen years older sister prior to her arrival. Marie and Josef Klima lived in an apartment house at 435 East 75th Street in Manhattan. Their apartment became the first stopping place of my other uncle Joseph and my aunts Barbara and Anastasia. The youngest arrival was my mother, Albina, who came to the Klima household in 1920 when she was eighteen.

Aunt Barbara

Some of the Vane children looked forward to coming to America, but others were simply "sent" because there was no way for them to make a living in the humble villages of prewar and postwar southern Bohemia.

One aunt in particular, my caretaker when my mother was at work, was Barbara, who married a widower with three young sons. She had one child of her own, but, all her life, strongly resented being sent to America. (Her husband, Mike, was a cooper. The marriage had been arranged because the widower needed an unpaid servant. [My mother's words.])

Barbara refused to learn English and, although she lived to be 87, never learned more than Pidgin English. Not that she was mentally incapable. She simply refused.

She was smart enough to be the recording secretary of the Bohemian Benevolent and Literary Association, a large ethnic organization that still owns the National Hall, later a Dvorak Museum on 73rd between First and Second Avenues.

Barbara, who was known to me as Aunt Levak, lived on East 75th Street. She was described as the "black sheep" of the family by her brothers and sisters. When I was about six or seven and an elementary school student at P.S. 158 at York Avenue and 77th Street, both my mother and father were working, so after school I went to Aunt Levak's house (apartment). I ate supper with the Levak family and my fondest recollection was that I could drink all the soda I wanted.

Often, when I got to my aunt's house, she would be ironing. She had heavy irons and heated one on the stove while using another. She also had small irons for more delicate work. She would often let me "help" her by allowing me to wield an iron that was cooling and iron handkerchiefs. I thought this was great fun. At other times, I was allowed outside to run around the neighborhood. There were interesting things to do, such as, jumping from barge to barge on the barges parked in the East River at the foot of 75th Street (that was before the FDR Drive was constructed) and running around on the roofs of the six story apartment houses playing chasing games. (On hindsight, those were years during a now much lamented musical education could have been initiated.)

I looked up to Aunt Levak's three stepsons, Bill, Emil and Charlie, who were in their twenties in 1933. I remember being particularly impressed by Bill, the oldest, because he had a car: a 1932 Ford. The two younger sons became career warehousemen but Bill, although not a mental giant was persistent. He went to night school at NYU for fifteen years and eventually got a degree. He became a clerk for the Union Pacific Railroad, in California.

The Levak daughter, Georgiana, was my favorite cousin because she spoke Czech (unlike the boys who understood the language but answered their parents in English), and at only ten years older than I, treated me like a kid brother. Georgiana's son Peter and his extended family currently (2012) live in the Los Angeles area. Peter is a retired sales engineer, divorced and enjoying his condo in Hawaii. Peter has come east to visit me a couple of times and takes pains to keep in touch.

Uncle Joe

My uncle Joseph Vane, a skilled woodworker, moved out of New York fairly early on and lived in middle-class circumstances in Linden, New Jersey. He had one son, Joe, who, unfortunately, didn't inherit his father's skills and spent his life as a warehouse worker. I never knew Joe, Jr. well and my last contact was with his widow Helen when she phoned me about his demise at the age of 90 (in 2010)

Uncle Joe was one of the few people we knew who actually owned a house. For many years he commuted daily from Linden to Long Island City where the Czech owned shop where he was employed built the fancy wooden insides of churches, board rooms and Fifth Avenue town houses.

Relatively speaking, Uncle Joe made a lot of money. He had a sideline of photographing and developing pictures of completed jobs for his boss. He invested the money earned in this way in Eastman Kodak common stock which had a meteoric rise at the beginning of the color photography age. He didn't know anything about the stock market but figured that since Kodak sold the best photographic paper, it must be a good company in which to invest. Pretty good thinking!

Aunt Stella

My mother's favorite sister was Aunt Stella (Anastasia), only seven years older. She married a man named Jaroslav Zoudlik, who worked off and on in a picture frame making shop. At one time they owned a twelve unit apartment house in Queens but lost it because of Uncle Jerry's poor management. They had no children and Aunt Stella became an expert seamstress, working many years for Henri Bendel, a 57th Street custom dress house patronized by the rich (in later years Aunt Stella helped my mother get a job at Bendel's).

In retirement, she and Uncle Jerry lived in a small house in Tampa, Florida for 17 years. When Jerry died in 1975, Aunt Stella came to live with Doris and me in Somerville, New Jersey. She spent the last five years of her life with us. At 84, as her life was ebbing, she was in a nursing home while I was engaged in a difficult legal battle (see my career chapter).

I came to see her three or four times a week and told her about the ups and downs of the struggle in which I was engaged. I later learned that she was kept up to date by the nurses who read her excerpts from the local Somerset County newspaper which followed the case.

When, after a two year fight, I finally prevailed, she said: "I was waiting until you won."

The next day she died.

My Father

My father, Anthony Trebat, was born as Anton Trebaticky, in 1889 a few miles north of the Slovak capital of Bratislava, probably in the town of Nove Mesto nad Vahom (Newtowne on the Vah River). An inspection of the Bratislava phone book turned up about twenty Trebatickys, but we didn't try to contact any of them. When I was a child, my father often told me stories about his own childhood. His people were migrant farm laborers who went south down into Hungary every spring and worked their way back to their home village in Slovakia in the fall. By all accounts, it was a life of poverty and ignorance.

One anecdote that stuck in my mind was my father telling me that when he was six he was left to take care of a one or two year old sibling. The child dirtied itself so my father took the child outside, it being winter, and held it under the spigot while he pumped water onto its backside. The baby died.

Another incident that might say something about my father's family in Slovakia occurred when my mother and I spent the summer in Bohemia, with her family, in 1930: My mother left me with my grandmother in Kocelovice and took a train to see the Trebatickys in Slovakia. She stayed about a week, and apparently had a bad experience. As a three year old, I would not have been privy to what she said about her visit, but in future years she mentioned her trip to Slovakia but refused to give any details. From various remarks that were dropped, I got the idea that the people she met were living in wretched circumstances and were less than welcoming.

My father had a very rudimentary education and wanting to leave for America was clearly more than just the adventure seeking of a 17 year old. He had several siblings, but the only one he referred to was an older brother who got on his motorcycle and one day took off for France. Nothing more was heard of him. In my files I have an undated picture postcard of three adults and four children.

The Immigrants' Son, An American Story

Maybe, if I were really ambitious, I could find these people or their grandchildren among the Trebatickys in the Bratislava phone book.

In 1995, Doris and I visited Ellis Island, a special thirty acre island in New York Bay, just a stone's throw away from the Statue of Liberty. This was the port of entry to America for millions of immigrants, mostly from Europe, from around 1880 through the 1930s.

It was special to me since among those millions were my parents. First was my father. He arrived from Slovakia on a ship named SS Kroonland which sailed out of Antwerp, Holland and arrived in New York on April 28th, 1906. According to our copy of the list of passengers, he was 17, had $25 in his pocket, and was going to join relatives in Bridgeport, Connecticut.

The "Kroonland"

Sailed between Antwerp and New York

In 1975 I got a copy of the manifest (from the Ellis Island Foundation) of the SS Kroonland, sailing from Antwerp, in April 1906. Among the passengers was listed a 17 year Slovak boy named Anton Trebaticki (note the unexplained last letter) whose destination was an aunt's house in Bridgeport, Connecticut. His occupation was listed as laborer.

According to my father, when he arrived at Ellis Island, the immigration agent examining him simply crossed out the last part of his name and changed the Anton to Anthony and, as he handed him his entry permit, said something like: "Okay, kid, Anthony Trebat will be your new name in America."

He had a train ticket to Bridgeport, which must have been sent to him by his aunt in Bridgeport, but, (and here's another of my father's favorite anecdotes) before getting on the train he went into the bar at the railroad station and loudly asked for rum. The people to his left and right politely moved away, thinking that he was asking for more room. It's hard to imagine a five foot four inch 17 year old commanding the attention of the patrons in a bar in this way, but that's his story and he told it to me more than once.

Another revealing, and ultimately sad, story my father told was that when he arrived in Bridgeport, his relatives celebrated his arrival by getting a barrel of beer and drinking themselves into a stupor. Someone in the family helped him get his first job, in a salt factory, where his assignment was to stand in a salt pit and shovel the salt into a wagon. He told me that he was not allowed to leave the pit for hours at a time and had to resort to relieving himself into the salt being shoveled. A great beginning!

I know little, or nothing, about my father's early life in Bridgeport, but can't imagine that it included any intellectual or uplifting activity. What I do know is that he came to New York sometime in the mid nineteen twenties and was introduced to my mother at a dance by a Slovak woman named Sophie (Novak) Swanson who was married to a Swedish sailor. When my mother met him, she still spoke heavily accented English, and he spoke perfect English. She was 23 and my father told her that he was 29. He was actually 36, but being short, round faced and handsome, he could get away with the deception. As a child, growing up, I knew about the age discrepancy but didn't think much of it. Later, after my father died in 1945, my mother told me that she only found out his true age after I was born. She was very unhappy to be deceived in this way, but she said to me: "What could I do? I had a baby and, what's more, I loved him."

After my father married my mother in June of 1926, he had little, or no, contact with his former life in Connecticut and it was a closed issue. He had some little contact with his relatives in Slovakia, as indicated by my mother's visit there in 1930, but never spoke of them.

When my parents were married, my father, in contrast to my mother, had a good ear for languages, and simply switched from Slovak to Czech. Among the Czechs in the Yorkville neighborhood, there was a sprinkling of Slovaks. The Slovak language, I should mention, closely resembles Czech. There is, perhaps, a 10% difference in vocabulary with Slovak having a somewhat softer inflection than Czech. Czechs and Slovaks can easily understand each other.

In the 1930s when he felt good my father would often burst into song, regaling my mother and me with Slovak drinking songs, some of which I still fondly remember. Mostly, my father had a sunny disposition but there were also dark times. About twice each year he would drink himself into oblivion much to the dismay and embarrassment of my mother. I remember once walking along First Avenue with my mother when we spotted my father reeling along, drunk, on the opposite side of the street. My mother grasped my hand tightly and said: "Let's just make believe we didn't see him." We kept walking, but that night, in a fit of exasperation, my mother broke a window shade rod over his back. In the morning, after he had slept off his drunk, my father wondered where the black and blue mark came from. Sometimes, when my mother was working, my father would take me with him to one of the several Slovak taverns in the neighborhood. There he would have a couple of beers and discourse in Slovak with some of his acquaintances, while I happily sipped on a soda. In this way, I picked up the dialect and some of the Slovak words that were different from Czech.

One of my father's favorite foods was pickled pigs feet, which he called, "sultz." It was very tasty, and the fat content must have been astronomical but, of course, nobody knew about cholesterol in those days. In the early to mid-1930s, before my father got sick in earnest, his five foot four inch frame was made to carry a full 190 pounds.

In later years, it occurred to me that my father must have had a good brain which was undeveloped because of his impoverished, mental and physical, environment. Maybe he was trying, but for some reason, he was never able to raise himself out of the morass of his early years.

Except for the Depression years, and when he was sick, my father worked as a radial drill press operator at a railroad parts manufacturing factory at 105th Street at the East River, in Manhattan. His job, which was considered semi-skilled, consisted of placing iron castings on a workbench and drilling holes in designated areas. Day in, day out, that was it. My father would leave our apartment around 7 a.m.; take the York Avenue bus for the thirty three block ride in twenty minutes. When he came home around 6 p.m., his hands would be grimy with dirt and machine oil. He got paid on a piece work basis with more pay for processing more engine blocks, a strenuous job. I remember him mentioning that the factory had overhead chains for transferring the 100 plus pound engine parts on and off his workbench, but he usually just hefted the iron castings because it was faster.

In his childhood, my father had suffered rheumatic heart fever, a viral infection affecting the heart valves. In the 1890s they did not have the necessary antibiotics and other medications. One summer during the depression, he was unemployed but had to lie in the sun. His illness slowly degenerated into a series of small heart attacks, and ultimately led to his early death. He died when I was eighteen and in the army. I was called out at the infantry training camp in Aniston, Alabama and put on a train for New York. I cried for an hour as I stood alone, in front of his open casket. It was in 1945 and I was given two weeks furlough to attend his funeral. He had been in and out of the hospital in his final year and succumbed to a cerebral hemorrhage in Bellview Hospital. As one looks back, it's amazing that he lasted as long as he did.

Being almost an adult, I stood there imagining the thoughts that must have been going through his head while I was an innocent, happy child. The resentment at being thrown in with "bottom of the barrel" relatives at 17 after an impoverished childhood; the hurt of being caught up in the Great Depression and being laid off from work for three years; the ignominy of having to send his wife out to work at a menial job; the concerns about his health, financial worries, and I don't know what else.

My Mother

My mother, Albina, joined three sisters and a brother already living in New York City. Later our daughter, Julie, using computer power found Albina on a ship manifest listed as Albina Vdnovd - as the feminine of Vane is written in Czech. We have her original passport as well as her birth certificate.

New York would have been a frightening place for a farm girl who didn't know the language, but, living in the Czech neighborhood, that Yorkville was in those days, she was surrounded by relatives and some 10,000 other Czechs who had already established fraternal and other organizations where a newcomer was welcome.

She lived with her older sister Marie, who got her a job as cook and maid to an uptown wealthy elderly family in the wall paper business. The Thibauts must have taught her the rudiments of English and she worked for them for at least ten years. She also attended night school to complete her English education.

My mother and her sisters wrote back and forth to their family in Bohemia. In 1930 the international postage to Czechoslovakia was fairly comparable to our 2¢ domestic rate. She soon began to learn English in addition to her native Bohemian, and kept in touch with her brothers in a regular correspondence that would last for the rest of her life, except for the years of the Nazi occupation during World War II.

The Thibauts took a parental interest in their maid and asked the oldest sister (and American matriarch, Marie Klima, 18 years older than Albina, if the man Albina was about to marry in 1926, Anthony Trebat was "alright." They were assured of his bona fides as a sober (mostly) hard working member of the community. A year or so earlier Albina had met Tony at a dance in one of the local Sokols, and, although short of stature, she was impressed by his good looks, charm, and excellent command of English.

Into this social grouping Anna Kubistova, MD in a third floor apartment on East 73rd street, brought me into the world at approximately 3PM on Friday, March 25, 1927.

I weighed in at seven pounds and a few ounces. Albina and Tony, a Slovak, decided to call me George because, their preferred name, Jiři, (pronounced *Yizhy*) after a Czech saint, did not sound American enough. Albina's three older sisters, who presided at the birth with hot water and clean white towels, recommended that they use the English equivalent.

In the first week of my life, I did not thrive; I lost three pounds because I could not digest my mother's milk. The doctor had to be called in again and somehow, she solved the problem, mentioning in passing, that "the boy will be alright because his eyes are bright." Indeed, after my initial setback, I did thrive and soon started responding to my mother's care and the attention of my father and extended family of aunts, uncles and cousins. In later years, my daughter Julie discovered, from Aunt Stella, that the doctor put me on a diet of goat's milk, which apparently was the right stuff.

The tenement buildings in which we lived, built around 1890, typically contained four apartments to a floor; sharing two toilets located in a central hallway. The bathtub was in the kitchen. As there was no central heat, the bathtub doubled as a heating device in winter for me, and probably for others, because it could be filled with hot water and was nice to sit on. Heat was provided by way of a potbellied coal stove located in the kitchen and supplemented by a small gas heater in the parlor.

My mother may have had a hard life, but she never complained. She took her responsibilities for a child and sometimes sick husband in stride. From the time I was two or three she made it a habit to have a little talk with me at bed time. Sometimes she would tell me of her life in the old country, at other times she would read Czech children's books to me, and as I grew older she would encourage me to do well in school. "Uc se, uc se, kluku", (study, study, my boy), she would often repeat. Somewhat to my regret, I never became much of a scholar, although I probably exceeded her modest expectations.

Etched in my memory is an incident that illustrated her tough mindedness: when I was seven or eight, I came running up to our apartment in tears complaining loudly that a neighbor boy my age had hit me. She listened to me, dried my tears, and then asked where she might find this boy. Thinking that she would go out and discipline him, I told her where he could be found. Then, much to my astonishment, she said, "Good, I'll go out and give him a nickel". Then in fear of the humiliation that would descend on me, I cried, "No, Ma, no, don't do that!!" She then sat me down and told me, in no uncertain terms, that I should not be a cry baby and should go back outside and take care of the problem the way all boys do. I never forgot that lesson.

As is noted elsewhere, my father died in 1945 when he was 56 and my mother became a widow at 43. She started working as a seamstress somewhere around 1948. She moved to her brother's house in Linden, New Jersey. The household consisted of my Uncle Joe, by then a widower, my mother, and Charles Holub, a bachelor and lifetime boarder with my uncle and aunt in Linden.

"Uncle Charlie", as I called him, had been a boarder with the Vane family since his early days in New York. He came from Cheb, a small town on the German border on the very western part of Czechoslovakia. My guess is that he came to the United States somewhere around 1915. I'm including the background of the Vane's boarder because he became an important part of my mother's life, and in my life.

Just after Doris and I got married in 1953, my mother and Charlie announced that they too were getting married. He was 72 and Albina was 52. Charlie was hard of hearing so he never drove a car but got around Linden, where he worked as a furniture refinisher, by bicycle. The generally understood idea was that my mother would take care of him in his declining years.

Sometime after Charlie and my mother got married,

The Immigrants' Son, An American Story

Uncle Joe Vane got remarried and moved to St. Petersburg, Florida. At first, my mother and Charlie lived with Uncle Joe and Bertha, his new wife, but soon bought their own house in Gulfport, a small city surrounded by St. Petersburg. Their house, on an unpaved road had two bedrooms, a small living room, one bath and an eat-in kitchen. It was a modest house but had a room sized screened in porch in front. Their blissful life changed radically in 1958 when my mother had a stroke which left her with a useless left arm.

Suddenly, Uncle Charlie, instead of being taken care of, became the caregiver. At 76, he was in perfect health, thanks in no small measure to his bicycling habit, and he did all of the shopping and cooking for the both of them. Although fate had dealt him a bad hand, he never complained. Charlie and my mother got along well and lived happily until she had a fatal stroke, at 66, in 1968.

When my mother died, Charlie was 85 and soon stopped riding his bicycle. Uncle Joe and Bertha took care of him until he died of congestive heart failure. I inherited more money than I had any right to expect ($100,000 – a lot of money in 1972), and their small Gulfport house which I sold furnished, brought me $7,500. Interestingly enough, he also left $25,000 to the Gulfport First Aid Squad.

When I was cleaning out his house of personal effects, Charlie's and my mother's lawyer, a courtly southerner named Noble Doss, suggested that I go in the house alone and determine if there might be any money hidden for safekeeping. Mr. Doss must have known their habit of keeping some cash hidden somewhere, When I entered the house, I immediately made for the closest hiding place, to which Charlie had earlier alerted me, and stuffed my pocket with $2,400 in $100 bills.

The lawyer was waiting for me outside and said: "You didn't find anything, did you." As the latter was a statement, not a question, I got the message and agreed that there was nothing there. That evening I got on the plane for Newark with a heavy heart and with an equally heavy suitcase filled with the best of Charlie's beloved woodworking tools. Soon after, Doris and I bought a piano which I've always thought of as the Charlie Holub Memorial Piano.

Anthony Trebat

Anthony Trebat about 1938

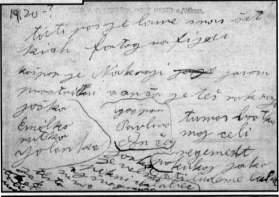

An undated postcard from Anthony Trebat's relatives in Slovakia. Those marked may be a sister and brother in law (front and back)

Pictures from 1930 and Earlier

Albina Vanova
Passport Photo 1922

Jan Vane
George's grandfather
Circa 1916

George (left of grandmother) and
cousins in Czechoslovakia 1930

George and Mother 1930

Growing Up

The Early Years

When I was conceived people were still riding around in the last of the Model T Fords. My parents didn't have a car, but, of course, we didn't need a car because we lived in New York, New York.

At my birth in 1927 my grandfather Jan Vane was, as they say, was 'long time dead'. My grandmother Marie was still a healthy 73 year old tending her chickens and milking her cow. She lived in a little house owned by the government and lived on a small pension because my grandfather had been a forester.

I don't remember anything in particular between the ages of three and five but I'm sure that even though I spoke Czech at home since my mother had only arrived in the U.S. in 1920 and Czech was the language of our house and all of our friends were of the same background. The storekeepers all spoke Czech too since our part of Yorkville was an ethnic neighborhood.

At that time, life was good and my mother was what they called an "ordinary housewife." We were poor but so was everyone else in the neighborhood populated by recently arrived Czechs, Hungarians, Germans and the ubiquitous Irish.

In 1930 when I was three years old, my mother, then 28, and working as a maid in New York, had saved enough money to take me to the 'old country' for the summer. She took me on a big ocean liner called the Leviathan to spend the summer with her 76 year old mother in her ancestral village in Czechoslovakia.

My father, a radial drill press operator in a locomotive parts factory stayed at home in the Yorkville section of New York that summer. I can't claim any real memories of that summer in Czechoslovakia, but I remember some stories of our visit that I heard over and over again in the ensuing years.

S.S. *Leviathan*, "queen" of the United States' merchant fleet

The most engaging story was that, at the shipboard bon voyage party in New York I was given a sip of red wine which had been diluted with a lot of water, I got up on a table and joined in the merriment by singing songs (in Czech of course, since that's the only language I spoke when I was three).

There was also a story about my falling in love with a little red wagon which I dragged around the courtyard most of the summer. I have one or two old photographs of my grandmother, several cousins, and me, which any interested reader may want to refer to. I didn't understand it at the time, but when we came home to our apartment in New York, my mother told me that that was the last time she would see her mother. Grandma died five years later.

When we arrived home after a summer of me playing with my cousins and cuddling on grandma's lap, we discovered that dad was "out of work". Something called the Great Depression had arrived. At three, this was not of great consequence to me but it did change my routine. For starters, my mother went back to her job as a maid and cook for a wealthy family, and dad took care of me during the day. He was out of work for three years, until 1933 when he got back his old job at the factory on 105th Street. Apparently, to make ends meet my mother decided to keep on working and eventually got a job as a seamstress in a fashion house on 57th street. They laid her off every summer, and this was great because she collected unemployment insurance for the six or eight weeks before she was called back.

Memories of a Funeral Experience and what I was told about Grandparents' Dying

My first experience with death was when I was five or six. A 37 year old man, the son of some friends of my parents, died of a heart attack and I can still remember being at the cemetery. Someone gave me a rose and I was standing at the edge of the opened grave with instructions to throw the flower in. My greatest fear was that I might fall in, but l didn't. After the funeral, the families met and there was much talk as to why such a young man would have a heart attack. This incident must have made a big impression on me because I've carried the memory of that funeral with me all my life.

As a small child, I remember being told that my maternal grandfather died at home in his village in Bohemia. It happened around 1912 or 1914 after he walked an hour's distance to treat a neighbor's sick calf. As I remember the story, he had some kind of heart condition and after coming home, he sat down at the kitchen table and simply keeled over. He was sixty two. My maternal grandmother, on the other hand, died at 81 in 1935. I think she died of congestive heart failure and I remember being told that she spent the last year of her life bedridden with her feet swollen. Of course in 1914, and even in 1935, the pharmaceutical industry had not yet discovered diuretics or things like beta blockers and other cardiac medications that would certainly have prolonged the lives of my grandparents.

Real Life

I was a skinny little kid running around the streets of New York making dugouts in the winter-piled-up snow and setting fires therein. My mother used to say that little boys sure do like playing with fires when I came home with red eyes and ashes smudged all over my face.

When I started kindergarten at Public School 158, at York Avenue and 77th Street, they say that I spoke no English but that I soon learned. By the time I started first grade I could get along pretty well and by second or third grade my language skills were much better than average. In this respect I took after my father.

Family stories aside, my earliest childhood memories take me back to Public School #158, my elementary school at York Avenue and 77th Street on the east side of Manhattan abutting the East River. That was in the days before the FDR Drive was built when kids could still run along the docks and jump from barge to barge and where the big kids swam, dodging the tug boats, over to Welfare Island. I used to watch the teenagers dive into the dirty water from platforms jutting into the river. There were a lot of dangerous things to do in the neighborhood but, even as a six or seven year old, my sense of personal survival kept me as a spectator. Well, maybe I did jump the three feet (without looking down) from roof to roof on the six story tenements now and then, but that was as nothing compared to diving into the river. It's a wonder none of the boys ever got crushed between the pulsating barges tied to the docks.

One of the first memories that actually made a strong

impression on me was when I was in the first or second grade. One morning my mother gave me an outgrown blue winter jacket with a hood and told me to take it to school; that it was for a boy in my class named Jimmy Macklin. She told me that Jimmy was "poor" and that I was not to give it to him directly but was to hang it up in the clothes closet to avoid embarrassing Jimmy. I was just to tell the teacher who it was for. I clearly remember puzzling over why Macklin would be embarrassed by being given a coat, after all, we were poor too, but I did as I was told. Now, as I look back on my childhood, I can still close my eyes and see Macklin's skinny Irish face and pale watery eyes staring at me and at the coat hanging in the closet. He saw me bringing it in, he knew.

Another vivid memory stored in my aging brain is of one particular story, and illustrations, in the reading primer we used in second or third grade. Although we lived in a mostly poor immigrant neighborhood, the pictures were of a house with a white picket fence and a family with a smiling boy and girl, a dog named Spot and a father who wore a suit and, after breakfast went to something called "the office". Maybe the reason I remember that storybook so well is because it described a lifestyle that was completely foreign to me and the story book was literal to the point of mentioning that the father's salary was $4,800 a year. When I went home and asked how much my father's yearly salary was I was told that he makes $16 a week and that that translates to about $800 a year. These may sound like miniscule numbers to a 21st century reader, but keep in mind, that we're talking about 1935 and the country was in the midst of the depression. For the record, our rent was $16 a month and all the people we knew were in the same boat; except one family friend who had a butcher store and a car; but that too is another story.

Why do I remember things like Jimmy Macklin's jacket and the stories in the primary reader? Obviously it's because these stories and events and maybe many similar ones made a strong impression on my young brain. Early on I wondered, for instance, why we were poor (my father got back his job after three years of unemployment) and lived in a very modest apartment while people in storybooks lived in houses with grass in their front yards. When I was nine or ten I started to notice the big black cars disgorging well-dressed people into big apartment houses, with doormen, on the streets leading to Madison, Park and Fifth avenues, as I passed on my way from my east side neighborhood to Central Park. I was only a kid in 1935, 6 and 7 and certainly knew nothing of economics or finance but I had the wonderful experience of growing up in Yorkville (and Manhattan for that matter) where I could take in the images that New York City provided; the rich, the poor, the pushcarts selling vegetables along Second Avenue, the grand ladies walking their fancy dogs along Park Avenue, the museums (all free) and I stored all this in my memory bank for future reference.

Face Times with Tony

At four, five and six, I never questioned why my father didn't go to work like my mother, but I liked that time because he would often take me to Central Park, tell me stories and buy me boxes of cracker jacks. The crackerjack box always had a small toy at the bottom, so, you can imagine the anticipation with which I gobbled up the caramel covered popcorn.

When I was about seven or eight, my father taught me

how to play his favorite card game, pinochle. I liked playing cards with him because he would always, somehow, make sure that I would win at least half the time. I would like to think that he was teaching me how to handle numbers, and I also would like to think that he was teaching me how to look ahead and make plans, but, most likely, he was just having fun and sharing some time with his little boy.

When I was 11 years old and of average size for my age, all the boys competed in various physical endeavors: numbers of basketballs thrown into the hoop in 30 seconds; broad jumping, chin-ups, 100 yard races and maybe a few others.

For excelling, we got little brass medallions that were proudly attached to and worn on our belts. Being reasonably athletic, I got my share of medals. The competition was structured in such a way that assured that almost everyone got something. At that age there is always a lot of hazing and bullying but I don't remember ever being picked on because I was not yet short, not yet fat, and not yet four-eyed. I struggled with arithmetic and that gave me a certain status with my classmates; and to complete the picture, I was good at reading, vocabulary and something called comprehension. At that point my relative size was not a matter of concern as it increasingly became about five years later.

A Happy Coincidence

Jumping far ahead for a few moments; after I retired from banking, Doris and I continued to travel, making many more friendships along the way. One of those friendships heightened our seeming gift for finding things accidentally – serendipity[2].you might call it.

During one of our frequent Elderhostel trips to what

---

[2] *Serendipity:* the faculty or phenomenon of finding valuable or agreeable things not sought for. Merriam-Webster

the English call 'the continent", Doris and I found ourselves with a congenial group exploring the museums and street scenes of Paris. On this particular trip around the year 2000 we were thrown in at dinner with a couple from Maplewood, New Jersey named Irene and Walter Sivek.

Dinnertime small talk led to my observation that our new friends' family name was a Czech name that meant grey-blue pigeon. Though obviously of Czech background, Walter did not speak Czech, nor did Irene. Also, they were not from New York but had grown up in the New Jersey suburbs. Walter allowed as how he was a retired insurance executive who had spent many years commuting to the New York downtown financial district, the headquarters of many large insurance companies.

During the next few days we got to know the Siveks better while discussing people, places and even venturing into religious preferences and politics. When I told Walter that I had grown up in the Yorkville section of New York and that I spoke Czech as did many of the people in my 'home town', his ears perked up. Irene, too, found my recollections of my early life in New York interesting. This discussion occurred in the course of our strolling along the Avenue des Champs-Élysées, and then the subject was dropped and we didn't see Walter and Irene anymore. During the next few days we lost sight of the Siveks as we continued our journey through France. Since I'll refer to it in the next paragraph I should note that both we and they had a list of the names and addresses of the twenty-eight or thirty Elderhostel trip participants.

At the end of the trip to France we flew home landing uneventfully in New York and returning to our own life in Edison/Highland Park. In the next few months, as winter descended, we pretty much forgot the names of our co-vacationers in France. Then, in December we got a letter from Irene and Walter postmarked from their home in Green Valley, Arizona. It was Irene who wrote. They had been window shopping at a bookstore in Green Valley when Walter noticed a book displayed in the window. The book was titled "74th and York, Growing up Czech in New York", and had been written by a local Green Valley author. Irene asked if we would like a copy of it. Almost immediately I sent the Siveks a check (I think it was about $16.00) and wrote, "Yes, yes, please buy the book and send it".

Olga's Book
The book, it developed, was written by a widowed, retired school teacher named Olga Leone. The name meant nothing to me at first, but as I scanned the first few pages I realized that the author was my childhood, and family friend, Olga Ceilnicky whose mother had immigrated to the United States with my mother and others in 1920.

Of course, it all came back to me in a rush. First, I had not heard or had even thought of Olga in more than fifty years. I had no idea as to where she was and what her life had been like. As it turned out later, she also had lost sight of me. More about that below, but the book itself was a very sentimental exposition of Olga's childhood experiences in Yorkville. She describes her parent's third floor apartment at 1382 York Avenue in considerable detail and tells about her father's shoe store on the street level in the apartment house, as well as her uncle's butcher shop in the same building. Reading on, sharp images of the shoe store and the butcher shop flashed into my mind. After all, Olga's mother and Olga's aunt (the butcher's wife), who was Olga's mother's sister, had come to America with my mother. They had been close friends of my parents throughout my childhood.

I hungrily read through Olga's book, and then gave

it a closer re-reading. I could almost smell the light scent of leather in the Cielnicky shoe store and the slight sweet smelling butcher shop owned by Olga's uncle, William Sterba. In my own recollection of that era, hardly anyone had a car, since we could easily traverse our whole neighborhood on foot in about thirty minutes. But Mr. Sterba had a car because he had to drive to the meat auction at 4AM to pick out the best cuts of meat for his customers, which included me and my parents. Naturally, we also bought our shoes at the Cielnicky shoe store.

As Olga lived in an apartment just steps away from her uncle and aunt, their families' interaction was intense. Olga's primary playmate was her cousin, Helen, who was some two or three years younger than Olga. In her book, Olga poignantly describes her love/hate relationship with Helen, who Olga describes as something of a beauty while Olga described herself incorrectly as plain.

Economically, Olga and Helen's parents were a step or two above my parents. Their father and uncle respectively owned good businesses and their wives and children were sent to 'the mountains' (the Catskills, I think) every summer while my parents soldiered on, respectively a factory worker and a maid.

Nevertheless they remained close friends with my parents. I recall that we once visited the Cielnicky and Sterba summer encampment. Somewhere, I have an old photograph of our families sitting in front of a cottage in relaxed mode. It is interesting to note that Mr. Sterba was the only person in our social circle to actually own a car.

It might also be evocative that, as a thirteen or fourteen year old I had a crush on Helen and I apparently wasn't the only one. (As I remember Olga either writing or telling me; Helen married an engineer, moved to somewhere on the west coast and died of cancer at a relatively early age.)

Getting back to Olga's book; when I got to page 27, Olga described a family dinner occasion where she was one of the younger children. She wrote "… *The only one anywhere near even my brother Ladi's age was Georgie Trebat. But on these occasions it didn't really matter. All of us were trained to be polite to one another, and here sitting at the table for hours, the age difference wasn't apparent since we didn't really play together. On other occasions, when we did play together, the older children treated me respectfully as an older sister or brother would, and the younger ones (Ladi and Georgie in this case) and I were sometimes allowed to participate in games. The point is that our childhood relationships made for happy memories.*"

A few paragraphs further on in describing a family get together, Olga wrote, "*But now, the formalities over, we could start enjoying the evening. Sitting at the table were Mr. and Mrs. Knizek and their son Pepi; Mr. and Mrs. Vodvarek, who had no children; Mr. and Mrs. Trebat and their son Georgie …*" And on and on Olga went to describe in detail the various family dinners and rituals that were observed in the 1930s.

Having been an English teacher for many years and then an Elderhostel instructor in the writing of personal histories, her book sparkles with self-revelatory feelings and the complications of family life in her close family circle.

Olga, or Ollie, as she signs herself, is 88 as of 2012, is physically frail, with vision problems, and never made it into the internet world. Consequently, after being re-introduced by way of the Siveks and Ollie's memoir she and I corresponded by ordinary mail and her handwritten letters. I call her about once a year near Christmastime and get the feeling that she is suffering the pangs of old age.

In reviewing my correspondence file, I noticed in a letter dated April 2008 that she was working on her third book, but basically we have lost touch again. Possibly for the last time, I'm afraid.

At any rate it was a wonderful trip into the past for me to re-meet Ollie after more than a half a century, albeit only by mail or telephone. It's a good thing that I'm not a mystic. If I were; I would be tempted to describe the serendipitous connection to some higher power. As it is, I'll record it here as a happy coincidence.

Kick the Can and Other Stories

I was eight years old in 1935 and we lived on the third floor in a red brick building on the corner of 75th Street and York Avenue. I was born only two blocks away on 73rd Street and I knew the neighborhood well. The streets of New York were not considered dangerous in those years as there were far fewer cars (at least in the residential neighborhoods) than later. It was a Saturday and all the kids on the block were out playing games. The girls were jumping rope and the boys were playing 'Kick the Can'. 'Kick the Can' was my favorite game because it involved a lot of running.

The way you play 'Kick the Can' is to put a can on a manhole cover in the middle of the street and everybody hides except the person who is 'it'. Probably about ten kids hide behind cars, in doorways and anywhere where they can peek out to see the can. Then the kid who is 'it' has to find the kids who are hiding. When 'it' sees one, he calls out his name and races him to the can on the manhole cover... and kicks it. Also, while the 'it' is looking around, one of the other kids can run out and kick the can. If the 'it' sees him running for the can, he has to try to beat him and get there first. If the 'it' gets there first, then the other boy has to be the 'it' and everybody goes to hide again.

I was hiding behind a parked car and the 'it' was looking

into a building across the street where he thought someone was hiding. So I saw my opportunity to run out and kick the can! My eye was fixed on the gleaming can only a few quick steps away. I jumped out from my hiding place and succeeded in reaching my objective. But wait, something else was going on... At the same time I started running toward the can, a black 1934 Ford driven by a man named Crandell was moving briskly along the street. It reached the manhole cover a split second after I did. I kicked the can all right but the car gave me a good kick and broke my left leg. It was a fracture about halfway between my knee and my hip. Everybody in the neighborhood came running out to see what happened. Mr. Crandell picked me up, put me in his car and drove me to the emergency room at the hospital. I never saw Mr. Crandell again but it occurred to me years later that I owed him an apology. The accident was very much my fault. His insurance company paid my hospital bills and they also put $1,500 into a trust fund. I got the money when I turned 21.

One of the neighbors, who saw the accident, ran to my house and told my mother. She came to the hospital just as the doctor was examining my leg and taking an X-ray. A piece of the bone had pierced my skin and was showing through my pants. It hurt. It hurt a lot but I tried not to cry because I didn't want my mother to get angry. But she didn't get mad. She kissed me and told me that the doctor would take good care of me and my leg would get better. I was scared; there were people and nurses taking my clothes off and washing my leg. When they touched it, it hurt and I started to cry. I don't remember what happened next, but I soon found myself in a hospital room with my leg raised up. There was a rope holding my leg up and it was tied to something over the bed. There were also heavy weights on the rope. Later, I found out that my leg was up in the air because they were stretching it so that my broken leg would come back into place. The next day, when my leg was straight, the doctors put a plaster cast on it. The mummy casing started at my foot with just my toes sticking out, and went all the way up over my hips. A nurse told me that the doctor had to put the cast around my hips and down to my toes to make sure I don't move my leg. She said that it had to be kept still and straight so that the bone could heal.

Of course, when my dad came home from work he came to the hospital to see me too but he wasn't mad either. He just said it was an accident and that it could have happened to anyone. I had to stay in the hospital about six weeks. While I was lying there, my parents, some friends, and my aunts and uncles came to see me but I was pretty bored because I had nothing to do. When I told my mother that I was bored, she brought me some of my school books so that I could keep up on my school work. I asked her to bring me some of my comic books but she also brought some books for bigger kids. I was proud when one of the nurses saw me reading a "big kids' book" and said that her ten year old still only reads comic books. The next day I asked my mother to bring me more books for bigger kids because I started to enjoy the adventure stories and I discovered that I really enjoyed reading.

When summer came, and my leg started to mend, I still had to keep the cast on but someone in the hospital's social work department told my mother that they would send me to a convalescent camp in the country for the rest of the summer. At the camp they had nurses and the doctor came only once in a while to make sure the leg was getting better. There was another, slightly older, boy from my neighborhood there too, but I don't remember his name. One day toward the end of summer, the doctor came and said that it was time for them to take my cast off. I thought that, once they took the cast off, I would be able to walk and run right away. But no! A nurse cut the cast off with big scissors and a small hammer but then I couldn't bend my leg. The knee was still stiff and my ankle was too. They told me that it would take another few weeks and that I had to do exercises every day to make my leg strong again. Even after they sent me home, I had to do exercises to make my leg stronger and it was another couple of months before I could run again. Of course, one of the biggest fears that my parents had was that one leg would turn out to be shorter than the other, but I knew nothing of their concern. Either because of good luck or because the doctors at New York Hospital were capable, my parents' worst fears were not realized. The most serious consequence of my broken leg, as far as I was concerned, was that my mother threw away my roller skates. I never did learn how to skate.

When I had to return to New York Hospital for a different kind of procedure there was an ambulatory patient on my ward who liked to walk around singing. He helped keep me from being bored. His favorite song was Pennies from Heaven. "Every time it rains, it rains - pennies from heaven. Every little cloud contains - pennies from heaven, etc." Another one of his songs was When the Merry-Go-Round Broke Down. "When the merry-go-round broke down - it made the darnedest sound umphpa, umphpa," etc. I didn't find his singing annoying, in fact, it was fun.

It seems like one hospital visit followed another. One of my memorable recollections is that just about that time the whole nation was following the fortunes of Joe Louis, the world champion heavyweight boxer. He was scheduled to fight Max Schmeling, the champion from Germany. The excitement was heightened by the fact that there was a lot of animosity between Germany and the United States. There were no radios in hospital wards and television was yet to be invented. A sympathetic nurse brought in her radio so that I could listen to the "big rematch fight." Joe Louis beat Schmeling and America was happy; at least for a while, until the war started.

Sundays in Pelham Bay Park

On Sundays, in the summer, my mother, father and I would walk to Lexington Avenue and 76th Street, a hike of 20 minutes, to take the Lexington Avenue Local to Pelham Bay Park. On several occasions, my father stopped and coughed up some blood, while telling us to go ahead and that he would catch up with us. He didn't go to see a doctor. Among the immigrants in those days, it just wasn't done. I had no idea what was going on with him and I don't think he or my mother did either.

Once we reached Pelham Bay Park, there was another 45 minute hike to a favorite place in the woods. There the men who were also from our neighborhood would play cards and the women, dare I say it ... gossiped. For me, it was a ball. There was swimming in the bay, lots of berry picking, and plenty of strawberries with cream. I don't know how they found it, but I'm sure they picked their favorite picnic spot because it reminded them of their home across the sea.

Some Random Thoughts

Some people would say that I was very lucky because I was brought up without any religious training. They might reason that this condition enabled me to study the options and make up my own mind as to religious preference when I came to the age of reason (whatever that is).

Most people, however, would express the belief that I was sadly neglected because I was not provided with a sound religious foundation and a belief in God. As far as my studies went, I was never too great at math, but reading and the manipulation of words has been the secret to whatever professional success I may have achieved in later years. My father spoke English like a native and my mother, 13 years his junior, went to night school to learn English. Yes, we were poor, but not poor in spirit.

I can't remember my father being involved in it, but my mother knew that I was a very good reader, and she wanted me to excel. Instead of just comic books she spent her grocery coupons at 25¢ per book, as part of a food store promotion at the local grocery store, to buy me the books that became my library.

She not only got a full set of classics, but in addition the coupons provided me with an opportunity to read the autobiographies of Benvenuto Cellini, and Ben Franklin, plus the "Last of the Mohicans" and the "Count of Monte Cristo". At first these books were difficult for a young mind to digest, but the challenge of reading them over and over brought me a lot of pleasure. So, by the time I was fourteen I had read many of the classics. My mother's encouragement was the key.

The broken leg at 8 was quite an experience and it made me more careful after that – at least for a year or two. Something else happened, however, when I was in the hospital and summer camp that changed my life. That summer I learned to read and really started to enjoy reading. It was not just the act of reading itself but thinking about what I've read. My reading program has always been what I call informational – in other words, very few novels.

When I came back to school after summer vacation, I was one of the best readers in my class. By the time I was nine, I could read almost as well as most adults.

By the age of ten I was reading at almost the high school level and they placed me in a special class for advanced readers. That meant that I could read any book I wanted and didn't have to do reading drills anymore. This gave me a lot of prestige among my classmates and was fun too because I was given the freedom to read any books I wanted.

In actuality, I was a reasonably curious child and around the age of eight, nine, or ten, I became painfully aware of the fact that most of the kids in school had a religious affiliation; Roman Catholic, for the most part, but also Protestant and some Jewish. Each new teacher would ask my religion and when I said I was "nothing," she (most elementary teachers were 'she's') would mark me down as a Protestant because' "You HAVE to be SOMETHING!" So, there you have it, there was a big "P" marked on my school chart and I was not inclined to assert my "rights" to insist that I be marked down as a "nothing." Much later, in the Army, where they had to know your religion in case you got killed, it was the same.

All of this fuss did, however, sensitize me to the fact that there were different religions and that there were certain practices like going to church, crossing yourself, taking Communion, memorizing the Catechism, counting beads, being circumcised and so on. Of course, I knew nothing of Islam or the other great religions of the world; that would come later. I didn't worry about my status too much but every once in a while I would get into a conversation with one of my religious schoolmates and was assured that there, indeed, was a God and that He would not look upon the likes of me with great favor. I was told that it was a "sin" not to believe in God and that there were a lot of sins such as eating meat on Friday, telling a lie, stealing and using bad words that I should watch out for. Some of this made sense to me, and some of it did not. My way of handling this dilemma was to observe what was going on around me, ask questions and, eventually, to read books about the philosophy of religion.

It distressed me to learn that there was a holy figure named Jesus who was sort of God but was also a person, at least for a while, and there was another something called the Holy Ghost and the Holy Spirit. God, the unsophisticated believers assured me, was an old man with a white beard, while Jesus "rose from the dead" and sat on his right hand. All this really blew my mind as it did not jibe with reality, as I knew it.

At the age of nine, I knew nothing of the concept of the trinity and transcendence and all of that I was hearing just confused me. When I added the Christmas story to the things I was reading in children's books on religion, I became convinced that my father was right and that it was all a lot of gibberish invented by priests and ministers to keep ignorant people enslaved (his experience with the church was not good. He told me of the fat priests in Europe who would babble in Latin and the people were told that they would go to hell if they didn't believe in God and give money to the church).

Because of the above, I decided at the age of nine or ten that I didn't believe in God although my parents did, mostly by example, stress the Protestant or Judeo-Christian ethic as a guide for living. But, as a nonbeliever, there was still something nagging on my mind, yes, the 'what's it all about" question. Who (or what) put people on earth? What made the sun come up? What made the stars shine? The seasons change? What was electricity? Magnetism? Gravity? And why does everything fit together so well? Is there a higher power, after all?

While I enjoyed a traditional New York childhood, played baseball, hide and seek and did reasonably well at school, I kept these questions in the back of my mind as

I tried to understand the world around me. My mother, a loving person, was no great help on the question of religion.

Being an indifferent athlete, not too well coordinated and four eyed to boot, my strong area, as I advanced into teenage-hood, became reading and comprehension. At first, I thought I was the only person in the world who questioned the existence of God, but slowly it dawned on me that those questions which I had so dimly framed in my child's mind were the same questions that all of the great philosophers and theologians of the past six thousand years, and more, had struggled with. It was a relief to discover that the more you learn about the thinking of the likes of Plato, Aristotle, Aquinas, Descartes, Kepler, Hegel, Kant, Locke, Newton, Voltaire, and all the rest, the more you realize that they didn't know the nature of God either. They can try, but no one can really tell you what it's all about.

Now, almost eighty years after I started to think about religion, God, and why people believe what they believe, I've come to some tentative conclusions. For instance, every religion has a creation story. Human beings need a creation story and most of them accept whatever story their particular religious tradition puts forth and they are certain that only they have the true "word". They will then fight to the death in support of their religion. Note the Serbs, Croats and Muslims of today, in the former Yugoslavia, all fellow Slavs, all willing to kill each other. Over what? Most people can't mentally or emotionally handle the vagueness of a creative force "out there" that cannot be defined so they need their understanding of the infinite to be personified – Jesus, Buddha, Mohammed, etc. The Jews, Muslims, Hindus don't believe in Jesus and they don't buy into the Jesus "myth" of Christianity. Why not? Look, the Christians are sure that their Lord and Savior is Jesus and that makes some sense as far as it goes. If my brain had been hard wired from infancy as an Orthodox Jew, a Muslim or a Christian, with all the trappings that go with each religion, surely I would be a strong believer in my faith and would reject the others.

As it is, I'm sure of only one thing: There, indeed, is a God. I know something about black holes and how an atomic bomb is made and I'm confident that the organization of forces that bring these miracles about didn't just happen by accident. Somewhere there is "something" and for want of a better word, I'm willing to call it God. I have a lot more that I could say on this subject, but a detailed religious exposition would be a whole book by itself.

The Adolescent Years

"Where are you going?" my mother asked.

"Out", I answered as I scuttled down from the third floor of our apartment house.

It was a beautiful Saturday morning in May and I had absolutely nothing to do.

My best friend was Johnny Kucera. He lived around the corner and, without being invited; I just went up to his family's apartment so that we could jointly make plans of action for the day. We had quite a few choices: go down and run around on the river barges until we were chased away; try buying a few cigarettes (they were sold individually for 1¢ each) at the neighborhood candy store and, if successful taking them to a secluded place in Central Park and "smoking"; we were only twelve years old. Another Saturday activity was to get on the subway and go somewhere.

Once, when we were, maybe 13, Johnny and I went to Central Park with Margaret Kral, a neighborhood girl. We hid under a small stone bridge, and took turns kissing her. Quite innocent – as I remember.

This day we decided to ask Johnny's mother to make two sandwiches and we took them with us on the downtown express. We each had a nickel and maybe another nickel in case of emergency. We lived at 77th street and hopscotched our way up to Lexington Avenue and took the downtown express at 86th and Lexington.

The train was about half filled with newspaper reading men and older looking women, probably around forty. They paid no attention to us, and we reciprocated. After about ten stops we got out at the last stop in Manhattan, which was called South Ferry.

At South Ferry we walked through the urine scented passageway to the west side of the street and started walking uptown. That is, back toward home. It was then about 10 AM and a beautiful spring day; the kind where you wear a cotton sweater and no hat and you feel 'good'. Our point of embarkation, from the subway, South Ferry, was the southern tip of Manhattan and about five miles from where we lived.

We soon found Broadway and noticed the sleepy looking maintenance people working around the big Wall Street buildings and we made our way to the easterly tip of New York.

There were the names of the big banks on the buildings, the New York Stock Exchange, and, as we walked, the fancy men's stores like "Brooks Brothers" and "Broadsheets". The little sandwich shops that serviced the financial district were all closed as were the discount electronics stores where we lingered with our noses pressed to the window glass examining the radios, shavers and record players.

We kept walking along for a couple of hours, reaching the Plaza Hotel (Fifth Avenue and Central Park South) and then the Frick Museum (1 East 70th Street at Fifth Avenue), and finally around to the Metropolitan Museum of Art

(1000 Fifth Avenue at 82nd Street) and then over to the west side and, my favorite, the Museum of Natural History (200 Central Park West at 81st Street). Unlike later, these museums were all 'free' in the 1930s.

These Saturday excursions were repeated by us many times over a five or six year period.

Johnny and I had a unique communication method. His apartment was across the back yard from mine and when I wanted to talk to him I would lean out the window and yell, "Johnnie" as loud as I could. Then he would yell "Georgie!" when he wanted to arrange a ball game or something else.

Although the whole neighborhood could hear us we had no inhibitions. Our families had no phones and a good loud voice was all that was needed.

Then there were the long summers when we'd hop on the back of a railway express truck (they had platforms wide enough to stand on and hold onto the door handles) and hitch the twenty or so blocks for the free swimming at the 57th Street YMCA. All you had to have was a towel and pair of trunks. On most days in July and August we'd go to Central Park, a twenty minute walk from the tenements in which we lived on the East Side. There my friends and I would play the chasing games of the day, the most popular being ring-a-leevio which involved a lot of running and lasted for hours. After running at flat out top speed for a couple of miles I remember sometimes getting a dull ache on my left side. This lasted for about two minutes. I now realize it was my heart getting stronger and preparing me for many years of good health.

Almost all year 'round my friends and I would play marbles on the very convenient iron sewer covers which were located in the street just off the curb. The sewer covers had a circle in the middle and raised lettering saying: Property of the City of New York. As a result of my marble playing skills, I wound up with almost half a shoe box of marbles; some of them the highly desirable "puries." Another favorite occupation of the 1930s was the building of balsa wood airplanes and boats out of kits sold in hobby shops. One would buy a box full of thin delicate balsa wood strips, some glue and colored paper together with some directions and a pattern. Now for the hard part: gluing those tiny pieces together and pasting the paper in the right places to make the semblance of a fighter plane was a detailed painstaking task. At least for me, it was. Some of the kids had their bedrooms festooned with an armada of airplanes hanging from strings tacked to the ceiling, but not me. The balsa wood pieces were much too delicate for my clumsy fingers and the wing struts never came out straight; the glue got all over my shirt and some of the pieces broke even before I got them glued together. What a mess!

But since I had pretty good powers of deduction, my lack of finger dexterity taught me that I shouldn't try for dental school and that I might not make it as a brain surgeon or ophthalmologist. So, when it came to choosing careers, there were, at least, three items I could cross off my list.

Playing Ball

It was 1940 and there was a war going on in Europe, I can still remember it as if it were yesterday. Pearl Harbor had not yet happened and there was not too much for a thirteen year old to do that summer. In those days, my mother, father and I lived in a small apartment above a barber shop and newspaper store between 76th and 77th Street on York Avenue on the East side of Manhattan.

On this particular Saturday in June all was well in my little world. After a breakfast of oatmeal, I went down to John Jay Park. I don't know why John Jay Park was "down."

The Immigrants' Son, An American Story

Maybe it was because the park was a twenty acre miracle overlooking the East River at 76th Street where one could go and always find something to do. The park consisted of a main building with toilets and a large room where unemployed artists were paid by the government to teach kids handicrafts, to put on playlets and to paint with water colors. This was part of the Works Progress Administration, a make-work program during the Great Depression but, of course, I didn't know much about its inner workings at the time. I only knew that the park was a good place to go. The park had a public swimming pool where one could go in the summer for a fee of something like a nickel. There were also benches facing the river where old men would congregate and talk about God knows what. The park was a ten minute walk, or five minute run, from our apartment and it was a prime destination of my early teenage years.

My mission on this brilliantly sunny warm day was to determine if any of the guys were there and maybe to get in on a softball game. When I arrived, someone had already checked out a bat and ball from the East Side House. I knew more about the East Side House than most of the kids because I remembered reading, in my father's newspaper, that a charity ball had been held at the Plaza Hotel for the benefit of the East Side House. I didn't know why some rich people living on Park and Fifth Avenues would stage a fundraiser for the East Side House, but I tucked this fact into my mind for later (much later) analysis. In my milieu, to borrow a word from the sociologists, the most important thing about the East Side House was that they would lend you a bat and ball, and that if you showed up with a sandwich and ten cents for the subway, they would take you to the Polo Grounds or Yankee Stadium to see the Giants or Yankees play. The newspapers called us "the knothole gang".

I got down to the ball field just as a group of boys, some of whom I knew, were choosing up sides. The way it worked was that by common consent the two biggest guys would hold the bat between them and thread their hands along it with the one whose hand wound up at the top getting to choose the first player. They would choose alternately until full teams were chosen for each side. If there were more than eighteen kids, that was no problem, they just assigned more outfielders. As best as I can remember, on this day there were just about enough for two teams. The first one chosen was the overgrown fourteen-year old who, at 150 pounds and almost six feet could knock the ball over the fence. Next came the little guy with his own glove and he got to play shortstop. A big skinny guy was chosen to play first base and from there it went downhill until I was finally chosen and assigned to the outfield between the centerfielder and the left fielder. In "real" baseball, the pitcher always bats last because he's not expected to be a good batter but in this game I was assigned the last position in the batting order because the pitcher, who was also the team captain and the best batter, took unto himself the fourth position in the batting order. In case you don't remember, that's the prestigious clean-up position.

I didn't much care because I was glad just to be playing in a game where I could possibly gain recognition and glory and be part of the gang. This could happen at any time when, at bat I would realize my fantasy of the night before and step into a fast ball and knock it right over the left field fence. Actuality, as was often the case, was a little more prosaic. My first at bat came with two out and no one on base in the second inning. Like Casey, I took a mighty swing. And then I took two more mighty swings, never even coming close to the ball. No harm done, my team was already ahead thirteen to nothing. The opposing pitcher must not have been very good because my teammates hit the ball almost at will so I got to bat again in the next inning. Again, I struck out to end the inning but no-one said a word as I jogged out to my assigned position in the outfield, thankful that no one had noticed. In that very inning I got my first chance to field a hard hit ball which came straight at me. It was a bouncer which I fielded flawlessly and threw to first base, a little late, while the runner, never stopping slid into second base.

After that, I got to bat seven more times and I stuck out seven more times, only once catching a piece of the ball which the opposing catcher snared as it made a feeble attempt to fly backward. My team won by a lopsided margin and, as the game ended; there were a couple of good natured remarks heaping scorn on the ability of my optometrist. I didn't think too much of it, but way down deep a little voice told me that I could scratch baseball as a possible career choice. Not worrying about what other career options this left me, I turned my mind to more important matters, like, how shall I spend the rest of the day? As the game broke up, I joined a small group walking over to the East Side House, just across from the park, to return the bat and ball and to see if we could sign up to go see the Giants. The answer was yes, and soon I was on the train to the old Polo Grounds in the Bronx.

When I graduated from high school in 1944 my father, who was then ill with heart problems, innocently offered to get me a job at his factory saying (and I paraphrase): "You now have a good education and probably can get a job as time keeper." I, of course, had been making plans to start at Columbia. In one of my relatively rare acts of discretion I replied: "Thanks, dad, but I think the army will get me first".

High School Years

While I was twelve and in 5th and 6th grade, I had been promoted into the superior reading group. I was an "A" student in reading but my arithmetic was just average. I was good at subjects like drawing, civics (I think they call it history now) and geography. We lived in an apartment only a block away from 158 and getting there involved crossing only one street. On the whole I enjoyed grade school and had good relationships with the other students.

Even in grade school romance flourished. The best looking boy in 6th grade, John DiVita and a girl named Helen (something) started "going together". At that time it meant nothing to me but a few years later I got the message.

After I graduated from P.S. (Public School) 158 on York Avenue and 77th Street, I started a longer trek to Yorkville Junior High School, also known as P.S. 30 on 88th Street between Second and Third Avenues. It was an all-boys Junior High School and covered the seventh, eighth and ninth grades. My grades were just average but I stood out in Art and Civics. In fact, on graduation I was awarded the civics medal which meant that I got the highest grade on a test which covered history, government and similar subjects. I was very proud of this distinction. As in grade school, my weakest subject was mathematics although I got decent grades in plane geometry and beginning trigonometry.

Being in the heart of the, so called, German part of Yorkville, the only language available for study was German. Despite the fact that my Czechoslovak parents, and me by definition, were not at all enamored with the Germans who had only recently taken over Czechoslovakia, I enjoyed studying German. We had an excellent teacher who started us out singing simple German songs and acting out playlets, such as, Little Red Riding Hood, in German. Since we all knew the story line, it was a lot of fun, and easy, to put German words to the action. Even though many of my classmates came from German-American households and therefore had a head start, I readily took to the language and got good grades. Later, in high school I took more German and actually learned more German grammar than English grammar. And much, much later, after serving in Germany for a year in the Army and using my rudimentary German to good advantage, I took more German in college and got to the point of comfortably reading simple books.

One of my schoolmates, whose parents were German immigrants, assured me that Hitler, having taken over Czechoslovakia, would soon be master of all Europe and the United States too. Of course, I disagreed and we did a lot of verbal sparring (on our own level) on the subject of European politics.

Sometime after I entered P.S.30 my parents moved to an apartment on 67th Street between York and First Avenues for about six months. When an apparently much desired apartment became available on 82nd Street between York and East End, we moved again. My mother was tipped off to the apartment at 514 East 82nd by her sister, my aunt, Barbara Levak, who lived in the adjoining apartment house.

While in the 67th Street apartment, my mother gave me ten cents a day to take the bus along First Avenue to school. I don't remember ever taking the bus but remember well the game I invented. The game was that I raced the bus from 67th to 88th Street, running all the way. On the days that I started out "even" with the bus, I started running while the bus was standing taking on passengers and by the time it came to its next stop on 69th it had passed me. But since it had to stop again for passengers, and sometimes for traffic lights, I was able to get ahead of it again. It seems strange recalling my bus racing experiences from a twenty first century perspective, but I don't recall that I was ever tired or even out of breath when I arrived at school with my books and brown bag lunch. Of course, the ten cents a day that I saved was generally spent on toys or candy.

The years when I was 12, 13, and 14 at P.S. 30 were also years of learning a lot of street language and something about sex, since there were a lot of older, and much more experienced, boys at the school when I first arrived. One of the boys in my class was named Frank Yost. The older boys in the ungraded class (a class for toughs who were not destined to go on to high school), took an interest in Frank Yost and it was a great mystery to me until someone told me that Frank earned money by going under the cellar steps with the older boys and "doing something." Later, someone told me that Frank was a "homo." That was a new word for me so I looked it up in the big dictionary in the library and slowly came to understand that Frank was not like the rest of us.

While in junior high, and even before when I was in grade school, I was a frequent visitor at the Yorkville Public Library which was located just across the street from my former elementary school. This library was special because, as it was in the middle of the Česka Čvert, or Czech Quarter, it had a large section of Czech books. I spoke Czech with a reasonable fluency, but I wasn't interested in reading Czech books but mostly used the library as a school research resource. Another great attraction of the library was that I could look up the "dirty words" in Chaucer, Studs Lonigan and other grown up books.

The Ceska Budova, a large five story building completed in 1896 during the high tide of the Czech immigration surge, was the center of the Czech social scene and was the place where immigrants went to see plays in their own language and where dances and celebrations were held. The Budova also had a busy Czech Restaurant, owned by my friend Rudy Cerny's father (he later lost it in a card game), and various school and meeting rooms. My aunt, Barbara Levak, who never learned how to speak English, was the long-time recording secretary of The Bohemian Benevolent and Literary Association, which owned the building at that time.

The Czech immigrants wanted to make sure that their children would not forget their "mother language" and the culture from which they came. For this reason, from about the age of eight until I was sixteen, I was enrolled at the Ceska Skola (Czech School), located in the Ceska Budova (Czech House).

Classes were held from about 3:30 until about 5 about three days a week. I liked going to Czech school because the teachers made it fun and because a lot of my friends were there too. It was there that I learned to read and write Czech, and it was there that I learned the words to many Czech songs and the steps to national folk dances. On May 30th of each year, Memorial Day, there was a large parade where the members of the various Czech organizations marched through the street to the sound of band music. Prominent in the line of march were the children from the Czech school as well as the gymnasts from the two Czech gymnastic organizations in the neighborhood. I've never seen any statistics on this, but my guess is that there were some 10,000 Czechs and their children living in the Czech Quarter.

After the parade it was the custom to take the elevated train to Astoria, across the East River in Queens, where there was another Czech Hall and one block square fenced in picnic ground. This was the place where we danced the national dances on the dusty picnic grounds and this is the place where my father, more than once, had too many beers.

When I was about fifteen, I could read Czech well enough so that I was chosen to act in plays put on by the Czech school, whose official name was the "Ceska Svobomyselna Skola v New Yorku" (The Czech Freethinkers School in New York). The plays were put on in full native costumes on a large stage in the main ballroom of the Czech Hall and were attended by some 250 or 300 paying patrons, including the parents of the actors. There was a makeup person for the actors and an orchestra in the pit to accompany the romantic and nationalistic themes. I was chosen for major parts in these plays mostly because I was able and willing to memorize extensive speaking parts. I pity the poor audience that had to listen to my singing in the few solo parts that I sang because I never did learn how to sing on key.

Again graduating from the Czech school, I joined the Klub Mladeze, or Young People's Club, which put on slightly more sophisticated plays in the same venue. As it was by then becoming evident that I was going to be vertically challenged, I no longer got the romantic hero parts but got to play the "wise old man" parts. I don't know how I did it, but I memorized pages and pages of dialogue and for this ability was awarded leading parts in several plays. To be sure, there was a prompters shell at the front of the stage which was a great help when I, or one of the others, flubbed a line or forgot which way to go. Sometimes the prompter could be heard halfway through the audience.

Along with the fun of acting in the plays and, not coincidentally, learning the language and culture, there was a lot more going on. The Czech school and, later, the Young People's Club were co-educational, which, to me didn't mean much at the start. At around 11, 12 or 13, I wasn't much interested in girls and we boys had special names for some of them. The two that I especially remember, were 'pig face' and 'piano legs'. Luckily, I no longer recall their real names or I would probably print them here for all posterity to remember. But that phase did not last. As I got closer to sixteen, for some reason, Miss Piano Legs, and a few others got much more interesting.

By the age of 14, when I was finishing junior high school, (similar to middle school) my graduation class picture shows me to be the biggest of the smallest third, and setting in the front row with a number of early spurt growth (or a little older) boys already scraping six feet.

The ethnic community my parents lived in was socially and culturally very active. There was a gymnastic association and social hall on 71st Street known as the T.J. or Blue Sokol, and another one at 72nd Street and the East River called the D.A. or Red Sokol. A third center of activity was the National Hall, built in 1896, at 73rd Street between First and Second Avenues. It was known, more simply, as Budova (the house) to several generations of Czech immigrants. These institutions were built in the 1890s, by Czechs who came to the US in the decades after the Civil War, for the purpose of helping new immigrants get their bearings in the new world. My parents sometimes went to various social affairs in the neighborhood, but, my mother's work schedule being what it was, they were not active in the various organizations.

Into the mid-1980s, and even through World War II, in the fall and winter social season, there were dances at all three halls every Saturday night featuring eight piece polka and waltz bands. This is where I learned to dance. I can still remember standing on the sidelines trying to memorize the steps of the dancers and, then screwing up my courage to ask someone to dance. Eventually, because I was blessed with good rhythm, I became a good dancer and spent many happy Saturday nights whirling around the dance floor. In those days it was not necessary to have a 'date' as young people would come to the dance halls just to dance and flirt. When I got into my middle and late teens, I would often go to sleep from 3 p.m. to 6 p.m. on Saturdays so that I could dance every dance from 9 p.m. to closing time at 2 a.m.

On Sunday there were often ethnic plays, put on by Klub Mladez, as well as dinners and other affairs. There were, at least, five acting groups in the neighborhood sponsored by one or another of the cultural, social or athletic organizations. Between the ages of fourteen and seventeen, I acted in some eight or ten plays on the stage at National Hall. For a while I was much in demand as an actor because I excelled in memorizing my lines. As I grew older and it became apparent that I was vertically challenged, I stopped getting the romantic leads and became a specialist in the 'old philosopher' roles. The plays to which I refer were put on in full costume and makeup with the musical numbers being accompanied by a respectably sized orchestra. There was always a prompter's shell at the front center of the stage which gave me, and the others, confidence in acting out our sometimes lengthy parts. I have copies of some of the old playbills and considered including some of them in this book. My mother and father took part in these activities only as spectators. My mother certainly didn't have the leisure time that other housewives had. Neither my father's health, nor his inclination led him in this direction.

Most of the immigrants in the Czech neighborhood, my parents included, were brought up as Catholics in the old country. When they arrived in the United States most of them dropped their religious ties in favor of the fraternal organizations described above. This was true of my parents and most of their close friends whose childhood experiences in the churches in Europe left them with a bad taste in their mouths. My parents told me that the Mass, both in Bohemia and Slovakia, was recited in Latin, often by a fat priest who threatened them with hell and damnation and urged them to have many children and give money to the church.

There was, also a very active Czech speaking Protestant church in the neighborhood, at 74th Street between First and Second Avenues. It was named the Jan Hus Church, after the Czech reformation hero, and had, perhaps, 300 members, most of whom were also active in the cultural life of neighborhood through the Sokols and other organizations. After the war I became a member of the Jan Hus Church....primarily because it had a young people's group, some of the female members of which claimed my attention.

This rounds out the life and activities of the neighborhood into which my mother was introduced when she got off the ship at Ellis Island. I've included my own experiences in the neighborhood because the neighborhood was not too much different in the 1930s from what it was in the 1920s. The really big changes came after World War II when there were few new Czech immigrants; the old people started to die off and others, like my mother, moved to Florida, while young people married and moved on, mostly to Long Island and New Jersey. Nevertheless, a few hardy Czech-Americans of my generation did stay in the old neighborhood and as of the year 2009 the National Hall was bought by the Czech government and remodeled into a museum, after many years of being vacant and neglected. The T.J. Sokol (the Blue Sokol) is still in operation on a small scale.

The main cog in running the Sokol organization seemed to be Norma Zahka who stayed in the old neighborhood and taught gymnastics at Hunter College. Blanche Ledeky

(Fiorenza), my onetime girlfriend stayed in New York too. Both she and her husband became art directors.

In later years, my ties to the remaining Czechs in New York became quite tenuous; and I meet my former friends only on a few reunions and funerals.

THE 1940S

Tensions in Yorkville – War Clouds in Europe

When I was a boy growing up in New York in the 1930s there were still a lot of old men hanging around whose quintessential moment in life came while serving in the American Expeditionary Force in France in 1917 or 1918. Mostly, they would bore me to death telling and retelling the same tale about the time Black Jack Pershing, the commanding General, came by on his white horse (yes, really!) on his way to the front. Sometimes, if the raconteur of the moment was a close friend of my parents, or some other person from whom I could not readily extricate myself, I learned to listen with half an ear and nod at the right time until the story was over.

In the 1930s, the neighborhood was the home base of Fritz Kuhn's German American Bund, the most notorious pro-Nazi group in 1930s America. As a result of their presence, Yorkville in this period was the scene of fierce street battles between pro- and anti-Nazi Germans and German-Americans. Tensions had escalated rapidly in our cluster of ethnic neighborhoods in Yorkville in September 1938 when we learned of the Munich Pact and what it meant. Czechs and Slovaks called it the 'Munich Betrayal'.

In those years I often argued with my schoolmate Kurt Helbig whose parents were German immigrants.

Kurt was "sure" that Hitler would become master of the world. Youthful friendships were severely strained. All we heard from our German neighbors was the marvelous things that would be done now that the Sudetenland was part of Germany. My family felt just the opposite. They understood that Czechoslovakia had been stripped of much of its industry, all of its border defenses; even many banks were lost. But that was then; retribution came later – and in spades!

As it was primarily a German neighborhood I studied the German language at the Yorkville Junior High School at 88th Street and Third Avenue. I often went alone to the German language movie theatre to get a better feel for the language. I estimate that I have retained a 20% command of German and have often made use of it in social contacts. German is much easier for the English speaker than is Czech[3]. The Slavic languages come from a different "linguistic root system" than English and German and the Nordic languages.

My parents were both working and even though the money was not much, my mother and her sisters kept up a steady correspondence with my relatives in the old country. Whenever possible my mother and her siblings kept sending packages overseas, and my Czech relatives would respond with bags of dried mushrooms.

The Second Czechoslovak Republic, (the second Czechoslovak state) lasted for only 167 days, from October 1, 1938 to March 14, 1939. The government was destroyed when Germany invaded it on March 15, 1939, and annexed the Czech region into the German Reich as the Protectorate

---

[3] **Czech** is a West Slavic language with about 12 million native speakers; it is the majority language in the Czech Republic and spoken by Czechs worldwide. The language was known as Bohemian in English until the late 19th century. Czech is similar to and mutually intelligible with Slovak and, to a lesser extent, with Polish and Sorbian.

of Bohemia and Moravia. The independent nation of Czechoslovakia disappeared.

In 1940 while I was playing marbles pretty well, and finding that I couldn't build model planes or play ball at all well, I was aware that there was a war going on in Europe and it was affecting my relatives in Czechoslovakia in ways I was too young to comprehend.

President Roosevelt changed from fireside chats to touting us as the Arsenal of Democracy, making it clear that we could not be complacent and that isolationism could be our downfall. His speech brought bitter memories to many in our Czech community, especially in the Sokols, and other institutions which were headquartered in the Bohemian National Hall.

Once hostilities started there would be no more letters or packages to Bohemia or any dried mushrooms in return for the next five years. For the next few years there was nothing but rumors.

In 1944 the war was in full swing and our high school history teacher kept a big map of Europe on one wall. Every day when we came to class he ceremoniously moved the pins and ribbons documenting the ebb and flow of battle as the Americans, British, and smaller contingents of other allies were driving their way up the boot of Italy and eventually across Europe itself. In the Pacific US Marine advances were shown on the little known islands of Bougainville and the Marianas, which were suddenly household names. The long awaited charge into France was building up as reports of 8th Air Force raids filtered back.

In subsequent years I've had to listen, patiently, for the most part, to many of my friends and acquaintances stretch the truth about the time they heard General Patton bawling out the troops for their slothful behavior and urging them to go out and to get some blood on your bayonets. Mostly

I just listened and nodded at the right time. Also, I came to realize that those infantry soldiers who participated in the Normandy invasion or got bloodied in the Battle of the Bulge seldom recounted their experiences around bars or at family picnics.

Getting Into College

I was seventeen in March of 1944 and was moving rapidly toward graduation in June and expecting to get drafted into the Army when I was eighteen. In the meantime I could start college, so I took a test at Columbia University and was accepted for the freshman class of September 1944 at King's College. My parents had just enough money to pay for the first semester, and, after that, I figured I would either work part time or the Army would call my number, but I never did enter that hallowed hall of learning.

While I was still finishing up at the High School of Commerce on 56th Street near Columbus Avenue (where Lincoln Center was later built), a notice was passed around announcing that one could take a test, and if qualified, would be accepted into the U.S. Army Specialized Training Reserve Program. This meant that the Army would send one to college at least until the age of 18 and then, one could probably get into the Army Specialized Training Program for further study.[4]

All this "free" college training was very appealing to me since we didn't have much money to pay for college anyway and, even if I started at Columbia, the chances were that I

---

[4] The Army Specialized Training Program (ASTP), started December 1942, was designed to provide a 4-year college education including Army technical training in an 18 month period to develop officers from current enlisted men. After D-Day these men were largely returned to infantry combat units in Europe and the Pacific. Some ASTP training in medicine and engineering still continued into August 1945.

would be drafted soon after my 18th birthday. So, I took the test and was accepted after a cursory physical exam. The catch was, that in volunteering after being accepted for the ASTRP[5], I was also volunteering to go into the regular Army the minute I turned eighteen. The situation, being what it was and with the possibility being very small of my not being drafted, the appeal of three "free" college semesters available before basic training was so strong, I signed my name and was inducted into the service on June 15, 1944.

From then on, things proceeded very rapidly, I was put into a size 36 regular (at 125 pounds and almost five and a half feet, I was a 'small', but 'regular' or 'long' was all that they had in sizes) uniform and they shipped me up to Hamilton College in Clinton, New York. I had never heard of Hamilton College, but I later learned that it was a top tier liberal arts college. At Hamilton I took another test and was placed into the middle range ability level. The only course of study available was engineering and since all of the courses were basic physics, algebra, geography, engineering drawing, trigonometry and chemistry with a large dollop of physical training and military drill, I was quite happy with the assignment.

My Time at Hamilton

When I was at Hamilton College, I remember one bull session where a few of my fellow trainees were discussing the progress of the war in Germany. One of the guys complained that he was getting tired of all this studying and was anxious to get into combat and get some blood on his bayonet. The

---

[5] The Army Specialized Training Reserve Program (ASTRP) served a similar opportunity for High School graduates before they reached the age of 18. It was also discontinued as the expectation of long term hostilities was reduced.

others all heartily agreed (they being immortal), except me. I shocked my fellow trainees by exclaiming: "You (expletive deleted) jerks are crazy! Don't you know that the Germans have had five years of experience and their bayonets are just as long as ours?" Well, needless to say, after that outburst, I was no longer "one of the boys" but it didn't bother me because, even then, I had an intimation of my eventual mortality.

In all, I spent six months at Hamilton College and the life was idyllic. All of the students who normally would have been at Hamilton were in the armed forces and, other than two contingents of regular Army pre-meds and Japanese language students we had the campus to ourselves. Hamilton continued to be run by the same instructors and professors as before the war and they often invited us into their homes for discussions around a blazing fireplace. Little did I appreciate what a rarity and privilege this was! This was really one of the most important periods of my early academic life and I've always regretted that Hamilton had no room for me after the war because their first responsibility was to their own matriculated students who were then returning in droves.

For the most part, the Hamilton faculty fit us into their regular academic routine and applied their high standards of scholarship. They operated under a Dean's List system which meant that the names of the top students were listed monthly. A Dean's List designation included the privilege of skipping study hall on Wednesday night. Maybe a regular student would have used the free Wednesday to do independent reading in his room, but the Army boys, as we were known, used the time to hitch hike the ten or so miles to Utica and check out the bars and night clubs, such as they were. I mention all this because I got on the Dean's List the first month at Hamilton. Then during the succeeding month

The Immigrants' Son, An American Story

I dissipated on Wednesday, slept through the lectures on Thursday and lost my position on the Dean's List. The next month, being confined to campus on Wednesday, my name reappeared on the list and I followed my earlier pattern of using my uniform to sneak some forbidden whiskey into my underage gullet on Wednesday night.

As I remember it, we had some courses or laboratory sessions and military drill on Saturday morning and then it was off to Utica to do some more pub crawling at night. I was 17, the war was by no means over, and who knew where we would be in a year or two? Sure, I passed all my courses and even got a couple of A's, but, in my heart of hearts I knew that I could have done a lot better and that a big opportunity had been missed.

Sundays at Hamilton were special days. Gone on Sundays were the tawdry bars of Utica and the ladies of the night to whom we did not want to disclose our inexperience. A Sunday morning was a blur but on Sunday afternoon we were exposed to the Clinton social register. First, let me explain that when I say "we" I mostly mean myself and a few likeminded friends because there were several hundred boys on campus and some of them were what they now call "nerds". They just studied and studied and studied.

One thing I became painfully aware of was that life was a lot more serious for the pre medical students on campus because they were mostly several years older than the ASTRP (my group) students and they had already been through basic training and knew that if they flunked out, they would be in France squinting through a gun sight in no time at all. Thus, the ASTP pre-med students kept their noses to the proverbial grindstone while some of us pre basic training students lived the Good Life.

Clinton is a one mile walk down the hill from Hamilton College and on Sunday afternoons I became one of the few, and there could not have been more than twenty, who regularly attended tea dances. What a contrast to Saturday night! The tea dances were sponsored by various "ladies clubs" active in this upper middle class town but I can't remember how or why I was invited but I do remember the small triangular sandwiches and long tables decorated with party paper. Everything was very, very proper with fortyish ladies bustling around introducing us to their daughters. The music was recorded and they seemed to favor a sentimental tune having to do with tying a yellow ribbon around something or another. When it was time for us to climb back up the hill for supper and Sunday evening study hall, the girls waved goodbye at the door and I always felt good about myself. Maybe it was all those Judy Garland movies I saw as a teenager. It couldn't have been my Presbyterian background because I had been brought up un-churched and only joined a church organization much later.

For the Christmas weekend of 1944, all of the Army trainees were given time off to be at home with their families and the place was virtually deserted. Only another boy and I stayed on campus and, in my case, it was because I couldn't afford the round trip train fare from Utica to New York City. (The 17 year olds were in uniform, but we were not being paid). The holiday was spent pleasantly enough in the company of one of the training officers, an older regular Army major. He was not considered fit for combat duty and was assigned to teach military history at the college. A bachelor, he had a house on campus and invited us to share his scotch and watch the flames dancing in his fireplace. The next week I came down with a strep throat and landed in the infirmary. When I got out I learned that my entire training group had been transferred to the Jerome Avenue campus of New York University in the Bronx. I joined my fellow trainees a day or two late, but without further incident.

As far as academic work was concerned, the third semester at NYU was more of the same except that I learned that I was not really cut out for an engineering or scientific career. This truth came to me while I was taking intermediate physics and something in math having to do with vectors. I really buckled down and worked hard on those courses and wound up with straight C's. My thinking was that if I work this hard and the best I can do is to draw a C, I'll never be a really good engineer and should think about another career path.

As spring of 1945 came into view and my third Army sponsored semester was ending (really a trimester), the word came that Uncle Sam needed us in a more active role. Since I was now a little over 18, on April 16, 1945, it was off to active service and basic training. We all went our separate ways and I saw only one of the other trainees again, but one whom I had completely forgotten. Much later he became the banking commissioner in New Jersey. He recognized my name on a list when I was made president of a New Jersey bank and called me up saying, "aren't you the George Trebat who ..." ... but more of that later.

The Events That Probably Saved My Life

The Smithsonian Institute opened an exhibition marking the fiftieth anniversary of the bombing of Hiroshima and Nagasaki in the summer of 1995, it is entitled "The Last Act: The Atomic Bomb and the End of World War Two".

The following historical and statistical references are from "Truman" by David McCullough, Simon & Schuster, 1992:

Truman

Unlike most decisions, the decision to drop the atomic bomb was not made by a committee, but, in the end by only one man, Harry Truman, the then President of the United States. Before the bomb was dropped there was anguished and torturous soul searching on the part of the scientists, who had created the bomb, and the politicians and military people who had to make recommendations to the president. In the spring of 1945 the president's mind was on plans for the invasion of Japan. He wanted to know the number of men and ships needed; he wanted an estimate of the losses in killed and wounded that would result from the invasion of Japan proper. A memorandum from a high official noted that it was the president's intention to make his decision with the purpose of economizing to the maximum extent possible in the loss of American lives. Based on American experience in the war with Japan up to that time it was thought that the Japanese would not surrender easily if their homeland were invaded but would fight to the death. The experience of the battle of Okinawa Island was on the minds of the American policy makers; an attack on the American armada by hundreds of Japanese suicide planes, the kamikaze, had had devastating effect--thirty ships sunk, more than three hundred damaged, including carriers and battleships. Once American troops were ashore on the island, the Japanese fought from caves and pillboxes with fanatic ferocity. In the end more than 12,000 Americans would be killed, 36,000 wounded, and, as later studies show, civilian deaths on the island may have been as high as 150,000, a third of the population.

With regard to the matter of dropping the bomb,

(General Marshall later explained) we had just been through a bitter experience at Okinawa which had been preceded by similar experiences in other Pacific Islands, (the first day of the invasion of Iwo Jima had been more costly than D-Day at Normandy), the Japanese had demonstrated in each case that they would fight to the death. It was to be expected that resistance in Japan, with their home ties, would be even more severe. Marshall said: "We had to end the war, we had to save American lives". Another estimate at the Pentagon said that America would save no less than 500,000 to 1,000,000 lives by avoiding the invasion altogether. Some critics and historians, in later years, argued that Japan was already finished by the time the atom bomb was dropped. Japan's eventual defeat, however, was not the issue. It was Japan's surrender that was needed since every day Japan did not surrender meant the killing would continue. Truman foresaw unprecedented carnage in any attempted invasion. "It occurred to me," he would remark a few months later, "that a quarter million of the flower of our young manhood were worth a couple of Japanese cities."

Initial Basic Training

The first atomic bomb was dropped on Japan on August 5th, 1945; unleashing, for the first time, the basic power of the universe. Excitement and feelings of relief swept the United States – especially among families with sons and husbands in the service. Surely the war would be over any day. To the millions of men serving in the Pacific, in Europe preparing to be shipped to the Pacific and those being trained for the invasion in infantry camps; the news came as a joyous reprieve.

One of them was me, an eighteen year old rifleman trainee at an infantry training camp at Fort McClellan, Alabama. All that spring and summer I had been marching up and down the red clay hills near Anniston, Alabama.

As the war in European War ground down I found myself shooting at targets that looked like evil looking Orientals as the European War ground down.

A Soldier in Training 1944
Fort McClellan, Alabama

Handling flame throwers was another interesting skill I learned – there were times in my later life that I wished I still had a flamethrower available (metaphorically, that is).

April of 1945 was momentous because President Roosevelt died, as did my father.

My basic training was interrupted. After an emergency leave to attend the funeral, I reported back to my training unit. Since they were already far advanced in the seventeen week infantry training course, of which I had completed about half, I started all over again with a new group. Never mind the glasses, I could hit the bull's-eye "pretty good" and, after a series of increasingly long marches, with rifle and full field pack, I completed the twenty-six mile final training march in fine physical condition. In fact, because my peculiar walk made me seem slightly out of step, I was made a squad leader so that I could march up front somewhat ahead of the others.

Although, at that time, my days were filled with preparations for cannonfodderdom, the news of the dropping of the atom bomb made a deep impression on my young consciousness because I had no lack of imagination as to the horrors of war that were awaiting me. A fact of life is that most seventeen and eighteen year olds think of going into war as a glorious adventure. After all, getting a gun in your hand and being called a "man" was a rite of passage. But not for me! I have previously mentioned an anecdote about mortality which I still consider appropriate.

I have often thought about what the dropping of the atomic bomb on Hiroshima meant to me, personally. To start with, I was scheduled to be part of the invasion force and there's no doubt in my mind but what I would have been one of the first ones to hit the beach and face a hail of fire from the enemy anxious to repel the invading Americans. Could it have been any different than the landing on Okinawa? No way, except it would have been a lot worse. Worse, because it would have been me scrambling up those rocks trying to secure a foothold so that the big guns and supplies could follow. What's the chance that I would have been one of the casualties? The odds against me would have been very high. No doubt about it, I could easily have got my ass shot off and wound up floating upside down in a pool of blood -- my blood!

As it happened, the first infantry training unit I started with, before my father died, was sent to Japan but as occupation troops, since the second atomic bomb, the one dropped on Nagasaki, convinced the Japanese that the game was over.

Second Training Group

Because of the surrender of Japan, my next training group was sent to Germany where I spent a not too unpleasant year as a replacement for the men in the famous First Infantry Division who had fought through Africa and then Normandy and lost a large percentage of their original men.

With the official armed combat being over in Germany I spent a year guarding SS prisoners and giving political lectures to the troops. At one point I was sent to Heidelberg University to learn how to be a discussion leader. I also lectured on venereal diseases and wrote the battalion newsletter. In my spare time I studied German and practiced it whenever I had a chance to go into town.

In subsequent years, I have had many occasions on which to reflect on my great good fortune at being born at just the right time to miss getting into the thick of combat either in Europe or Japan. It has often occurred to me that the last great battle in France, known as the Battle of the Bulge, where the German Army breathed its last breath, was fought by soldiers just one or two years older than I.

In later years, when I accidentally came upon a German graveyard in a little town called Grosssteinhausen, I shed a tear for the German boys, just my age, who lost their lives in the last days of the war. On another occasion, the ten thousand Christian crosses and Stars of David at the American Cemetery in Normandy stopped me in my tracks; this could easily have been me!

Some Historical Perspective

In 1945 as World War II was winding down the victorious British, French, Russian and American Allies agreed upon post war spheres of influence. The western countries were given everything west of Czechoslovakia, Poland and Hungary with Germany split into East and West Germany.

Edvard Beneš and other Czechoslovak exiles in London had organized a Czechoslovak Government-in-Exile. One of its demands to the Allies began in 1943 and was culminated at the end of the war through the Potsdam Agreement completed August 2, 1945 when Czechoslovakia, after four years of occupation by the Germans had its borders restored.

Czechoslovakia suffered relatively little physically from the war. Prague was freed on May 9, 1945 by Soviet troops. Both Soviet and Allied troops were withdrawn in the same year.

The German annexations were reversed and the Germans were forcibly expelled from Czechoslovakia. Some wild expulsions occurred from May until August directed by groups of armed local Czechs. Several thousand Germans died violently during the expulsion and more died from hunger and illness. Once the agreement was in effect the expulsion was done in a more orderly manner. Even over that winter there were some minor clashes, but none that affected my 'extended' furlough.

Beyond the day to day humiliations of the conquerors, the Czechoslovak military guerilla efforts caused the greatest physical damage to the Czechs. We didn't learn until after the war that the most horrid part of the German occupation was more psychological than physical.[6] In 1942 all the villagers of Lidice, Ležáky,[7] and later Javoříčko were

---

[6] Heydrich's brutal policies quickly earned him the nickname "the Butcher of Prague". In 1942, sweeps against Czech cultural and patriotic organizations, military, and intelligentsia resulted in the practical paralysis of Czech resistance. The terror also served to paralyze resistance in society, with public and widespread reprisals against any action resisting the German rule.

[7] A British-trained team of Czech and Slovak soldiers attacked Heydrich in Prague on 27 May 1942. He died one week later. Intelligence falsely linked the assassins to the villages of Lidice and Ležáky. Lidice was razed to the ground; all adult males were executed. All but a handful of its women and children were deported and killed in Nazi concentration camps.

executed in retaliation for the assassination of Reinhard Heydrich[8] by Czech and Slovak commandos.

The Third Republic was formed in April 1945, but despite the euphoria of freedom from the Germans, there were storm clouds of the strengthening communist menace. The Communist Party of Czechoslovakia (KSČ) grew strong because of new popular enthusiasm evoked by the Soviet armies of liberation, and old remembered disappointment against the West following the 'Munich Betrayal'.

Reunited into one state after the war, the Czechs and Slovaks held national elections in the spring of 1946. President Edvard Beneš hoped the Soviet Union would allow Czechoslovakia the freedom to choose its own form of government and aspired to a Czechoslovakia that would act as a bridge between East and West. Communists secured strong representation.

Occupation Duty in Germany

Despite the official armed combat being ended in Germany I spent most of that year in Regensburg, Germany guarding SS prisoners and giving current affairs lectures to my fellow soldiers. At one point I was sent to Heidelberg University to learn how to be a discussion leader. I also lectured on venereal diseases and wrote the battalion newsletter. In my spare time I studied German and practiced it whenever I had a chance to go into town.

By late 1945 the American troops were allowed to fraternize with German girls. We were billeted at a former

---

[8] Heydrich was a high-ranking German Nazi official and a main architect of the Holocaust. In 1942 he laid out plans for the final solution to the Jewish Question—the deportation and extermination of all Jews in German-occupied territory. He was Deputy Reich-Protector of the Protectorate of Bohemia and Moravia and military dictator. Historians regarded him as the darkest figure within the Nazi elite; Adolf Hitler christened him "the man with the iron heart".

German compound called (by us) Fort Skelly. Periodically a truck was sent into town and the girls (aged about 17 to 24) would hop on and be taken for dinner, drinks and dancing to a live band. Of course, I used the opportunity to practice my German since I already was a good dancer.

Six Weeks Furlough

My second visit to my ethnic roots occurred in late 1945. After that I did not make a third visit to see my relatives again until 1974 when I came with Doris and our two daughters, then 13 and 18. The first visit happened in 1930 when as a three year old, I stayed for the summer with my mother visiting my grandmother, uncles and cousins.

Since we were now allowed to fraternize and to travel away from the base, I requested and was given a 10 day furlough, with travel time, to go see my Czech relatives. At that time there were no organized travel arrangements in war-torn Europe and since there was no direct transportation to Prague, the "travel time" was left open. As it turned out, the trip from my base camp in Regensburg to my uncle's village took me only two days, but that was because I was very opportunistic and lucky.

As it happened, I hitch-hiked a couple of truck rides to Nuremberg and easily found an east bound train to the south western border of the reconstituted Czechoslovak Republic. The German train only went as far as Furth im Wald where I looked around for a train to Bohemia. I was told that the only train going east would be a milk train leaving at 5AM the next morning.

In a restaurant, however, I met a man traveling by motorcycle who offered to let me ride with him. So off we went with me sitting above the rear wheel of the motorcycle, knees locked on to the fender guard and my hands curled around the two small duffle bags I was carrying.

It was a harrowing ride through a mountain pass and into the westernmost Czech border town of Domažlice, where an express train going to Prague was waiting ready to depart. In a couple of hours I was in the capital city where I picked up the required food ration card and stayed the night.

From Prague I took another train to the small town of Breznice, some twenty kilometers from Jan's house in Životice. I checked into a hotel to wait for the mail wagon which would take me to my uncle's house in the morning.

Around midnight, a loud knocking at my door woke me and three big policemen demanded my identification. The problem, I soon found out, was that earlier that evening, as I sat in the hotel lobby I picked up a German newspaper. The ever alert room clerk noticed this and reported to the police that an escaped German soldier in an American uniform who spoke Czech was hiding out at the hotel. The police called my Uncle Jan to check out my story.

The next morning I rode with the mail wagon to my uncle's village. When I arrived, much to my surprise my Uncle Jan, the local forester, resplendent in a grey uniform with green epaulets, was waiting for me at the post office. It was then I learned that the police had contacted him to check out my "story".

I asked him, "How did you know I was coming on the mail wagon?"

"That's easy," he replied. "The hotel keeper became suspicious when he noticed that you, an American soldier who spoke Czech also picked up a German paper in the dining room."

By 1946, the Viennese gentry for whom my uncle had worked, had long been dispossessed of the chateau, well-kept gardens, forests and carp ponds. They lost them after World War I when the Czechoslovakia Republic was established and the Austro-Hungarian Empire was broken up. The chateau and surrounding property, by then was owned by people named Vaňícek, a family of wealthy lawyers from Prague.

To back up a little bit, in 1918 the main house at Lnáře, a small town, and the estate became the property of the Czechoslovak government. Uncle Jan, still the forester, became a civil servant. The State permitted him to stay in the cottage he had long occupied to grow vegetables and maintain farm animals for the family's use on the adjoining plot of land allotted to him.

So, in 1946, at 18, I spent six glorious weeks with my cousins in the bosom of "my family", since by then Uncle Jan had long been married and had three children: Jiři (25), Jarmila (19) and Miroslav (13). The Catholicism and annual pregnancies of my grandparent's generation had given way to a more modern way of life.

Thinking that I might never get to see my relatives again I stayed six weeks after which I decided to return to Germany. Upon arrival I was called into the Colonel's office. The colonel, a lawyer in civilian life, towered over me and put his hands in his hip pockets saying, "You were given a 10 day furlough and returned in six weeks. Exactly what is your excuse?"

Sensing that I had to have a legal explanation, I reached into my pocket and pulled out the 'orders' and said, "Sir, my orders read 10 days plus travel time and the travel time is not specified."

Realizing he had lost this one, and suppressing a smile, the colonel said, "OK, Trebat. I see you're something of a wise guy so I'm going to reduce your rank to private and you'll have to clean out the orderly room toilet for ten days. Now go back to your barracks."

Upon hearing this I saluted, saying, "Thank you, sir." I wheeled about smartly in the best military fashion and with a feeling of great relief reported to my sergeant. The sergeant, not much older than I, told me that I was really lucky – that if it was not for the fact that the fighting was over, I would have been charged with desertion.

Since I was the information and education specialist for the First Engineer Battalion, charged with teaching corporals and sergeant's basic algebra and chemistry to qualify them for higher rank, my corporals stripes were quietly restored within a month. No more was said; my gamble had paid off.

A regular soldier Schweik,[9] don't you think?

Later, when I was returned to civilian life, effective October 29, 1946, I noticed that the good conduct medal[10], given to almost everybody, was not among my array of war medals.

A Short-lived Freedom

The Czechoslovak government had a brief period of relative freedom; however in 1948 a Russian sponsored Communist government took over. For the next forty years Czechoslovakia existed under a Communist dictatorship, taking its orders from Moscow. While the West prospered in

---

[9] *The Good Soldier Švejk*, also spelled Schweik or Schwejk, is the abbreviated title of an unfinished satirical/dark comedy novel by Jaroslav Hašek. The original Czech title of the work is *Osudy dobrého vojáka Švejka za světové války*, literally *The Fateful Adventures of the Good Soldier Švejk During the World War*. He has become the Czech national personification.

[10] There is some question as to the good conduct medal having been withheld since my friend, Ron Littlefield, after research, told me that the medal required three years of honorable service, which I did not have.

the post-war years, Czechoslovakia sank deeper and deeper into a totalitarian malaise.

'BLACK HUMOR'

I learned later that based on Communist ideology everyone was paid the same and everyone was employed I quizzed my Czech cousin Miroslav on this subject and he told me that there were differing income levels; however the spread was quite narrow. For instance, as an experienced physician, he got paid about twice as much as an unskilled laborer but just one-third more than a nurse or an office clerk. Thus there was very little incentive for anyone to work hard or produce quality manufactured goods or services. None but the most necessary repairs were made. Retail clerks, waiters, teachers and even doctors performed their duties in a surly manner. How could it be otherwise when everyone was paid almost the same and there was no reward for quality performance? Buildings were left to crumble, store windows were left unwashed and people one would meet in the street would not make eye contact. Every apartment house had an appointed minor functionary whose job it was to report anyone who spoke against the government or committed other infractions.

In those days and years, the people went "underground" by minding their own business, keeping out of the way of the authorities and living for the weekends when their retreated to their cottages in the country. When we visited our relatives in 1974, with Communism in full power, we found my cousin Miroslav to be super cautious and seemingly afraid of his own shadow. Later, we learned that as a host to visiting Americans, he was being watched closely and that his position as a hospital department head could have been compromised if he was perceived by the authorities to have stepped out of line. People seemed to be living on two levels – one was the day-to-day world of compliance with the dictates of those in power – and a second was an inner life that concerned itself with the welfare of the immediate family and simple survival.

The Communist time, as it was referred to, was not a happy time and there was a lot of black humor being whispered among family and close friends. The one example I remember is: "*they pretend to pay us and we pretend to work*." It's hard to imagine the level of repression and control that the Communist government exercised. It was a time when contact with "the West" was, at the very least, frowned upon and books from the West had to be smuggled into the country. Such books were often copies in samizdat (self-publishing, "*The secret publication and distribution of government-banned literature in the former Soviet Union*.). These books were hidden in bookcases behind "approved" books such as "The Life and Works of Comrade Stalin" and similar titles.

People resorted to "black humor" to show their intellectual superiority to the communist regime with jokes. These samples came from an Article about the feature-length documentary "Hammer and Tickle".

People cracked jokes:	
Why is Czechoslovakia the most neutral country in the world?	Because it doesn't even interfere in its own internal affairs
Are the Russians our brothers or our friends?	Our brothers—we can choose our friends.
What would happen if they introduced Communism to Saudi Arabia?	Nothing at first but soon there would be a shortage of sand.

Why, despite all the shortages, was the toilet paper in East Germany always 2-ply?	Because they had to send a copy of everything they did to Moscow.

| And one proud dissident said proudly, "We showed our intellectual superiority." ||

This is not to deny that the communist joke was often at its best in its dissident form. When Russian tanks rolled into Prague in 1968, the population fought back with wit. Graffiti appeared every night in Wenceslas Square with lines like *"Soviet State Circus back in town! New attractions!"* and *"Soviet School for Special Needs Children—End-of-Term Outing."*

College Graduation

Back home and an Army veteran in 1947, I planned to go to Columbia University where I had been accepted in 1944 but never actually started. But there were two million other veterans returning at the same time and many of them had already started college when they were drafted, so they, naturally, had first call when they came back. It was the same story at NYU, but I hung around the admissions office so long that a sympathetic secretary finally suggested that I start in the evening for a semester and then apply for transfer to day student status. This worked out fine, and soon, I was a sophomore, having received credit for my engineering courses, a lot of which were basic chemistry, physics and mathematics. The U.S. Government generously picked up the tab for all my college tuition and even paid me $105 a month to live on. (Don't laugh, that was a tidy sum of money in those days). I majored in banking and finance, mostly because I was not smart enough to be a rocket scientist and didn't even consider medical or law school. My richest relative, Tony Pospisil, at that time was a head teller in a bank, had a nice house in the suburbs and seemed to be doing well. So, in a small way Tony was sort of my role model. I was a good student and found that I could get fairly good grades while pursuing an active social life. I minored in fine arts and psychology, areas of study that added a lot to my subsequent quality of life. Later, being endowed with 20-20 hindsight, I wished I had worked a lot harder in college and played a little less.

Together with the notification of my eligibility to attend the graduation ceremony at the Polo Grounds, the office at NYU that handles such things sent me six tickets for my family and friends. I was advised that I could rent a cap and gown and would stand with my graduating class when those being awarded BA degrees from Washington Square College were called upon. Even back in 1949, NYU was a big university with some 65,000 students scattered among the various colleges and professional schools at the main "campus" surrounding Washington Square which sits at the foot of Fifth Avenue and abuts Greenwich Village in downtown Manhattan.

I don't remember how many people were being graduated from WSC, the liberal arts college of NYU, but a safe guess would be about five or six hundred. From the University as a whole, and that includes the Law School, Medical School, Graduate School of Business and assorted other schools, I think there were some six or eight thousand graduates who were invited to sit in designated rows, in the infield of the Polo Grounds which was then the home field of the New York Giants. Not wanting to get caught in the crush of graduates out on the playing field, my mother, Albina, by then a widow since 1944, and my Aunt Stella, mother's closest friend, older sister and fellow seamstress and I used the tickets to sit in the bleachers. We watched as the 1949 graduates of WSC jumped to their feet and accepted the mild applause of the gathered multitude of some 30,000 parents and friends, and then sat in the hot sun for another hour while the other schools called upon their graduates to do the same. I don't remember applauding on the exact moment when I became a graduate but I do know that it was a lot easier for the three of us to get to the subway and back home to our apartment on East 82nd Street than it was for the people who had rented caps and gowns for their moment of glory.

In her own quiet way, my mother was proud that she, an immigrant from Czechoslovakia with a sixth grade education, had encouraged her only child to look beyond the blue collar world she lived in. My father, who died in 1945 while I was in the Army, an immigrant from Slovakia, had spent the latter part of his life as a semi-skilled factory worker at the Nathan Manufacturing Company, a locomotive parts plant located at 105th Street at the foot of the East River.

When I was graduated from high school, he thought I really had it made and offered to introduce me to "the boss", and since I had "an education", my father opined that I could become a timekeeper; that way I wouldn't have to get my hands dirty. I didn't take advantage of his well-meant offer.

So, with the graduation ceremony my early career at NYU was over. Actually, I had accomplished quite a lot for one just 22 years and three months old.

So there I was at the end of June 1949, with a shiny, new college degree in my pocket and contemplating the wide open future. My cousin, Georgiana Sindelar, ten years my senior, had moved to Los Angeles several years before and I conceived the idea that, as a first step toward finding a job, why not move to California? Why not indeed? I could live with my cousin and her husband George until I found a job and an apartment somewhere in Los Angeles and then, who knows?

Good Advice and Legal Details

It just so happened that a friend of mine, Dick Penkava, recommended that if I decide to fly, I should sit in the back of the plane because in his experience, most people who survived plane crashes during the war were sitting near the tail. Since I had a lot of respect for Dick's opinion I asked for a seat in the back of the plane which was to deliver me to my cousin's house in San Gabriel, a suburb of Los Angeles.

So it happened that on the 11th day of July 1949 I became a passenger on an airplane owned by Standard Airlines, a so-called non-scheduled airline with two planes, with a ticket from La Guardia Field in New York to Burbank, California. The plane was a C-46, the workhorse of the U.S. Force and both the pilot and co-pilot were war veterans with thousands of miles of airtime flying over France, Germany, Burma, China and who knows where. Now I quote from the tenth paragraph of the complaint filed in New York Supreme Court by Charles Evan, Attorney for Plaintiff in the case entitled GEORGE TREBAT, Plaintiff vs. STANDARD AIRLINES, INC., Defendant:

"That on the 12th day of July, 1949, while the said airplane was still continuing said flight, and plaintiff was still a passenger thereon, and the personal effects of plaintiff were still being carried thereon at about 0743 A.M. of Pacific Standard Time of that day, the said airplane crashed near Chatsworth in the vicinity of Burbank both in the State of California, and that as a result of said crash out of the 48 passengers, including its crew, 35 were killed and 13 others, including the plaintiff suffered serious injuries, and the plaintiffs personal effects transported by said airplane had been destroyed and lost."

And the complaint goes on and on reciting how negligent, careless and reckless the airline people were and in paragraph thirteen recites that "plaintiff received great bodily and mental injuries and sustained, among others concussion of brain and a severe shock to his whole body, spine and nervous system, about one hundred severe cuts, lacerations, contusions, bruises and scratches extending over the plaintiff's body; severe contusions of his head, injuries of his face, both arms, hands, back, thighs, knees, legs, feet and body, many of which injuries were and are of so severe a nature that they probably will and are reasonably certain to be permanent ..." And the complaint continued in this vein in dense legalese for several more pages and ended as follows:

"Wherefore plaintiff demands judgment against the defendant in the sum of One Hundred Thousand Seven Hundred Sixty Three ($100,763.00) Dollars, with interest from the first day of June, 1950, together with costs and disbursements of this action."

If $100,000 looks like a fairly small number, I would note for the record that we are talking in 1950 dollars and well before the explosive inflation in damage judgments that juries started to award starting in the 1980s. To put into context, that's when a cup of coffee or a beer was 5¢ and tuition at a major university was about $800 a year. The rent in our rent-controlled apartment in Manhattan was $24 a month.

The Crash

The case never went to trial as I accepted a total of $5,000 of which $2,500 went to the lawyer. Why so little? Well, let's look at the story as it actually happened and contrast it with the lawyerly briefs and newspaper reports. As noted above, the plane did indeed, crash at the time and place indicated and newspapers the next day carried banner headlines and gruesome pictures of dead bodies and the broken up plane on the front page. The headline in two inch high capital letters in the Wednesday July, 13th Los Angeles Times read: "CAUSE OF L.A. AIR CRASH UNDER PROBE "and the story headlines, also on the front page read: "35 Die as Transport Rams Mount after Cabin Fight" and "Full List of Dead in Crash" and, finally "Crash May Mean End of Airline—Company Already Under CAB Orders to Quit Business."

Somewhere there is a scrapbook full of deteriorating newspaper clippings reporting the accident and its aftermath. At the time, reading all of this stuff in my hospital bed, I quickly learned that newspaper reportage is only about 50% accurate and that when reporters don't have the exact facts or the right name, they don't hesitate to make up details to fill out their story. For instance, one of the pictures that were in newspapers all over the country showed me on a stretcher being wheeled into a hospital with the caption: "George Trebat, 22, a New York student seeking summer employment on the coast was dragged from the wreckage of the big plane. His condition was described as serious." Luckily the caption was wrong.

The crash was, to say the least, a shocking experience and the details are still burned into my memory. Since I asked for a seat near the rear of the plane I was assigned a window seat, third from the back. After refueling in Albuquerque early that morning we had come through an electrical storm with a lot of turbulence but, now, it was almost 8 A.M. and the plane was cruising smoothly toward a landing in Burbank in about five minutes. The seatbelt light was on. Our trays were in an upright position; I had no premonition that anything was going to happen.

There was no warning.

As the wingtip of the plane hit the mountain and the front of the plane was rammed into the earth, the plane spun around and the tail section broke off just about where I was sitting, with the rest of plane splattered over another thousand feet or so. I knew nothing of this because the initial shock knocked me unconscious and I could have been on my way to becoming an angel.

When I regained consciousness, I was lying at the side of a firebreak without shoes (they were blown off) or glasses, and my pants were in shreds. About fifty feet up from where I was lying, parts of the plane were in flame. As my mind cleared I tried to get up to get away from a seemingly imminent explosion, but I couldn't move. I have no recollection of how I got out of the plane or how I happened to be lying flat on my back ogling a 23 year old actress, whose dress was around her hips, lying in a daze about ten feet away from me. (Yes, even such details did not escape me.) A few other people were stumbling around in shock further up the mountain near the remains of the plane. That's all I can remember, but as it was later reconstructed, I was apparently thrown free of the plane as it broke up on the mountainside.

I don't know how long I was unconscious as there is a half hour, more or less, gap in my memory. Some of the other survivors told the press that I was walking around immediately after the crash pulling out people still strapped in their seats. I don't remember any of this but neither can I explain why my trousers were torn in shreds from the brambles or how I got to where I was, If I was actually doing something heroic and was helping the other passengers, I'm glad, but I certainly don't remember it.

> *As a further note*: News stories later recounted how: "Trebat and passenger Judy Frost helped pull four passengers through the plane's split belly. 'What I remember, I was sitting on a fire break about 50 feet from the plane and it was burning,' Trebat recalled. 'I was told, but I don't remember, that I helped pull people out of the plane'"

As far as there being a fight on the plane as was reported in the newspapers, that was an exaggeration of the wildest kind. The simple fact was that there was a disturbed passenger who had to be calmed down by one of the pilots; the whole thing took about a minute and the pilot returned to the cockpit without incident.

I was kept in the hospital for about a week and had every conceivable part of my body x-rayed and tested. I gave a radio interview from my hospital bed. My most severe injuries were a number of surface cuts on my legs and one scratch on my face. Not too bad considering that my seatmate and most of the people directly in back and in front of me were killed. In addition to the scratches, I did have a 'charley horse' in my legs and back, apparently from the plane suddenly coming into contact with an immovable object. The pilots were both killed as were all of the people in the front and middle sections of the plane. Only some of the people in the tail section survived, and of those only one or two came out without any broken bones or serious injuries. To say that I was lucky is an understatement of monstrous proportions!

As near as anyone could figure out, the plane had been

roughed up quite a bit passing through a storm somewhere over Arizona or Nevada during the night. The altimeter was later found to be off by about a thousand feet, enough to give the pilots a false sense of security in approaching an airport into which they had flown a thousand times before. There was reportedly some fog or a small cloud covering the mountaintop just at the point where the plane had to make a turn to swoop down into the Burbank airport. Since the pilots could not see the mountaintop, they had to rely on their instruments for the two minutes, or so, that it would take to make the fatal turn.

After some massage therapy, a lot of sitting in the sun and a few nightmares, I got over the effects of the plane crash in about six weeks and resumed my life. In actuality, Georgie and George Sindelar (there are a lot of 'Georges' in our family for some unexplained reason) saw me through my recuperation, taking me to the necessary therapy and integrating me into their little family. Life in Los Angeles was not all I had imagined so I returned to New York in about a year. It was time to start my career.

At that time they had a two year old son, Peter, with whom I reconnected almost 60 years later. Although he still lives in California, I've re-formed a close family bond. He used to call me "Uncle George", but after he turned 65 he acceded to my entreaties and calls me George (as of 2012.)

Reflections on the Crash

These are my later reflections on why I received such a small judgment when I sued the airline, and how it affected my determination to succeed.

It's not that my lawyer wasn't competent or that the airline had a big Wall Street law firm defending it (which it did). I had to submit to neurological and physical examinations two years after the accident and since I was healthy and leading an active work and school schedule, there was precious little that I could talk about in terms of permanent injury. I found it quite sobering to discover that the 65 year old retired man, sitting next to me, whose life was snuffed out, only qualified for an award of $5,000 to his estate. The legal principle involved, is that since he was retired the "economic value" of his life was zero and, therefore, his family was awarded the $5,000 as a sort of gratuity. In the years since 1950 the social and economic values have changed radically so that years later I would probably have received at least $1,000,000 for my troubles.

After the accident I avoided flying on airplanes for a long time until I was forced to fly to Florida in 1958 because of my mother's sudden serious illness. The flight there and back was traumatic for me on several levels but it did help change my mental focus to the point where I eventually accepted flying as a regular part of life. I no longer sat in the back of the plane and my experience had a profound and not always subtle effect on my subsequent life. For one, it gave me the courage to live my life in a more open way and to become something of a risk taker with strong entrepreneurial tendencies.

For instance, I determined early on that the bank's president and most of the top executives were, or had been, commercial loan officers so that's the job on which I set my sights. When the Chase bank (by then Chase Manhattan) did not recognize my sterling qualities, I did not hesitate to change jobs. In all, I worked in seven banks in the next 42 years. I did become a bank officer on my third try, and later still, president of two small banks in New Jersey. Making all of these changes, I did not build any great pension rights, but that's where my entrepreneurial bent kicked in. When I got a little money together, I started investing in the stock market and then some real estate. Doris taught school for some 14 years which paid college expenses. Her salary enabled me to build up some capital.

The point of all this is, that I had absolutely no background that would have led me to achieve even the modest successes that I have spelled out here. I'm sure that the July 1949 air crash caused me to take a longer view of life and made me into a more assertive and ambitious person than would have been the case if I had landed without incident at the Burbank airport.

Time and time again, over the subsequent decades I have recalled with gratitude Dick Penkava's prophetic advice; "Sit in the back of the plane". Dick's career kept him in Europe for some thirty years, teaching in the American overseas school system. He eventually became a reserve Army Lieutenant Colonel. We kept in touch for many years until his death in 1997.

In August 1999, Annette Kondo, wrote an article called "**Survivors' Tales**" for the Los Angeles Times.[11]

> Ask about that day five decades ago, and they'll calmly tell you they easily could have been among the 35 who perished.
>
> One survivor credits a guardian angel, a divine protector that followed him from rescue to hospital recovery. Another says it was a gift from her Lord.
>
> The newspaper headlines have long since faded from most memories. And the boulder-strewn mountainside just east of Simi Valley is now silent and peaceful except for an occasional jack rabbit.
>
> But for several of the 14 who survived the July 12, 1949,

---

[11] For pictures of the crash go to Google and click on "Remnants of a deadly crash - Framework - Photos and Video ..." Jan 26, 2011 – **July 12, 1949**: Wreckage of Standard Airlines C-46 is examined following **crash** killing 35 passengers and crew. Fourteen survived.

crash of a Standard Airlines plane — at the time, the Southland's deadliest aviation accident — each day is still precious; each year is still a gift.

"When you come that close to not being here, or being told they are going to take your foot off, it changes everything in your life," said Caren Marsh Doll, who was known at the time as Caren Marsh, a stage and screen actress who was Judy Garland's stand-in on "The Wizard of Oz."

The Hollywood native was one of 49 passengers and crew members flying from New York's La Guardia Airport to the Lockheed Air Terminal, known today as Burbank Airport.

The Civil Aeronautics Board had ordered Standard Airlines of Long Beach to shut down its business by July 20, the result of regulation violations.

The plane was a C-46 or Commando--a popular military workhorse and the largest twin-engine transport plane used during World War II.

About 45 minutes before the crash, two passengers brawled. Over Riverside, about 7:35 a.m., Pilot Roy G. White radioed the Lockheed tower, asking police to meet the plane.

To keep the peace, stewardess Vicy Zelsdorf, 25, offered to change seats with one of the men. She was 4 1/2 months pregnant and heading home.

During the flight, Zelsdorf had chatted with Marsh, 30. Marsh sat about three rows from the back of the plane. She had been working in New York and was flying home to attend a cousin's wedding.

The petite, brown-eyed brunet, a talented dancer since childhood, was already a familiar face on stage and film. Fresh out of Hollywood High School — where Judy Garland was a classmate –Marsh won an MGM movie dance role.

In 1946, she was cast as Winifred McMasters in "Navajo

The Immigrants' Son, An American Story

Kid," a western starring Bob Steele and filmed in the Chatsworth hills.

A year later, she was voted Miss Sky Lady of 1947. The prize: free flying lessons. After she had soloed, Marsh printed up leaflets listing her credits, then took off in a two-seater to shower MGM, Paramount, RKO and other studios with the fliers.

The publicity stunt worked, and more roles followed, including "Wild Harvest" with Alan Ladd.

"She was cute," recalled George Trebat, then 22, and fresh out of New York University with a degree in banking and finance. Like Marsh, he was seated about three rows from the back of the plane.

Young, single and curious about the other coast, Trebat was headed west to look up relatives in San Gabriel and find a job.

Also in the rear of the plane, on the right side, was Pvt. Robert E. Steinweg, 21, who looked forward to 30 days of furlough at home in Petaluma, Calif. He had just finished a three-year stint in the Army and left Camp Kilmer in New Jersey.

*

Seated near a window exit, Larry Bettis, 29, and his wife, Mary, 36, were on their way home to Long Beach after visiting relatives in Missouri. A thick fog enshrouded the plane, he recalled.

That's all anyone remembered of the flight before the C-46 slammed into a peak in the Santa Susana Mountains north of Chatsworth.

"I remember going through the seat right in front of me," Larry Bettis said.

With a gash across his head, he ended up beside a cabin door near the pilot's compartment. Flames licked the battered plane.

"I crawled out on the wing," he said, "then fell, I don't remember how many feet, to the ground."

Mary Bettis was still in her seat when she regained consciousness, then quickly climbed through a window. She found her husband outside and used his shirt to make a bandage for his head.

Trebat remembers little that happened immediately after the crash--the third deadliest in the nation in 1949. Federal investigators later determined the plane had been flying too low and that pilot error caused the crash.

News stories recounted how Trebat and passenger Judy Frost helped pull four passengers through the plane's split belly.

"What I remember, I was sitting on a fire break about 50 feet from the plane and it was burning," Trebat said. "I was told, but I don't remember, that I helped pull people out of the plane."

*

The pregnant Zelsdorf can never forget the dead, including two young children.

She was seriously hurt; her lower back and ribs were broken and her pelvis was fractured in three places. "I was told not to have the child, because I was so severely injured," she said.

*

Steinweg was just plain lucky.

A July 13, 1949, Times story described how he staggered from the wreckage down a fire trail to a Mesa Drive home.

"I was walking down a road and some lady stopped me," he recalled. "And I said I better go to Petaluma."

That lady may well have been Winifred Steele, now 86, of Lilac Lane. She and her husband, Jim, are now the only residents of the lane who were living there in 1949.

Steele and a neighbor saw a man resting under an oak tree with tickets in his pocket. "He didn't know what was happening," she said.

That day, Steele helped guide ambulances on the narrow dirt road near the isolated crash site. One of those ambulances carried Marsh, whose foot was crushed by the plane's collapsed seats.

"Red hamburger with white noodles sticking out, that's what my foot looked like," she recalled.

After climbing out of the wreckage, she said she thought for a moment she had died because men in long robes were walking around her. Angels, perhaps.

But the bearded and barefoot men in old newspaper photos of the crash were Krishna Venta, a leader of a monastery in nearby Box Canyon, and one of his disciples, Brother Paul. Both had rushed to the mountain to help victims.

Later, at a Van Nuys hospital, a doctor told Marsh her foot would have to be amputated.

*

The injured and expectant Zelsdorf and her husband never gave up hope for their baby. Four months after the crash, their son, Gary, was born, and the Walter Winchell radio show and the Los Angeles Times heralded him as a miracle crash baby.

Zelsdorf, now Vicy Young, 75, of Cathedral City, stopped flying as a stewardess but remains an active advocate for infant seats on planes.

"A baby can go flying in the air and even kill a passenger," she said. "It's like a suitcase loose in the air."

Now 71, Robert Steinweg is retired from the construction business and living in Santa Rosa. After the crash, he was on newsreels in theaters and on TV news. While recuperating in a hospital room, he said, he had a vision of two heavenly visitors. "You always got a guardian angel," he remembered.

George Trebat

He eventually returned to the Army, serving in the Korean War. But he said he never flew again, turning down opportunities to visit Europe.

The brush with death made George Trebat more daring in business, he said, pushing him to reach his goal of becoming a president of a small New Jersey bank.

"I decided I'd rather live 10 minutes like a lion, rather than 100 years like a mouse," said Trebat, now 72 and living in Edison, N.J. "In other words, I got a feeling that life is short and it can be vicious."

The crash influenced the career of Larry Bettis, now 79 and a Laguna Niguel resident. As a firefighter in Long Beach, he rose through the ranks during 25 years of service. "When rescuing the elderly or young children," Bettis said, he understood their helplessness because "you realize what position they are really in, because you have been there."

Desperate to save her foot, Marsh sought another doctor at Cedars of Lebanon, now Cedars-Sinai, where a surgeon promised she would be able to walk but probably not dance again.

"I refused to accept that," she said. "I was in a hospital for a month. And I refused to picture myself not able to dance."

Tap was out, but eventually Marsh took up Hawaiian dance, then belly dancing. Today, at 80, Caren Marsh Doll lives in Palm Springs and teaches country and western and ballroom dancing.

For the last 10 years, she has set aside the last Monday of each month to volunteer at a Palm Springs stroke center, where she coaxes patients to try to stand up, sway to the music and forget their troubles.

"I was so thankful to just be alive. Things that bothered me before . . . nothing," she said. "I have become much more peaceful and less worried about anything."

(It might be noticed that in the foregoing pages Caren Marsh's age was variously listed as somewhere between 24 and 30. This discrepancy, I later found out, was because she, like many another entertainer, fibbed about her age to qualify for better movie parts.)

Early Career

After my return from California I found a job in a large downtown bank while enrolled in the NYU Graduate School of Business. I went to school, four nights a week while The Chase National Bank of the City of New York picked up the tuition and paid me the princely starting salary of $25 a week (plus free lunch). Even in 1950, $25 was a miserly salary for a college graduate.

I was not being discriminated against because of my lack of Ivy League credentials since that's the same salary that the Harvard and Princeton graduates were getting. For them, the $25 a week was pin money since they were being supplemented "from home" while they were in training. Most of the so called college trainees at the Chase National Bank were sons of captains of industry who were there to get well rounded and make some connections.

When I first joined the Chase National Bank, I was 23, a World War II veteran (of 2 years standing, if you counted my reserve status from age 17), and a year out of New York University with a degree in banking and finance. Other than a few basics, I knew almost nothing about banking. I was there to try to get my hand on the first rung of a career. The low pay seemed to be the price of admission to the executive suite, so I did my job, went to school and lived an active social life on weekends.

Before entering into the details of my banking career,

please enjoy some historical perspective and my personal recollections of two of the giants of my industry.

Some Historical Perspective

The Chase National Bank, formed in 1877, was named after former United States Treasury Secretary and Chief Justice Salmon P. Chase, although Chase did not have a connection with the bank. The Chase National Bank acquired a number of banks in the 1920s, which made it the largest bank in the world. It was primarily a wholesale bank, dealing with other prominent financial institutions and major corporate clients.

Chase traces its history back to the founding of the Bank of the Manhattan Company by Aaron Burr in 1799. After an epidemic of yellow fever in 1798, during which coffins had been sold by itinerant vendors on street corners, Aaron Burr established the Manhattan Company, with the ostensible aim of bringing clean water to the city from the Bronx River.

> "…Within six months of the company's creation and long before it laid a single section of water pipe, the company opened a bank, the Bank of the Manhattan Company… New York's second bank, rivaling Alexander Hamilton's Bank of New York. .—*The Economist* {Gerard T. Koppell (16 March 2000). "Soaking the poor"}

In addition to being fierce political and personal rivals, Aaron Burr and Alexander Hamilton competed in business, with Burr's Bank of the Manhattan Company competing against Hamilton's Bank of New York. In 1804, their rivalry erupted into a duel, leading to the death of Alexander Hamilton. Over two centuries after their duel, it can be said that the Bank of the Manhattan Company ultimately

The Immigrants' Son, An American Story

won the "business" side of the rivalry. In 2006, the modern-day Chase bought the retail banking division of the Bank of New York, who then only months later merged with Pittsburgh-based Mellon Financial to form the present-day BNY Mellon.

The following is an illustration of the company's major mergers and acquisitions and historical predecessors to 1995 (this is not a comprehensive list):

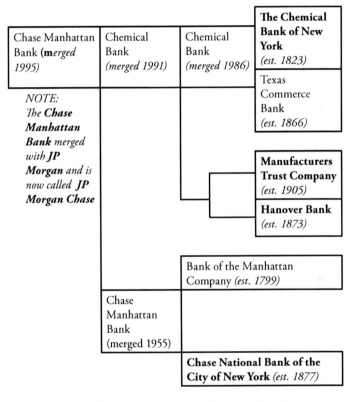

In 1955, Chase National Bank and The Manhattan Company merged to create. Chase Manhattan Bank. As Chase was a much larger bank, it was first intended that Chase acquire the "Bank of Manhattan", as it was nicknamed. However, Burr's original charter for the Manhattan Company had not only included the clause allowing it to start a bank with surplus funds, but another requiring unanimous consent of shareholders for the bank to be taken-over. The deal was therefore structured as an acquisition by the Bank of the Manhattan Company of Chase National, with John J. McCloy becoming chairman of the merged entity. This avoided the need for unanimous consent by shareholders.

For Chase Manhattan Bank's new logo, Chermayeff & Geismar designed a stylized octagon in 1961, which remains part of the bank's logo today. The Chase logo is a stylized representation of the primitive water pipes laid by the Manhattan Company, which were made by nailing together wooden planks. Under McCloy's successor, George Champion, the bank relinquished its antiquated 1799 state charter for a modern one. In 1969, under the leadership of David Rockefeller, the bank became part of a bank holding company, the Chase Manhattan Corporation.

McCloy's Tip

Just after the Second World War, maybe 1949, John J. McCloy was appointed by President Truman to be High Commissioner for Germany. McCloy was a senior partner in a large Wall Street firm; Milbank, Tweed, Hope, Hadley and McCloy, to be exact. His mission was to organize a democratic government structure and negotiate the terms of occupation with Russia, Great Britain and France.

After his mission was completed in 1952, McCloy became Chairman of the Board of the Chase Manhattan Bank. This coincided with the time I was working at the

The Immigrants' Son, An American Story

bank as a trainee and attending graduate school at NYU four nights a week.

Upon my earning my MBA degree, for which the bank paid my tuition, a group of twenty or so trainees getting advanced degrees were invited to a dinner at a prominent midtown hotel. The dinner speaker was the board chairman John J. McCloy. "Mister McCloy," as he was known to us, was a short dapper man dresses in the best ivy league fashion – a navy blue sports jacket, grey trousers, white shirt, his Harvard tie and brown slip-ons. McCloy was clearly relaxed and in a good mood as he started to address the trainees.

After a few congratulatory remarks and a reminder of the great bank by which we were employed, he started to wax eloquent in an avuncular tone. Then he said, "I'm going to tell you about an experience that has served me well in my Wall Street legal career. When I was young I lived in Forest Hills, Queens; an outer borough of New York City and near Forrest Hills Tennis Stadium where the annual tennis championships were held."

Getting into his subject he continued, "While I was a teenager, after school I used to hang around the tennis courts watching the professionals practice. Now and then I would shag balls for them. On several occasions when one or another of the pros came early they would hand me a racket and let me help them warm up."

McCloy then got to the point of his story. He condensed his experience by jumping ahead a few years and telling us that when he got to college and tried out for the tennis team he was readily accepted, because he was one of the best players in the freshman class.

He then continued, "What my forest Hills experience taught me was that to get to the next higher level you have to play against competitors who are better and more experienced than you are. In other words gentlemen the lesson to be learned is that to excel in your career you have to run with the swift."

He ended his talk by telling that if we remember his motto, that is, to "run with the swift," our careers are sure to take off.

Since that time I have been to many pro forma dinners which I don't remember, but I took McCloy's dictum to heart and, with mixed success, have always tried to run with the swift.

Retrospective – G. Champion

Recently, when I got to the obit page of the New York Times, there, staring at me was a face from the past: George Champion, 93, head of Chase Manhattan Bank in the 1960s. His picture brought back a rush of memories.

When I was a trainee at the mighty Chase Manhattan Bank in 1955, George was 51, my department head, and an Executive Vice President. He was in charge of dealing with major corporations the likes of IBM, General Electric and U.S. Steel. He was also six feet three, a broad shouldered former Dartmouth football player with steely, piercing, eyes that would look right through you. George was clearly a rising star, soon to be president and later the Chairman of the Board, a position of great prestige and power among the elite of Wall Street and international banking.

George, and he encouraged all of us to call him George, would occasionally leave his well-appointed office and come down to the Credit Department where we were learning the nuts and bolts of banking. On one particular day that I remember as if it were yesterday, he called all the credit analysts together to give us his "once a year" pep talk. As we thirty some odd aspiring bankers sat in rapt attention, George started out by telling us of his vision of great growth for the bank and how we, in the not too distant future, would be called upon to provide financing and give advice to the corporate elite of the United States, and, indeed, of the world. As I sat there listening to his wonderfully delicious word picture of my future, I imagined myself, invited to address the Board of Directors of a large corporation, telling them how, of course, I could provide financing for them to buy other companies.

Then George Champion, warming to his subject started to describe his vision of the Chase executive who would be sent out to represent the bank. He said that when a Chase man walks into a room full of people, he will be immediately recognized and a momentary hush will envelop the room. He said that the captains of industry will make their way to the Chase man's side because of his commanding presence and stature as a leader of men.

That night, just before going to bed, I weighed myself as I was brushing my teeth. There it was, the scale did not lie. I was 125 pounds, almost five feet six inches tall, and, at 28 still looked as if I were in high school. The moment of truth suddenly hit me in the face: why, that son of a bitch was not describing me, no, not in a thousand years would I fit into Champion's scenario. Maybe I would have quit the Chase sooner or later anyway, but that night I realized that I would never be on his fast track and I had better make my future somewhere else. Sometime later, when I resigned, I passed George in the hallway. I don't know if they had told him, but there wasn't a smile or even a flicker of recognition.

He never knew, or cared, and right then I knew I had made the right decision.

In retrospect, after more than 20 years of retirement, I am not so sure. Maybe I should have been more patient and waited for Mr. Champion to look down and tap me on the shoulder. As I later found out, the world "outside" was not always good to me either.

Size Matters

In November 2006, going through my Sunday morning ritual of carefully studying the New York Times, while the rest of the world was at church, I got to the Book Review section and the review of a book entitled "Size Matters" caught my eye.

It was by a science reporter named Stephen S. Hall and promised to tell how height affects the health, happiness and success of boys and the men they become.

> NYTimes 10/05 excerpt:
> "There is a considerable literature suggesting that taller men receive higher pay than shorter men, and one recent study concluded that economic discrimination against short adult males was equal in magnitude to racial or gender bias in the workplace."

Within a few days I had a copy of the book in my hands. The cover had Mr. Hall's photograph and noted that he is 5' – 5 ¾" tall, almost exactly my own tallest height (as one gets older the spine contracts so that in old age I receded to about 5' – 3"). I found the subject matter going to the very core of my being. As I got into the book I found myself nodding and reflecting that, at last, someone in the world understands and has been able to articulate the dilemma of the short man.

Unlike me, Mr. Hall has a 5' – 9" wife and two normal sized children. My wife, Doris is (was) 5' – 1" and my three children, especially my son, are clearly shorter than normal.

Mr. Hall reports that he was always the shortest in his class as a child, with 99% of all children his age being taller. My experience was somewhat different in that I was of average height all through grade school and only became aware of being shorter than normal around the age of 15 when all of my friends were having their adolescent growth spurt while I languished at less than five feet and one half feet.

The book, for those of you who are vertically short changed, can be easily obtained. It goes on to trace the history of society's bias against shortness and explains why one child's shortness may lead to anguish while another child develops an emotional resilience that will enrich his later life. I'm not going to quote Mr. Hall's book here but I know that my own shortness played a very large part in my social development, career and, eventually, my self image.

This is only one of many very authoritative documents that consistently report that not only do taller men receive higher pay, but that the degree of economic discrimination against short males was equivalent to racial or gender bias in the workplace.

I could bore you by writing a whole book on my experiences and reaction to shortness but I'll spare you and limit myself to relating just a few of my memorable reactions, not all of them negative.

As a teenager, on the days that I did not run the two or three miles to my high school from York Avenue and 82nd Street to West 66th Street, I would take the York Avenue bus. At 15, I didn't pay much attention to girls but I noticed that a small girl named Shirley, who was about my age and another shorty named Helen were there very often at the same time that I was there. Being naïve about such things, it took me a long time to "catch on" but one morning when I found them sneakily jockeying for a seat next to me, I became aware of why the small ones were, in my teenage vocabulary "hanging around me" while the taller ones were not even aware of my existence. It took me quite a while to figure out the boy/girl dynamic that was at work – I think that at that age, girls become socially mature much earlier than boys do.

During my 2 ½ year tour in the Army (starting at 17), height made little difference as I was tall enough to qualify as cannon fodder and it did not bother me one bit that the bigger men were chosen for the more physically demanding assignments. In fact, I was quite happy to be a discussion leader and mail clerk (among other things) before I was discharged at age 20 to go to college.

It was only after I started my career in banking that the matter of relative size really started to bother me. When I was a so-called executive trainee, and subsequently, I found that the six foot plus guys were chosen for key assignments. It was not that I was discriminated against; it was only that I was simply ignored. I was anxious to get onto the fast track of executive stardom but found myself first . . . . not . . . . chosen. It has occurred to me that if I were an intellectual superstar I would certainly have pulled away from the pack. For good or evil, in my own evaluation, I was just a little better than average in intelligence (among the college graduates) and I had no connections (among sons of business leaders) and was, apparently, the shortest executive trainee that the Chase Manhattan Bank had ever put into their training program. Thus, when I found myself in the slow lane I decided that competition in a less intensive environment than the New York big bank scene of the 1950s might be more fruitful.

When I complained to some of my taller acquaintances they usually said something like: "Oh no, your size doesn't matter; you're just oversensitive, George." After a while I learned to keep my thoughts to myself.

Early Investment Success

I got interested in securities in 1946 while studying for a banking and finance degree at New York University. During one of my securities analysis courses, a professor who was also a partner in a large New York investment banking house, used a small growing company as a case study in class. The investment prospects for the subject company evoked so favorable a response, that I was impelled to ask the professor if this was not a good stock for a young man to buy. At that question the professor got a little embarrassed and said he could not recommend the stock since he was only using it for case study purposes.

Well, needless to say, I took the $1,000 I had saved while in the Army and bought a hundred shares. As it turned out, the stock, a small electric utility, doubled and then doubled again and raised its dividend every year for the 10 years I owned it.

Though my first stock market investment was admittedly a lucky break, it helped finance my way through graduate school where I picked up a master's degree in banking and finance and it also financed my honeymoon. Instead of becoming a stock broker, as some people might have expected, I went into commercial banking, starting as an executive trainee with the Chase Manhattan Bank in 1950. I became a loan officer handling business loans - a job which involves accounting, law, economics, financial counseling and, most of all, a lot of psychology – all attributes needed later in managing investments.

Starting in the Loan Department

Having no better way of entry into commercial banking, I applied at the personnel department and was assigned to the main office loan processing department. I made a mental note of the fact that the personnel interviewer called the manager of the loan department and told him that he had a boy with "some education" for him. I thought that this comment was off-putting, but, I took the job anyway.

One of my first insightful acts was to read the bank's annual report where I learned that, of the 15,000 employees, there were several hundred vice presidents listed. Since the loan department where I was put to work, had about eighty clerks headed by a low level officer called an assistant cashier, I asked one of my fellow clerks where all of those vice presidents came from. He told me that most of the vice presidents were commercial loan officers who came up through the credit department.

With that information in hand, I screwed up my courage and marched over to the assistant cashier in charge and reminded him that I was a college graduate. I wondered if I could not be transferred to the credit department. The boss told me that the trainees in the credit department all come from Ivy League schools and had "connections" at the upper levels of the bank. In other words, he said I wouldn't have much of a chance of being transferred to the credit department because a New York University degree didn't mean much when compared to Harvard, Yale, Dartmouth and the like; and besides, I came from a working class background which was not what they were looking for. He was polite enough not to mention my inauspicious appearance. He added that everyone knows that the credit department is the training ground for the future leaders of the bank but suggested that if I stayed put and worked hard I might someday become a senior clerk. And all the time I would be accruing pension rights. I didn't say anything but thought that this was not quite the future I had in mind.

Nevertheless, he was a kindly old guy and I talked him into putting in a transfer request. A week went by with no response, then three weeks, and all the time I did my job and waited.

Access to the Chairman

At around six weeks I noticed an interesting article in the bank's in-house employee bulletin. The article was written by Mr. Winthrop W. Aldrich who served as president and chairman of the board of Chase National Bank from 1930 to 1953.

The chairman evidently was on an employee morale improvement kick and wrote in this vein: "I want the bank to be one big happy family and if any employee has a work related problem, my door is always open." Eureka! A light went off in my head. I picked up the phone and called the chairman's number. The secretary asked, "Who are you and why do you want to see Mr. Aldrich?" I referred her to page one of the bulletin and his "my door is always open" article. She said she would let me know. I heard nothing. After about three more weeks, the assistant cashier called me over and asked, "What's this about you calling the chairman's office?" Someone had apparently called him. I was ready for him and pulled out my copy of the article and said that since I had not heard about my transfer request, I wanted to talk to Mr. Aldrich. The assistant cashier, who had already spent forty years at the Chase and had never even met the chairman, was quite taken aback and said, "You're a feisty little bastard, aren't you?" Full of politeness, I stood my ground. About a month later, he called me to his desk again and said, "Ok, your transfer has come through." I never did get to see the chairman.

In order to get into the executive training program I had to take a test and be interviewed. The first time I took the test I came in at #2 out of 1,500 applicants, but I failed the interview because I wore white socks. I took the test again and again I was #2. They decided that it was no fluke. I passed the interview. This time I wore black socks.

At 128 pounds and of less than average height I didn't exactly fit their profile for a credit trainee, but the risk I took in insisting that I wanted to see the chairman paid off. Later, after finishing the training program, while working at the bank during the day and going to graduate school four nights a week, I was transferred out of a large Wall Street branch to a smaller branch office. I quickly figured out that I was not on the fast track, so I talked to one of my professors, who happened also to be an executive at The Bank of the Manhattan Company.

Before long I left Chase National and became a credit analyst on the Manhattan Bank's headquarters staff with a small increase in salary. Six months later, Chase National and Manhattan merged to form what became The Chase Manhattan Bank and, later, JP Morgan Chase (2000). So I had taken another risk and landed in a greatly improved job in Chase Manhattan's head office credit department.

When the Chase Manhattan Bank did not recognize my sterling qualities, I did not hesitate to change jobs. In all, I worked in seven banks in the next 42 years. By 1955 it was time to switch my loyalties. By that time I had become a solid family man.

The 20-30 Club

Back in Yorkville, after returning from California I joined the Youth Group at the Jan Hus Bohemian Brethren Presbyterian Church (a Czech-English speaking neighborhood church) for social reasons and which included a group of other neighborhood boys and girls. I knew them from public school, from the ethnic Czech school, from the

The Immigrants' Son, An American Story

Sokol organization (a Czech gymnastic group) and from the neighborhood at large.

At the beginning of 1953, I was attending graduate school four nights a week at the NYU business school while working as a credit trainee at what was then the Chase National Bank. My social life, what there was of it, revolved around the 20-30 Club at Madison Avenue Presbyterian Church (MAPC) at 73rd Street and Madison Ave. in Manhattan. The latter was a club for young people in their 20s and 30s. It was sometimes jokingly referred to as the marriage bureau for the church because of the numerous couples who found romance there.

The Yorkville Czech neighborhood where I grew up is about a fifteen minute walk east of the Madison Avenue Presbyterian Church, but it might as well be on another planet socially and financially. Seventh-third and First Avenue, where I was born, and Madison and Seventy-third, the church's locale on upscale Madison Avenue were as different as night and day.

As many of the young people at Jan Hus paired up, I found that there were slim pickings among the girl members (as the most attractive were either too tall or were getting married at a rapid rate).

So, as I've said over the years, I joined the 20-30 Club at MAPC because "that's where the girls were". And this is not just an exaggeration since I was not, what they call, "religious" and my motivations were strictly social. The proximity of so many "church people" did, of course, have an effect on me and many of my "churchy" friends have remained friends for life. Almost as a footnote I should note that in those days (the 1950s) young people of moderate means could meet members of the opposite sex in only four venues: church young people's groups, bars, or fraternal or political organizations. As my ethnic fraternal group thinned out, I chose to look for a mate among the girls in the church young people's group. I made the right choice.

The club itself has maintained its storied existence long since it helped me meet that "special girl". It is still serving as the marriage bureau, among other things. My special girl and I had little to do with it once we were married and settled down, until some 40 years later.

For the first five months of 1993 Doris and I were part of a group setting up a reunion for the 20-30 Club. Some 120 people, most of whom are now over 60, met for a weekend of fun and nostalgia at Lafayette College in PA. They came from as far away as California, but most were from the east coast and many of them had not seen each other for thirty years or more. Long forgotten relationships were rekindled in a flash ... we could go on and on but suffice it to say that warm memories of that event will last for many years.

A Special Girl

At one of the 20-30 weekly meetings, where putting on skits and dancing to recorded music was the norm, I spotted an attractive girl. Her name was Doris Jones. Being somewhat vertically challenged I usually drew the attention of girls who were five feet two or thereabouts. Doris fit the bill on that score and as I got to know her I discovered she was "something special" – we clicked. She was a teacher in the church's day school and had come from Oregon, after college, to study at Columbia University and, as she said, "To see the world."

As you can imagine, one thing lead to another and before long we knew our relationship was getting "serious". During the fall of the year I popped the question and fitted her ring finger with a $200.00 (1953 money) diamond engagement ring bought through Teddy Janacek at a discounted price.

Teddy was one of my close friends, whose father owned a Jewelry store. Doris and I were in love.

At this point you may well ask: "What about Doris, George's wife and the future mother of their three children?" Doris' forebears also came from Europe but came to the United States long before Ellis Island was in use. She can trace her ancestry in America to a man named Jedidiah Strong[12], who arrived in Nantasket, Massachusetts, in May 1630, from Plymouth, England. Doris (Jones) also has family names such as Craw and McMaster in her background but we haven't researched anything about their presence in America except that they all seem to originally have come to the New England area.

Doris' Notes

Starting in 1992, (I wrote this memoir bit by bit over a period of many years) I would write of some facet of my life and then put the copy away and write nothing for two years. Then I decided to continue with the story of my life and inevitably repeated parts of what I had written previously. Bit by bit, however, I moved through my early years, career, and so on.

All the while I was urging my loyal and beloved wife, Doris, to also submit her life and feelings to the printed page. As she was a professional reading specialist and longtime teacher and literacy volunteer and tutor, I hoped that she would write her own memoirs. But no such luck.

As I am writing this paragraph in 2012, Doris has been recently admitted to the Skilled Nursing Facility at Moravian Village; a community where we have lived for the

---

[12] You can find out a lot more about the Strong family by looking up a book entitled "strong Family History" published by the Strong Family Association of America, Inc.

past eight years. She is stricken by Alzheimer's disease and can no longer handle pen, pencil or computer.

A few years ago she did, however, put a few notes onto a yellow legal pad. We can no longer change, augment or expand on her musings of her early years, which I am adding to my own writings in an "as is" form. Here it is:

Doris at Six

"The house was a small, worn – looking one set back from the road, out in the country from a tiny hamlet in eastern Oregon, where our family had moved when I was 6 years old.

"Several vivid memories remain with me from the few months we spent in that remote place. The warmth of kerosene lamplight left a pleasant memory – the bitter cold of tramping through the snow in the dark to use the 'outdoor toilet' was not so pleasant.

"Bath-time on Saturday nights meant clearing out the kitchen of all except the child to be bathed and the parent; water was heated on the wood cooking stove, and a galvanized tub set in the middle of the kitchen. There was no running water; water was pumped up from a well.

"Homework was also done at the kitchen by my brother, a second-grader, while I spent the time writing numbers and letters, anticipating my entrance into first-grade that fall.

"This activity eventually earned me a special spot in my first-grade class when, on the first day of school, the teacher sent the new 1st-graders to the board with the instructions, 'Write all the numbers you know.' Many minutes later as I was left alone at the board, continuing to follow her orders, and proceeding to write higher and higher numbers, she finally suggested that I take my seat.

"I can still remember my anxiety when she called us in

a circle in the front of the room to begin our first reading lesson. I could not read, and didn't know what would happen when she called on me to read the unknown words from the primer. But lucky me, I was near the end of the line, and by the time my turn came, I proudly 'read' the sentences I'd heard the others repeat over and over. (To digress: I later became a reading teacher, and this keen memory of my first reading lesson helped me understand how scared most little kids are when they start school.)

"Another memory, a pleasant one, is of my father pulling us on a sled down the snowy country road to school, on the days when we couldn't walk or go by car. That was great fun, and we looked forward to those days.

"Our tiny house was heated by two wood stoves. One, in which a fire burned through much of the night on the coldest nights, was located in the room adjacent to the bedroom where I slept with my sister. Flickering flames reflected on the wall terrified me because I thought the house was afire. My parents had quite a job convincing me that my fears were unfounded."

No Television

"When I was a child, there were no television sets, but we did have a movie theater in our little town. Every Saturday afternoon we went to see the latest chapter of a serialized short subject. Although I can't recall their titles, these serials specialized in suspense, and it was hard for us to wait out the week for the next Saturday's episode. Western movies were also favorites, but the musical extravaganzas and romances were popular, too, especially with the girls.

"Our beloved cowboy movies provided us with another favorite pastime, as we re-enacted the dramatic scenes. Using our skates as horses, we sped over sagebrush prairies and up rocky mountainsides to capture imaginary cattle rustlers and bank robbers.

"Radio serials, like the Green Hornet and Jack Armstrong, provided excitement and entertained us through long winter evenings. Our imaginations provided the vivid pictures we needed to visualize the actions of these heroes.

"Most of the programs which appealed to children offered 'premiums' for which we saved coupons and box tops. 'Little Orphan Annie' promised to mail you a special trick ring for an emblem from an Ovaltine can, but to our disappointment, our mother staunchly refused to buy Ovaltine for us. My best friend was luckier – she got the ring, but then, she had to drink the Ovaltine. When I finally tasted it, I could hardly believe how bad it was, and perhaps that was my first lesson in understanding how deceptive advertising can be!"

Visiting My Grandparents

"Once a year our family was loaded into the car for our annual trip to our grandparents' home, some 300 miles away. 'Going to the Farm' was something we kids anticipated all through the year.

"Grandma was famous for her fried chicken. One day she invited me to accompany her to the chicken yard. As I watched her capture an unsuspecting victim, skillfully chop off her head and carry her back to the porch to be prepared for the frying pan, I felt a little sick to my stomach. However, an hour later hunger and the delicious smell of the brown crunchy chicken overpowered my earlier queasiness as I joined the family in a feast.

"I never could believe that Grandma could turn out delicious bread, rolls and pies from a woodstove with no thermostat or controls. Somehow she knew just how many sticks of wood it took to keep the oven at the right temperature.

"She never used measuring cups and spoons – her eyes and the 'feel' of the dough guided her turn out perfect products every time.

"Dinner was always at noon because breakfast was early on the farm, and hearty appetites came from lots of hard work accomplished before noon.

"Grandpa was up before it was light; milking the cows and separating the cream into large cans for the trip by horse and wagon to the creamery in town. When we kids were younger, we popped out of bed quickly every morning to accompany Grandpa to town. The excitement we felt during those years dimmed as we became teenagers and preferred sleep to the wagon rides we'd previously enjoyed. I think Grandpa was disappointed in us, tho he never said so.

"Grandpa never did say much, but he did what he wanted to even tho' Grandma tried hard to boss him around. As he got older he used his hearing as an excuse and a protection against her attempted dominance and verbal rejoinders. Yet somehow, he'd miraculously recover his hearing when someone across the room was discussing a topic of interest to him.

"Grandpa always kept a car in the barn, but he rarely drove it except to church on Sunday. We were allowed to sit in it and pretend/drive as it sat regally in its appointed spot in the barn. But of course we had to be careful how we treated it. We'd have been in real trouble if we fooled around or scratched up the paint."

Finishing College

"When I was finishing college, I had no definite idea about what I wanted to do as a lifer-work. Having majored in psychology no ready-made job classification arose to attract me.

"One thing I did know for certain: I was determined not to settle down, at least not right away, in one of the few larger cities in the state (Oregon), as most of my fellow students were planning to do. I knew, for sure, that I wanted to see more of the world and enlarge my horizons of experience beyond the provincial boundaries of my home state.

"It was scary, but I went ahead to search for an opening that would help me to 'get out'. It came in a bulletin board ad for a YMCA student program in New York for the summer following my graduation. I packed up, and wearing a wool suit that had been comfortable in cool western Oregon, and a 3-days/3-nights trip by train (chair car, of course), descended on New York in mid-June. My discomfort in my in- appropriate clothing for the 90° heat, combined with the noisy hustle of a city much larger than I'd ever imagined, made me wonder what I was doing there. After all, I really was a country girl, having spent all my childhood years to the age of 15 in tiny towns in eastern Oregon.

"Never had I seen so many people in one place before! The streets teemed with bodies; walking, sitting in front of buildings, fanning themselves. Everywhere people! Busses were packed, subways jammed, sidewalks almost impassable. It was confusing to me, yet unbelievably exciting. Here I was: in that city of cities that I'd read about, heard about, dreamed about.

"I'd hardly ever met anyone truly different from me. Oh, I'd met a few Negroes, a few Jews, some Catholics, but only in passing. My life experience had only included white Protestants - and there I was, suddenly immersed in a city of people from everywhere.

"My roommate in the settlement house where we lived was a Jewish girl from New Jersey with a distinct accent. A close friendship developed with a black girl in our group who took me home with her to White Plains and, for the first time in my life, I became a minority and experienced the feelings of isolation that go with that.

"The settlement was located on the lower east side of New York in a neighborhood of tenements, so I was confronted with a level of life I'd only read about before.

Marriage

We were married on December 19, 1953, not too much more than six months after we met. The ceremony was performed in the church chapel at Madison Avenue Church (as we called it). A young staff minister, Victor Baer, performed the ceremony assisted by the Reverend Arthur Jones, Doris' father.

At that time Doris' father, a widower had remarried. He was living in a trailer on his new wife's (Pauline Fouts) family farm in Indiana. It is notable that at our first meeting, some months before the marriage, he pronounced me "acceptable" as a potential husband for Doris because I was "well spoken, had a job and appeared to have good prospects."

Arthur Jones was then about 60 and, what you might call "a serious type." He was a small town minister, originally from the Chicago area, with roots in Oregon where he moved his family when Doris was two.

Luckily, as it turned out, Doris was born in a big Chicago hospital. They were quickly able to break and reset the club foot with which she had been born. This operation would not have been possible in 1923 either at home or in a small rural hospital in Oregon.

Arthur was very impressed by the Madison Avenue Presbyterian Church, which was one of the premier churches in New York City. The lead minister was the nationally known George Buttrick, who was a co-author of the Interpreter's Bible among other writings.

Because Doris was an employee we got a special priced reception in the church school's main lobby. There was a large wedding cake and the reception for about two hundred people was completely documented in black and white candid photographs by Doris' then roommate, Bethli Durst. Bethli was a Swiss girl who also was in New York to "see the world." Bethli worked as an economist for Standard and Poor's.

In addition to Doris' father, Arthur, the reception was attended by my mother, Albina, step father Charlie and many family friends from the Yorkville neighborhood, many of my boyhood friends and, of course, almost the entire 20-30 club membership which numbered about fifty or sixty.

Immediately after the wedding we took off for a honeymoon in Florida. We drove south on Route 1 through New Jersey spending our wedding night at the Swan Motel in Linden, NJ. (Many years later, as New Jersey residents we often passed the Swan on our way to and from an evening in New York City.)

A minor disaster overtook us on the outskirts of New Bern, North Carolina. As we were making a downhill turn, flashing red lights flashed in my rear-view mirror. We were reportedly doing 80 and the arresting officer led us into town where we were taken for $90.00, a princely sum at that time. As we left the courthouse, the arresting officer, sort of apologized and let on that we were caught in a speed trap. We decided to put the matter out of our minds and continued on our way south. Since that encounter, maybe unfairly, New Bern has been my most un-favorite town.

In Florida we had an uneventfully, pleasant time, winding up at Doris' brother's house on an Air Force base somewhere in north Florida. Don, her older brother, was an Air Force pilot who after the war decided to make his career in the Air Force. He had a beautiful wife and three even more beautiful daughters. Unfortunately, Don inherited the wrong family genes and died of a heart attack and stroke at the early age of 56 as a retired Lieutenant Colonel. (Doris' and Don's mother, Violet, died many years earlier of a heart attack or stroke.)

Getting the First House

Doris and I made our first home in the Woodside section of Queens, New York. The apartment, pleasant enough, was in an attached two family house where I had been a tenant for about a year, sharing the rent with two other boys. The other tenants moved out and Doris moved in. The landlord was an elderly widower named Hughie Wilson, who loaned us his car for our honeymoon trip to Florida. His primary claim to fame was that he was entrusted with an important message that he carried through enemy lines in France during World War I.

In that apartment we made plans for the future, which included the almost divorce-provoking exercise of teaching Doris to drive a stick shift car. I commuted to my job as a credit analyst at the Chase Manhattan Bank by subway and Doris finished up her job as a pre-school teacher at the Madison Avenue Presbyterian Church in Manhattan. We also decided to start a family and buy a house.

Noticing that my Woodside landlord had supplemented his income by renting the apartment in his house, we looked for a similar situation and we found it in Elmhurst (also in the borough of Queens in New York City). We soon bought a nice house town house (row house to be exact), a half hour commute to Manhattan where I then worked.

Noteworthy about our first house is the fact that we had a tenant who occupied the lower floor of the house. Our mortgage payment was $60 a month and, conveniently, the tenant paid us $60 a month rent. The house cost us $14,000, which in 1997 dollars would be about $140,000, and the rent and mortgage payment can also be multiplied by a factor of ten. My salary as a so-called college trainee was then about $3,000 a year.

Since I was taking some real estate courses at NYU at the time, and financing through my employer was readily available I got the idea that I, that is, we, should buy up the houses on one block as they came on the market and rent them. (1955 was a tight housing market with not too many rentals available. If we continued along this line for a number of years, so I calculated, we would soon build a real estate empire.

There was only one problem.

Since I commuted into New York daily, Doris would have to collect the rents, call the plumber as needed and otherwise deal with the tenants. This plan, unfortunately, was not going to work as Doris had no business background. She soon got into a squabble with our tenant as to who had first rights to the washing machine which we shared with the tenant.

Thus, my grand entrepreneurial plan went up in smoke. (Those row houses became very valuable as the boomer generation arrived in force and being near a subway to New York, they became even more desirable). But never mind, it did not wreck our marriage as we started having children and I soon left the Chase Manhattan Bank to join a fast-growing suburban bank on Long Island.

Expanding the Family – Betsy Arrives

The most important event involving the Elmhurst house was the arrival of our first baby, Betsy, at the Flower Fifth Avenue Hospital (on the corner of Fifth Avenue and 105th Street in Manhattan, NY). She was born without a hitch somewhere in the evening of March 1st 1955, after an uneventful nine month pregnancy; not a premature birth as a first born child often is.

Since my office was an hour away from our house, I had made arrangements for a neighbor to drive Doris into the hospital in the event that she went into labor. Around noon I was sitting at my desk scribbling some numbers and ratios when I got a call from my neighbor that nature was calling and that they were about to start the drive into the city.

I looked at my watch and pretty much knew how long it would take and the fact that I could get to the hospital in about twenty minutes. So I put the papers I had been working on into a cabinet, put on my hat and coat and breezily told my co-workers that I was on my way to have a baby. Upon returning to the office, after a pre-arranged week off I was surprised that the young women at the office expressed amazement on my cavalier attitude. They had expected me, as a first-time expectant father to be in a frazzle like new fathers are in the movies. I patiently explained to them that I had calculated the timing, had notified the hospital that she was on her way and got to the hospital a good half hour before Doris arrived.

My Job at the Meadow Brook National Bank

Back at Chase Manhattan Bank and competing with other young men with their Ivy League pedigrees, football player physiques and social connections, I was not exactly a star player, but I had better than average writing skills. After a couple of months I found that some of my analytical memos had been retyped over the signatures of several of the junior officers. At the bank, as in the Army, it is difficult, if not impossible, for a corporal to complain that a lieutenant is taking credit for his work. So, what to do? Not being the most patient of people, and having developed some pretty good job interview techniques, I sold my five years of Chase training and experience (coming from the Chase had a high cachet in those days).

With growing responsibilities and still a bank salary of only $100 a week I started looking around for greener pastures. In 1955 I went to work for a fast growing suburban bank on Long Island – the Meadow Brook National Bank (long since merged out of existence).

The president of my new bank was also a Chase graduate, some twenty years my senior. His name was Walter Van der Waag. Within a year I was made an officer of the Meadow Brook National Bank and was functioning as credit manager and junior commercial loan officer. My direct boss there was Ben Peticolas, Executive Vice President, a very competent banker. Unfortunately he was a member of a religious sect that did not believe in medication - he had untreated high blood pressure and died of a stroke at 49.

Meadow Brook had been put together in the early 1950s by way of some twenty mergers, and part of my job was to convey and interpret the president's directives to the thirty branch managers, most of whom were former presidents of small community banks. I also was the president's and executive vice president's assistant and took on customer relations duties and some lending and administrative functions for the 30 branch system. At this job, I learned a lot about how to run a bank because I was given a lot of responsibility and had access to the top people.

At Home on Long Island – Alan Arrives

So I started commuting east to West Hempstead Long Island instead of to New York and it made sense for us to look for an unattached house and bigger back yard nearer my work. In addition, at that time, one could get a lot more house for the money further out on the island.

By 1956, Doris, Betsy and I had moved to our second house. Doris was greatly relieved, because she did not get along with our tenant in Elmhurst. Now we did not have to share a washing machine. We found a nice little Cape Cod in Bellmore, just a few miles from my office. The house was on the south shore of Long Island about an hour's drive from New York City. The new bank was only fifteen minutes from home and convenient to our house. I was now solidly ensconced as Assistant Manager of the Bank's credit department.

After we moved to our new house, Doris and I decided that it was time to provide Betsy with a brother or sister. As was the case earlier, we had no trouble conceiving and, pretty soon Doris was suitably pregnant. We used the services of the same doctor who had brought Betsy into the world and, again, like clockwork we timed it right and drove into Manhattan for an uneventful birth – the best kind there is. Alan, our son, was born on September 26, 1956.

As I remember it, this time my mother came up from Florida and helped Doris and Betsy in their new roles. Naturally, since Betsy was being pushed out of her royal princess position, she did get a little antsy at times in showing her resentment at this new strange being over whom everyone now oohed and aahed.

Leaving Meadowbrook

I could have stayed at the Long Island bank forever, but my prior experience in New York got me to thinking, sometimes a bad habit, and I became convinced that if I didn't put myself on the line now and then, my chances of advancement would be limited. I wasn't about to take needless, senseless, uncalculated risks like running with bulls in Spain or trying to swim the English Channel, but I was restless. I came to firmly believe, and still believe, that one has to learn how to live on the edge and enjoy the element of risk and a certain kind of danger. What is it? - The thrill of victory and the agony of defeat.

In making my career plans, I discovered that most bank presidents got to that exalted position by first being commercial loan officers and I developed what some people thought was a quaint notion: that I too could someday be a bank president. Therefore, to get on the path I wanted, I had to become a Loan Officer instead of a leg man for others. Not being blessed with too much patience, around 1959 I started by talking to people and through my network at the Chase, I was put in contact with several large banks in California.

So, after five years at Meadow Brook, and since I had not burned my bridges at Chase, I had someone there put me in touch with the Executive Vice President of a large California bank which was growing rapidly and patterning itself on The Chase. I could well have stayed on Long Island, but I thought that I wanted to play in the big leagues and California's sunny climate and rapidly growing economy were irresistible. Doris went along with my thinking. This, I thought was an intelligent calculated risk and, I figured my new mentor would have a vested interest in me. I was only 32 and I planned to become an officer in a major west coast bank. In those days, it usually took college graduates ten to fifteen years to attain "officer" status in the big New York banks.

Going to California – Julie Arrives

So, in the spring of 1959 we sold the Bellmore house, packed up the car and I drove to Los Angeles while Doris flew out a few days later with Betsy and Alan to meet me. With Doris and our two children in tow, I got into a phone booth to call the Executive Vice President, Darwin Holway, to let him know that I had arrived. The telephone operator said, "Mr. Holway is no longer with us." When I heard this, I stood there for a couple of minutes, feeling as if an eight hundred pound gorilla had punched me in the stomach. After examining my options and pulling my thoughts together, I called the personnel department vice president who assured me that my job was secure. Sure, secure, but I had lost my mentor. I thought of Robert Burns who wrote: "*The best-laid schemes o' mice and men gang aft a-gley.*"

California Bank, as it was then called, paid for our move west and our first stop was a motel in San Gabriel, a Los Angeles suburb.

That motel became famous in our family lore because it was there that Alan, then three, turned on the spigots of the bathroom sink. Workmen were repairing the plumbing system and turned off the water without notifying anyone. Unbeknownst to Doris and me, Alan left the spigots in open position and we all went out to a park. When we returned, three hours later, the place was in turmoil because the plumbers had turned on the water in our absence and the motel room flooded. Of course, it was not Alan's fault but the motel owner tried to sue us. I reported my problem to the bank's legal counsel and with a couple of phone calls from him the problem was resolved. I didn't ask for details.

Some of the people at the new bank advised me to look for a house in the more genteel east side of Los Angeles and we soon found a nice house in the "executive section" of Arcadia which is a bedroom community about fifteen miles east of downtown Los Angeles. After the cold, damp climate of Long Island, Arcadia with its lush vegetation seemed like heaven. After an extended indoctrination period at the bank's main office I was assigned to a large branch in Hollywood because management figured that my New York experience would be useful in the fast paced hustle and bustle of west Los Angeles.

They were right, but living in Arcadia subjected me to an hour and fifteen minute twice daily commute. Not only that, but we found out that the reason the houses in Arcadia were relatively inexpensive was because that's where the smog settled each afternoon. Nevertheless, we loved Arcadia and made good friends there.

As the saying goes, we weren't getting any younger and after a couple of years decided to go for it. We didn't drive into Los Angeles but had Julie delivered in Arcadia. As in the prior two births, Julie's arrival came off on schedule, on December l, 1960. My mother and a neighbor helped us get through the postpartum flurry of sleepless nights (mostly Doris'). This neighbor had about five kids of her own and was well experienced in helping our little brood. I was then commuting from Arcadia, which was East of Los Angeles, to Hollywood, which is to the West side of the city. As in the past, my bosses were very tolerant in giving me a couple of weeks off and my co-workers helped me celebrate.

A California Curveball

I started at California Bank with no complications, but just as soon as I could take a day off, I flew up to San Francisco, where Darwin Holway was now the president of another large bank. I asked if he would take me up there.

But no, the two banks had close relations and he said it would not be politic for him to "steal me". He urged me to stay at the bank in Los Angeles, and counseled that "things would work out." Little did I know that there were some big mergers in the making. The job at the Los Angeles bank was okay, but not great; I had given up my official title and was just another one of the East Coast recruits. Fate had thrown me a curve ball. I had put my family through a lot of trouble, and I didn't feel too smart. The bank had 140 branches and was building more. I found myself sitting in a branch manager pool. That reminded me that Theodore Roosevelt once wrote: "The credit belongs to the man who is actually in the arena, who errs and comes up short again and again, because there is no effort without error and shortcomings. Who at the best knows in the end the high achievement of triumph and who at worst, if he fails while daring, knows his place shall never be with those timid souls who know neither victory nor defeat." In those days, and for most of my life, I was a self-improvement book addict: Aphorisms, the power of positive thinking, helped keep my mind focused.

After three years at California Bank, a move to a house on the west side of Los Angeles, and a promotion to Assistant Vice President, that bank formed a holding company which included the San Francisco bank where my hoped for mentor, Darwin Holway, was president.

He moved his office to Los Angeles and arranged for my transfer from a West Los Angeles branch to the Los Angeles Main office of his bank, called First Western Bank. So, now I was on the fast track, a loan officer in the main office of a major bank. Then things started to work out, just as Holway had promised, with my getting increasingly more responsibility. Until my friend was suddenly – retired. He was not yet 60 and I think "fired" would be a more accurate description, because powerful financial interests took over the holding company and wanted to put in their own management team (eventually, all the banks in the holding company were put together under the name First Interstate Bank which had subsidiary banks in some fifteen western states). I was coming up short again, and my hope of a vice presidency of a major bank was fading.

Subsequently, I was transferred to another office on Wilshire Boulevard in west L.A. and was promoted to Assistant Vice President. Since it was pretty clear that my future seemed to be on the west side of Los Angeles, and with the constant reminder of the smog in Arcadia, we found a suitable house in the Baldwin Hills section of L.A.

In Baldwin Hills we lived on Cochran Avenue in a predominantly Jewish business/professional neighborhood. By now our housing pattern was pretty clear. We moved in tandem with the ebb and flow of my banking career, and this pattern was to continue. In Baldwin Hills we lived on a secondary hill about two miles from a big hill which was crowned by a large earthen dam. The dam became very important in our lives.

Somewhere around 1963 the dam burst, causing a cascade of water which brought down some twenty or thirty houses. The water made a furniture-filled river out of Rodeo Road and surrounded our house on all four sides. We escaped the flood unscathed but there were a few scary hours when we piled our kids and the neighbors' kids in our car in preparation for a quick trek to higher ground.

After a merger of California Bank with First Western Bank and a spinoff of part of the merged bank into the newly named First Western Bank, I worked out a transfer to the downtown main office of the new bank on the theory that it's better to be working at the main office than at a branch.

A Finale in the Silverlake District

After three years at California Bank (which after a merger became the United California Bank) I was approached by a group of investors who wanted to start up a *de novo* bank in downtown L.A. I was Senior Vice President, Senior Loan Officer and a member of the Board at the new Silverlake National Bank.

With the several moves I had already made, my career was starting to take on an entrepreneurial patina. My business philosophy started to be: "Win or lose, be in the ring where the action is, make decisions, take the calculated risk!" With the help of Darwin Holway, who wrote a flattering letter on my behalf to the Controller of the Currency in Washington, I left the bank to help start a brand new bank in downtown Los Angeles – Silverlake National.

I was Senior Vice President, Senior Loan Officer and a member of the Board of Directors and I worked hard trying to get the new bank off the ground. There were a million things to do and everything had to be done "Yesterday". I expected to become president in a year or two. I had to do all of the organizing work and a group of Hollywood people put up the money. The start-up work was tough, but it was what I wanted! This job sounded like my dream come true. I was only 36 and was on my way! Was there risk? Yes, starting a new organization is always risky.

Fast forward six months. I was working hard, stealing accounts from the large established banks in town. With the help of Jim Garner, an actor who was a Board member, and some others, we were getting a lot of Hollywood big names as depositors. The president who was mentally "over the hill," was hired for one year because his reputation as a former bank president in Pennsylvania was helpful in getting the charter. Ray Talbert, was in poor health and was coasting waiting for Social Security and his pension from Pittsburgh to kick in so the future was mine.

Then fate intervened to make my life difficult again. The board chairman, a supposedly prosperous Beverly Hills builder, dropped dead with a heart attack at 50. That alone would not have derailed the bank but it was quickly discovered that his estate was insolvent and that he had filed false financial statements with the government to get the bank charter. A number of the Board members, it turned out, were "straw men"; local businessmen who had borrowed money to buy their required shares in the bank and had a secret deal with the chairman to sell their shares to him at a nice profit. In quick order, the board members panicked; sold the bank to a large chain bank and I was fired. Just like that! In this turn of events, all the fine quotes from Theodore Roosevelt couldn't help me.

It was 1965 and I was persona non grata at the large banks in Los Angeles because, as noted, I had been rather aggressive in soliciting their accounts. But in the meantime I had three children, a wife and a mortgage to support.

I took an interim job as Investment Specialist for the City of Los Angeles, handling their day to day cash flow. Because of my veteran status, which added 10% to the score, I got 105% on the civil service test. This job paid well enough and was secure, but the work was boring. I was not cut out for working for the City and wanted to get back into banking. I was becoming a battle scarred veteran of the banking industry. I had to find a way to land on my feet.

While working for the City of Los Angeles, I spent my evenings and weekends sending out resumes and flying around the country, being almost hired several times until the prospective new employers checked me out. My reputation was tarnished by my connection with a failed bank. I put an advertisement in a banking newspaper and received thirty replies; fifteen of them were from the State of New Jersey.

LIFE IN NEW JERSEY

The Highland Park Years

In the spring of 1966, as a result of the situation wanted ads I had placed in the "American Banker," and after many false starts, I met Gene Parker; a Harvard trained banker/lawyer who was chief cook and bottle washer to Emlen Roosevelt (a grand nephew of Theodore Roosevelt and cousin to Franklin D). Roosevelt was running a family owned bank in central New Jersey. Gene answered my "American Banker" advertisement and we met for lunch during one of his business trips to Los Angeles. Gene Parker was also an alumnus of The Chase and I frankly disclosed my bad experience with the Silverlake bank. We got along well.

Parker recommended me to Roosevelt who flew me to New Jersey for a weekend in May at his suburban mansion. We drank scotch together, discussed banking, philosophy and history; he showed me family artifacts. More important he offered me a job with his organization. With precious little bargaining power, I took a big cut in pay to be a branch manager for the National State Bank in a small town named Highland Park, New Jersey, one hour's drive south and slightly west of New York City.

I had to be in New Jersey in 30 days, so that left the responsibility for Doris, with our three children, to sell the house in Los Angeles, pack up, and get to New Jersey. I stopped off at the farm at Deer Creek, Indiana to visit Doris' parents during my drive of the family chariot east.

While I was looking for a house in New Jersey, Gene Parker's wife, Jane, offered to let me to stay at their large house for a few days. The few days stretched into two months and the Parkers treated me like family. They made a tough transition easy and offered their friendship. Janie and Gene are still among Doris' and my closest friends and we cherish the close relationship that developed between us.

In the summer of 1966, three months later, amidst a monumental airline strike, Doris and the children made the journey east with a lot of luggage, on a train, which was dusted off for the occasion. On their way east, Doris and the children detoured first to Seattle to see Doris' sister and family, next to several other points in Oregon, and then across country to Deer Creek, Indiana, where they spent a week with Doris' parents. In September my parents visited from Florida for a week so the children had the rare pleasure of seeing both sets of grandparents the same year.

Working with Roosevelt

Roosevelt, it turned out, was not the captain of industry I had expected but was a nice man with superb credentials, who had dropped out of Princeton and traded on his family name while running his family owned bank in a profitable but unspectacular manner. I liked Emlen, who, although tall and possessed of the Rooseveltian good looks, was actually somewhat shy and retiring. When Roosevelt took vacations, he used an alias: Mr. E. Rose of Bedminster, New Jersey. I ascribed his standoffishness to his protected upbringing and the fact that many people treated him like some kind of royalty. He held weekly branch managers' meetings and all but the most senior of his employees called him "Mr. Roosevelt".

After a couple of months, to differentiate myself from the

herd, I started calling him by his first name. To Roosevelt's credit, he didn't mind at all, and my peers thought I had some kind of special relationship with him; he became something close to a friend. In due course, I learned that "the family" had put him into the bank because they thought it would be a safe place for him. And it was not until later that a wave of bank mergers swept him into retirement in Bay Head, New Jersey.

I worked at the National State Bank in Highland Park for almost five years and was one of the more productive bank managers. Each year I got a plaque celebrating my business development prowess, but when it came to pay increases, Emlen was not very forthcoming. Over the years, he had lost some of his best branch managers, several of whom went on to become bank presidents, because, in his mind working for a Roosevelt was apparently pay enough. He figured that his name could always attract new employees, as it did me, and for a long time, he was right. He prided himself on paying his executives less than what other banks had to pay and he never tired of pointing out that his personnel expenses were lower than those of most banks. After the disaster in California, however, I was happy enough to find a hospitable place in which to relocate my family and start rebuilding my career and life.

An Entrepreneur Arises

During our stay in Highland Park, I became friendly with a group of men in town who were putting together a group to buy a small shopping center. The down payment was $100,000 so they asked ten men to put up $10,000 each. I came up with $10,000, which was a pretty good chunk of money in those days, and became a member of a partnership called the Park Ten Company. Compared to my prior jobs, my duties at National State Bank were not too challenging and I had plenty of time to pursue other interests. The real estate group consisted of two builders, a commercial realtor (who was also mayor of Highland Park), a lawyer, a dentist, a CPA, and several businessmen. My new partners were very well connected and knew their way around New Jersey. Not incidentally, they referred a lot of new business to me at the bank. That initial real estate investment grew as properties were improved, traded and sold with the group reinvesting in other properties and office buildings in succeeding years. In addition to contributing some money, I participated in the management of the various properties and learned more about real estate than I could ever have learned by limiting myself to the lending side of banking. As it would have been unlawful for me to make loans to the group from the bank in which I worked I became the point man for them in obtaining loans at other local banks. All the while I was enlarging my contacts in the New Jersey banking arena.

Of the forty seven branch managers at the National State Bank, I was apparently one of the few who became a part time entrepreneur. To his credit, Emlen Roosevelt looked kindly upon my efforts to be more than "just a bank employee" and later even loaned me money for a real estate investment. Back when I made that first $10,000 investment I was taking quite a risk because I had little beyond a down payment for our house and I didn't know my future partners very well. Several of my partners later told me that they really hadn't expected me to become an investor with them.

I discovered that you have to make irrevocable decisions based on incomplete facts in personal investing, much like I was lending money on behalf of the bank. Things could have gone wrong. The men with whom I invested could have been scoundrels, but they weren't. They helped me build financial assets which later became my unofficial pension plan. Doris took a job teaching school in Highland Park, became active in the community and our children gradually became easterners.

Life in Highland Park

In August we bought a split level house at 418 S. Fourth Avenue, Highland Park and because we couldn't sell our old house in Los Angeles, for a few months we were the proud owners of a house on each coast. While the Los Angeles house stood empty it was attended to by a gardener and the inevitable friendly realtor.

Betsy (11), Alan (10) and Julie (6) adjusted very well to Highland Park and each developed a coterie of friends. The children were absorbing all manner of middle-class suburban standards. As a further means of assuring a smooth transition for them, in August we acquired a young beagle. The pet was from Irene and Hilton Lee, longtime friends from our New York 20-30 Club days. This was the first dog for our children and they were just thrilled for a while. We parents, however, had never been quite as thrilled. Once they got tired of the dog we thankfully returned it to Irene and Hilt who were happy to have it back.

For all of us, this was the first time we've lived in a "town" and the experience was very pleasant. There were 15,000 people in the town at the time, no industry to speak of, a high tax rate, good school system, hardly any new houses and no open land areas. Houses didn't change hands too often in Highland Park and most of the people one met had been around for a while.

Highland Park is 50 miles from New York City and just across the Raritan River from New Brunswick, the county seat and the home of Rutgers University. The University was a magnet for a rich variety of social and cultural activity in which we joyfully participated.

Because of my position as head of the only commercial bank in Highland Park, we were rapidly assimilated into the stream of political, business and social life (for a night out, however, Manhattan was still the place to go). When we left New York and moved to California, we were pleased because we "were there for life." Now we had found a comfortable home in Highland Park and we were pleased because we felt we were there for life. Making new friends and getting reacquainted with many old friends in New York and New Jersey made our lives interesting.

Doris began taking courses at the local university, doing good works, and working part-time as a reading teacher in an elementary school. She progressed in the outside world to teaching remedial reading three hours a day, taking courses, and putting in time with the PTA, church, and League of Women Voters.

During my years in Highland Park we completed an expansion of the physical facilities at the local bank. For exercise I walked a lot and continued reading on a wide variety of subjects – scientific, religious and otherwise. I served on several charitable and civic boards and became chairman of the United Fund Drive.

A Bank President

I could well have stayed in Highland Park where I had a secure position, but I wanted to be a Bank President and had to take the risk of moving to yet another job. My career challenges toward becoming a bank president gave me a large pond in which to swim. Using my well-honed entrepreneurial skills, I was soon in the corner office with my own private parking spot.

The Immigrants' Son, An American Story

The job became available to me, as follows:

Around 1970, having established myself in central New Jersey banking circles, I had a customer who operated a financial personnel service (a head hunter). Through him I found the small bank in Raritan, which had hired him to find a chief executive. The State Bank of Raritan Valley needed a president for its three branch system. With Emlen Roosevelt's backing and strong recommendation, I was soon running the small suburban bank and getting paid enough to move my family into a bigger house in Somerville which was contiguous to Raritan and some twelve miles west of Highland Park.

The Board of Directors of the State Bank of Raritan Valley had made our moving to the immediate area a condition of the new position and, after some months of commuting from Highland Park we moved into Somerville, to a green colonial house at 179 Middaugh Street, Somerville. We enjoyed our big house in Somerville with its four bedrooms, heated garage and large, well landscaped lot. Surprisingly, it was socially acceptable for me to continue mowing my own lawn – a point of pride for the local gentry.

Doris kept her job as a reading specialist in the Highland Park school system – a wise decision as the perusal of future events will reveal. Doris had a 13 mile commute to Highland Park where she ran a training center in an elementary school. I had a quick five-minute drive to the neighboring town of Raritan.

1970 to 1974 were the years when all of the children became freshmen at different schools. Betsy entered the U. of Wisconsin in Madison. Alan enrolled in Connecticut College in New London. Julie was at Somerville High School, soon to enter Vassar in Poughkeepsie, New York.

More Historical Perspective – The Prague Spring

The high drama of the Cold War (often dated 1947–1991) assigned Czechoslovakia nothing more than a supporting role; a spear carrying puppet for the Soviet Union. The superpowers, USA and the USSR had nuclear weapons, so the Cold War was fought in the economic and propaganda trenches.

In July 1947 Stalin ordered his puppet states to sever economic ties with Western Europe. Instead of being a democracy, Czechoslovakia was one of the five Central European Russian satellite states.

As I mentioned at an earlier stage, the newly formed nation of Czechoslovakia now fell into a 'malaise', but that discomfort became apparent only gradually and most sharply after the Prague Spring of 1968. Then the decline was more abrupt and became all consuming.

In February 1948, when the Communists took power, Czechoslovakia was declared a "people's democracy" and launched its first step toward socialism and, ultimately, communism.

Periods of high tension mixed with cycles of relative calm swirled around Czechoslovakia; none of which the puppet state could control or greatly impact. Over the next twenty years the world struggled through the Berlin Blockade (1948–1949), the Korean War (1950–1953), the Suez Crisis (1956), the Berlin Crisis of 1961, the Cuban Missile Crisis (1962), the Vietnam War (1959–1975), the Yom Kippur War (1973). Any greater detail recounting my past would not be germane to this memoir.

Independent thinking was crushed.

Even while their 1960 Constitution was declaring victory for socialism and proclaiming the Czechoslovak

Socialist Republic, the Czechoslovak economy began to 'tank'. The industrial growth rate became the lowest in Eastern Europe. As a result, in 1965, the party reformers introduced some free market elements into the economy. Democratic centralism was redefined, placing a stronger emphasis on democracy.

Step by step, Alexander Dubček, the party secretary and a liberal communist, carried out reforms in the direction of liberalism to give socialism "a human face". Censorship was lifted. The press, radio, and television were mobilized for reformist propaganda purposes. The movement to democratize socialism in Czechoslovakia, formerly confined largely to the party intelligentsia, acquired a new, popular dynamism in what became the Prague Spring of 1968. Public participation increased and the population gradually started to take interest in the government. Dubček became a truly popular national figure. This was a period of political liberalization in Czechoslovakia during the era of domination by the Soviet Union.

On August 20 the Prague Spring died when Moscow ordered thousands of Warsaw Pact troops and tanks to occupy the country. They met only passive resistance. Popular opposition was expressed in numerous spontaneous acts of nonviolent resistance.

A program of "normalization" entailing thoroughgoing political repression and the return to ideological conformity followed.

(1) A new purge cleansed the Czechoslovak leadership of all **reformist** elements. Top levels of government and the leadership of social organizations were purged.

(2) Publishing houses and film studios were placed under new direction. Censorship was strictly imposed, and a campaign of militant atheism

was organized. There was no longer a Prague Spring to inspire music and literature such as the work of Václav Havel, Karel Husa, Karel Kryl, and Milan Kundera's novel *The Unbearable Lightness of Being*. Organized protest was effectively stilled.

(3) (3) In May 1971, Czechoslovakia and the Soviet Union signed a treaty which incorporated the principle of "limited sovereignty." Soviet troops remained stationed in Czechoslovakia.

A large wave of emigration swept the nation. Several of the émigrés were kissing cousins who settled in Canada, and with whom I am still in touch.

While there were many non-violent protests in the country, there was no military resistance. Czechoslovakia remained occupied until 1990.

In contrast to all of the internal repression, the US and the USSR sought to ease strained relations, especially in a political situation. In 1971, both sides agreed on a period of Détente, a thawing at a period roughly in the middle of the Cold War.

Any visitors to the communist countries received a mixed message, since the thought of Détente was highly unusual to the communist mind. Doris and I saw this during our extensive tour of the communist countries in 1972, and even more so with our 1974 Czech trip. Both of these experiences we now describe in detail.

An Emotional Trip

Doris and I enjoyed numerous trips, mostly to Europe, during a period of about thirty years. We started these international travels in the summer of 1972. At that time,

Betsy (17), Alan (16) and Julie (12) were busily engaged in the teenage social life in Somerville, New Jersey.

Although this was the first trip of many; to me it was the most memorable, and the one that made the biggest emotional impact on me. This commercial tour was designed to take us through southern and eastern Europe.

We boarded a plane in New York and after the usual long flight, landed in Zagreb, in what was then Yugoslavia. Our one day stopover in a 1930s style luxury hotel was made delightful, by an excellent dinner accompanied with a romantic dance band, muted lights and a smooth red wine. (All of this opulence was provided in spite of the fact that Yugoslavia was a communist country, and the cold war was still raging.)

The next day we were bussed back to the Zagreb airport. Along with thirty fellow American tourists, we were unceremoniously ushered into a large departure hall. While we were waiting in line to board, we noticed two short, swarthy and unshaven men carrying small black bags go past us. These were the pilots of our small, dirty two-engine per-war transport plane. Luckily our two-hour flight to Belgrade was uneventful.

Over the next few days we traveled in a grimy, but serviceable bus. (Everything in these communist countries was 'grimy'.) With local guides at all of our stops, our tour took us north to Budapest (in Hungary), then through Bratislava (the capital of Slovakia) and eventually to Krakow in Poland. We made a brief trip to Warsaw before our bus turned west toward East Germany.

Before leaving Poland we stopped at the infamous Auschwitz I concentration camp. The first stop is at the Auschwitz-Birkenau State Museum. It serves in part as a memorial to the 1,500,000 people killed here by the Nazis, during the four years of its existence. The 2.5 hour Museum tour included a documentary film about the history of concentration camps in Poland. (Later we saw the shower rooms at Mauthausen, near Munich, where people were gassed with a cyanide-based pesticide called Zyklon B.)

Our Polish lady tour guide wanted urgently to bypass Auschwitz II- Birkenau. Many of us in the tour group insisted on visiting the death camp. This was widely regarded as the most terrible Nazi extermination center of World War II. Whereas Auschwitz I was an administrative center, just 2 km away, Auschwitz II was designed strictly as a concentration camp, with gas chambers and crematoria. The history and facts of Auschwitz are extensively covered on the internet and in numerous books.

A shiver went down my spine as we entered through the entryway which was topped by the notorious inscription **"ARBEIT MACHT FREI"** (labor makes you free).

The entire killing camp was laid open for visitors to see and I was particularly struck by several images. First were the heaps of hair, eyeglasses, and false teeth from the victims gathered in piles and displayed behind glass for the entire world to see. Then there was another huge pile of luggage, still inscribed with the victims' names. Most of the names were Jewish.

We also saw the ovens in which the victims were incinerated. I gazed in shock and wonderment at the actual ovens, with the swinging iron doors which we were allowed to inspect in detail. I poked my head into one of the ovens, all the better to imagine the horror of it all.

For me, however, the most staggering sight was a seemingly innocent Christmas letter from one of the Nazi officers to his family back in Germany. The letter was displayed prominently under glass on a small table. Relying on my fairly good command of the Germany language, I've long remembered the gist of the letter which went something like this:

"Dear Gretchen and children,

I regret that I am so far away during this most holy of seasons. Please convey my very best of the Season to Aunt Lisa, Uncle Gerd and, of course, a great big hug for little Elisabeth and Gunther.

I have been very busy during the past several months carrying out the grand vision of our esteemed leader. Just last month we almost reached our goal of 1,000 units a day, recording 967. Major Helbig has promised us a grand dinner celebrating our achievement when we reach our goal. An additional oven has been ordered from Hamburg and will go online soon.

With best wishes for a blessed and joyful Christmas holiday, your loving husband and father of our dear children.

Heinz Guderian
Heil Hitler"

Seeing the actual letter displayed in what was the administrative office at Auschwitz produced in me a sadness in the realization of what killing machines we human beings are and how coldly and callously we can say, "It is not our fault, we were only following orders".

I use the word "we" in the preceding paragraph because I blame all humanity for the terrible crime of the Holocaust and regretfully it appears that the world has not changed too much. This is not to nullify the wonders produced by people active in the arts and sciences as well as the many, many wonderful people that I have had the privilege to know throughout my life.

After viewing the horrors of Auschwitz, we continued

our trip through the communist countries, traveling westward from Poland first to Dresden in Germany and then north to East Berlin.

I went through the famous "Checkpoint Charlie" to West Berlin and marched down "Unter den Linden". This was the infamous German boulevard where Hitler had his mass parades.

After we reached Vienna, our next stop, we left the tour group. Doris and I made our way to Prague and South Bohemia to see my Czech relatives, before we returned to the United States.

The Two Sides of Prague

While Alan worked at a summer job, the rest of us flew off to Czechoslovakia in July of 1974 and enjoyed a wonderful visit. The stewardesses on the Czech airline are about ten pounds heavier than the local product, but we soon discovered that their bulk is only reflective of the excellent food with which we were regaled by our hosts.

We arrived in Prague on July 8th with a scheduled departure on August 1st. Despite the recent tensions the Czech Travel Bureau was obviously delighted to be able to promote tourism and bring in hard currency to a depressed economy. Our American dollars were more welcome than we Americans were, at least to the petty officials.

Without going into too much detail, suffice it to say we thoroughly enjoyed the two weeks we spent visiting friends and relatives I had not seen since my extended furlough in 1945-46. Betsy was the designated camera operator, with considerable help from Julie. Neither they nor Doris spoke the language, so they all nodded and smiled a lot, while I used my rusty Czech to converse with all and sundry. We spent much of one week in Prague with relatives of my Aunt Stella Zoudlik.

Our rental car took us to a number of ancient castles, and more than a few ancestral villages; our feet took us up and down the pathways of the not always 'golden' in "Golden Prague." My command of Czech improved with usage and it was adequate enough to enable all of us to jump the communications gap. The girls were often bored while waiting for me to do my double-speak translation function.

A favorite picture of the Charles Bridge adorns my den

We walked our feet off visiting some of the key historic spots in Prague as well as a quaint night club reminiscent of American movie night clubs of the 1920s. Even though Praha – Prague to you – had by then been under Nazi occupation and a communist form of government virtually since 1938 its castle, national theatre, main squares, old town and other landmarks were breathtaking. Later, under a democratic government the city was totally renovated from a sort of 'middle ages' dinginess to the beautiful and sparkling tourist mecca it would become.

Our Prague adventure was punctuated by a singularly poignant incident that occurred on our very last day before our flight to New York and home. For some technical reason, our visa clearance expired one day before we had booked our flight home and we were directed to the Prague central police station to get our visas extended – seemingly a very simple matter. Remember Czechoslovakia was still a communist country and despite their wanting tourist income, the government officials were still suspicious of foreigners.

When we got to the police station we were sent down a dingy hallway (reminiscent of Vienna in the Orson Welles movie, '*The Third Man*'). Since I was the only Czech speaker in our little contingent, Doris and the girls were seated on a wooden bench in the hallway, and I was asked to go into an interview room. The door was closed behind me and I was suddenly alone in a windowless room with no furniture except for a small table and two chairs.

In about a minute a stern looking official who was holding our passports, came into the room; sitting down at one side of the table and motioning me to take the other chair.

He started out right to the point and said quite briskly: "Why are you in this country?"

"We're visiting relatives in Praha and other places in Bohemia," I replied, all in Czech of course.

After some further routine, but not particularly friendly questions, he came out with his main question: "How come you speak Czech, and why is it that you speak it almost like a native?" (I had encountered that same question in 1946, when I visited Czechoslovakia, while on my Army furlough.)

The Immigrants' Son, An American Story

Then I had to explain that my parents were immigrants to America of the World War I era; that I spoke the language from birth and also attended a Czech language and culture school in New York, after my regular American school classes. My interrogator did not write anything down but had more and more questions centered mostly on my rather deep knowledge of the Czech language and culture. He seemingly found it difficult to understand why I spoke Czech as well as I did.

The entire interview lasted about twenty minutes during which I was painfully aware that the interrogator (he did not try to be my friend) kept his hand firmly over our several passports. Finally, and without a smile or comment he slid the passports over to me and said, "You may go."

Doris, Betsy and Julie had spent the same twenty minutes sitting on a cold wooden bench in a half-lit dingy hallway (they were saving on electricity) wondering what was going on and if and when they would see me again. When I collected the passports, which were already stamped with the appropriate extension to our departure time, they greeted me with sighs of relief. I was pretty tense myself but I did not let on to Doris and the girls.

I just said, "OK, there's no problem." We hurried back to the hotel to pack for the trip home.

In October our family was enlarged by the addition of my Aunt Stella Zoudlik, my mother's next youngest sibling (there were five of them) and by then a childless widow. She moved up from Florida after having spent twenty of her almost eighty years there in retirement. She lived with us for over five years before her death at the age of 84. She and her pet cat, called Kitty of course, became a familiar sight in our living room as Aunt Stella sat reading and dreaming.

Returning a Favor

Several years before I took the job in Raritan, my friend, Gene Parker, got himself enmeshed in a bad loan situation which resulted in the loss of several million dollars for National State. Emlen Roosevelt, pressured by family and others of his bank directors, had no choice but to fire Gene, who then became president of a small bank in Florida.

With their children (all five later became professionals with multiple college degrees) in private schools, Jane Parker, a staunch New Englander, refused to relocate the family to Florida. Gene was running the Florida bank out of a motel room and family tension reigned supreme. At the same time as I was considering the job in Raritan I was also offered the presidency of a similar bank in Washington, New Jersey. After deciding on the Raritan position, I had a final meeting with the Board of the First National Bank in Washington and told them that I had a friend in Florida who wanted to return to New Jersey.

Shortly thereafter, they hired Gene Parker who was reunited with his family and went on to several significant successes. He merged the Washington, New Jersey bank into a bigger one and then merged the combined banks into what became First Union, the sixth largest bank in the United States. A few years older than I, Gene eventually retired from First union as a vice president. In a continuation of the nationwide bank merger frenzy First Union became Corestates, then Wachovia and in 2009 Wachovia became part of Wells Fargo (I wound up with a modest pension and an attractive medical benefit package as a Wells Fargo retiree).

A Friendship Renewed

When I joined the State Bank of Raritan Valley, my name came across the desk of Roger Wagner, the Banking Commissioner in New Jersey. Out of the blue, he called me and asked if I was the same George Trebat who was his roommate at Hamilton College in the Army Specialized Training Reserve Program. Frankly, after infantry training, going overseas for a year and then pursuing my education on the GI Bill, and the passage of thirty years, I had never connected his name with the Roger Wagner I had known for nine months in 1944. We renewed our friendship and, subsequently, this connection became very valuable because soon my banking career was to take another turn.

Not to get ahead of my story: at the Raritan bank the Board consisted of a group of retired squires, one a former Chase Manhattan Vice President; another a retired Vice President of the Federal Reserve Bank of New York, and the bank chairman, a then 76 year old former president of the Singer Company, a large industrial conglomerate that made the famous Singer sewing machine. The chairman, Wilfred Langille, was a tough, bantam sized, MIT trained engineer who had more than 10,000 employees making small motors for the Government during the Second World War. In my opinion, Langille and the other Board members looked upon the bank as sort of a club and didn't see what was happening around them. The bank's service area was growing rapidly but the bank was not expanding to meet the needs of the population; as a result, the New Jersey Banking Commissioner strongly recommended that they either sell the bank or hire a banking professional to run the sixty-some-odd employee organization. They enjoyed the prestige of being bank directors and didn't want to sell, so they settled on hiring me as president. They were hiring trouble both for me and themselves.

Based on my accumulated experience, I changed the bank's operating policy and we began opening the bank on Saturdays, an unheard of event in 1970. We started a business development program and invested the bank's deposits in business loans, instead of the safer, but less profitable, mostly mortgages and bonds. In the process I doubled the bank's earnings and size in two years, attracting many new customers and expanding the branch system. I was in a really nice position as president and Board member of the bank, with membership in a county club, active in the community as chairman of the United Fund Drive and treasurer of the YMCA. All of this and I was still only 43! That should have been enough to fuel a comfortable and productive lifestyle. Read on.

Everything was going well at the bank but I was rubbing some of the more conservative board members the wrong way because I was moving them along too fast in trying to bring the bank into the modem era. They gave me a set of golf clubs and expected me to be part of the country club crowd. But, that was not my style. The Board's average age was about 75 and their idea of a bank community activity was to take a booth at the Somerset County Fair and hand out a few flyers and balloons.

One of the Board members, however, was a man of a different stripe. His name was Edward Chandler. In about 1946, after having built landing strips for the Army during the war, Chandler, an engineer, started accumulating land in Somerset County with the idea of building an industrial park. He had the vision and foresight to foresee the future. He started by building garages, a modest enough business. When he started to buy land and build industrial buildings he went to the local banks to borrow money and was turned down by all of them.

Relying on money he had saved while working as a

contractor during the war, and using the down payments as he build garages, Chandler succeeded on his own financing. Eventually he built a large industrial park consisting of some fifty buildings; some almost as big as a football field. The park covered many acres straddling a main highway and was worth about a hundred million dollars (in 1970 dollars), and had no loans against it. He built this empire step-by-step without help from any of the local banks; who only offered him financing after he proved that he didn't need it.

Edward Chandler was financially successful because he had a lightning swift mind, fierce powers of concentration, an evil ruthlessness and a very high energy level. He was also 6 feet 4. His hobby was gambling, mostly in Las Vegas. When he gambled, he did not often lose. Due to his early experiences, he developed a special hatred for the people at The State Bank of Raritan Valley and vowed to someday own the bank. He knew how to bide his time.

The Raritan bank's Board members looked down on him. They invited him to be a director because he was, by far, the largest depositor in the bank and they wanted to keep his accounts. At the same time they let him know, in various ways, that he was not really one of them.

By the 1960s he was very rich and accepted the cynically proffered Board seat at the bank. Chandler, however, was not a forgiving man and, true to his vow, started buying every share of the bank stock that came on the market. There were only 500 shareholders. After a few years he also became the largest individual shareholder, but the old line directors were still very much in control.

Chandler was a risk taker of the first order and was also a maverick that pined for acceptance among the Bradys and Dillons of Somerset County. Considering his wealth, this would not have been difficult except that he was rumored to be a black man. He built his industrial park in the 1940s

-50s and 60s when attitudes toward blacks were different than they later became, especially among the horsey set in lily white Somerset County. Chandler had a light but slightly dusky skin and he colored his hair and thought he was passing himself off as white.

His habits did not help him either. He openly kept a mistress (his wife and children lived in Florida) and he was a big time gambler winning or losing $100,000 at a sitting in Las Vegas, and not blinking an eye. His wife and mistress were both white.

He was not invited to the "right" places, however, and there was a lot of whispering behind his back. I didn't like the community's attitude toward Chandler but I said nothing as I was a newcomer and I, too, wanted to be part of the "in" group.

As noted above, I was pushing the Board to become more progressive and Chandler strongly agreed with me. Without my even realizing it, Chandler started to draw me under his spell, his purpose being to promote his own well-thought out, agenda. First he would invite me to dinner; then, proudly showed me through his buildings, financed by the way, by my old boss Emlen Roosevelt, with whom Chandler by then kept his really big accounts. Ed could be very persuasive, and he turned his charm on to me for reasons of which I, only gradually, became aware; like a fly getting caught in a spider's web.

After I entered the scene and began to making changes Chandler saw his chance. He started cultivating me and I was flattered by the attention despite Chandler's "bad" reputation. Prophetically, after meeting Chandler at a Christmas party at my house, my aunt Stella said, "George, don't mix with him, he's a bad person." I think she had ESP, and how right she was!

Slowly I learned of his plans to gain control of the bank

and the sly fox hinted that he would sell me one of his buildings at "a price you can't refuse." Moreover, he said that he would sell it to me with no money down and set it up so that it would yield me $60,000 a year; tax free (a tidy sum in the 1970s). When I asked if he would consider putting our arrangement into written form, he fixed me with his steely eyes and acted insulted saying, "Don't you know that my word is my bond?" He ceremoniously showed me through "my" building and repeated the commitment in front of his two adult children. I was lulled to sleep. I was still only 48 and his offer sounded too good to be true, as indeed, it was.

The Board members, being sly foxes themselves tried to warn me that I was getting too close to Chandler, but they still wanted his very profitable deposits at the bank. As time went by, Chandler asked to see the stockholders list, which as a director, was his right. The Board members refused to show it to him because they knew he would use it to buy as many shares as he could. They suspected that he wanted to gain control of the bank and then sell it to National State.

Chandler was known to have a close personal and business relationship with Emlen Roosevelt. Emlen wanted to extend his branch system to the rapidly growing and rich Somerset County. The Board members had been right with their warnings, of course, but I was in the middle because I knew that, by law, Chandler had every right to a copy of the stockholder list. His cultivation activities had paid off and, for better or worse, I was on his side.

Covering My Bases

My prior experiences had not completely gone unheeded, however. Sensing that there might be trouble, I decided that it would be wise to diversify my sources of income. Around

1974 I applied to the Bureau of Securities to be named a Registered Investment Adviser and was licensed, without the usual examination, based on my experience and education. In time, I built up a small coterie of clients. The stock market was in the doldrums in the middle 70s but I managed the money of my five or six clients with reasonable success and started to build my own stock portfolio. I brought this side business along to the point where I was pretty sure I could make it into a fulltime occupation. At any rate, that was one of my several plans for a possible future full time occupation - another being that I would be a senior executive with National State Bank after Chandler completes his takeover and sale.

If I had really wanted to remain a country squire and run a nice sleepy country bank, I would have listened to the Board members and given Chandler the cold shoulder, law or no law. But something in my risk taking nature, my liberal background, some greed, and maybe a certain perversity, urged me on to feed stockholder names to Ed so that he could buy stock and, hopefully, gain control of the bank. The thought occurred to me that maybe he could realize his ambition even without my help, and then I would be out of a job for siding with the Board members.

So I gave him the stockholders list and, on a bright Monday morning as I returned from a banker's convention in Bermuda, the board chairman met me in my office, closed the door, and read me a prepared statement telling me that the Board had a meeting (a secret and possibly illegal meeting, without Chandler) and had lost confidence in me. I was to clean out my desk immediately and leave the premises forthwith.

I was in shock. After a few days, when I regained my composure, I met with Ed Chandler, who reiterated his intention to get control of the bank, and since he now had the complete stockholders list asked me to help him buy up the outstanding shares. My reward was to be reinstatement as president and, of course, to get the building he had promised. He did not, however, offer to take care of me financially in the interim, even though he could easily have done so. He suggested that I should take a temporary job in banking and work with him to buy up the outstanding stock. Chandler, of course, had more than enough money to buy all the shares of this small bank, but needed me because many of the stockholders were antagonistic toward him and refused to sell to him, at any price.

Doris kept working after we had moved to Somerville, which was a very good thing. The next few years turned out to be tough ones for Doris and the children. All went well with their home life, largely because Doris had her steady income. Were she not working, I would not have dared take the financial risks involved.

One of my banking friends was Tony Schoberl who was president of Franklin State Bank, a large aggressive central New Jersey bank. I went to Tony and told him what had happened. Franklin State had recently acquired a bank in neighboring Union County and he hired me as regional Vice President in charge of the fourteen branches in that county. My office was in Scotch Plains, a twenty minute ride from our house in Somerville. A true banker, Tony Schoberl offered me a modest starting salary, and I took it without negotiating.

The job at Franklin State was not my cup of tea as I had to spend a lot of my time on personnel matters and straightening out computer related customer relations problems. Whenever I was not tied down to my desk, I found time to work on the State Bank of Raritan Valley matter. Edward Chandler sent a solicitation offer, brushing aside my suggestion that we run it by an attorney in the securities regulation field.

As Chandler soon found out there is a large body of law having to do with disclosures that must be made when making a tender offer for stock held by the public. (The Williams Act, if anyone is interested.) I spent all of 1977 working with lawyers pursuing a "tender offer." In plain language this is an attempt by our side to buy enough stock in the bank to throw out the rascals. Needless to say, the rascals didn't agree with our point of view.

Some people immediately sold their shares to Chandler because he offered a price much higher than the going market price. The Board members immediately sent out a solicitation letter of their own and hired a big law firm which got an injunction against me and Chandler, forbidding us from buying any more stock than we already had, pending a hearing.

In short order, we hired a lawyer, and we countersued. The legal costs and other costs of solicitation were paid by Chandler and, here again; he brushed aside my suggestion that we hire a major law firm that knew its way around in the world of securities litigation. The result was that a large, well connected, Newark law firm buried our singleton lawyer in paperwork and I spent many hours in attorney Milton Diamond's Highland Park office writing briefs.

Getting control of the Raritan bank became an obsession with me. Parenthetically, I should record a special note of thanks to Ed Chandler who gave me a course in tough love I could never have gotten in graduate school. He taught me how to fight, and survive, in a Darwinistic world.

A Full Time Legal Struggle

After about a year of depositions, suits and countersuits, the New Jersey State Court mandated an eighteen month cooling off period. At about the same time, Franklin State

Bank replaced Tony Schoberl with a new president friendly to the Raritan directors. I was ordered to stop helping Chandler in his effort to get control of the Raritan bank, but I was too deeply committed and refused and he asked me to resign.

The Banking Commissioner put me in touch with a number of banks looking for chief executives (Roger Wagner's recommendation was like an anointing by the Pope), but they were all out of the immediate area. In short order, Chandler, not wanting me to desert him, asked Emlen Roosevelt to hire me as an officer of National State Bank. Emlen gave me an office and secretarial help in Highland Park but no duties. Emlen paid me just enough to get by; the idea being that after Chandler got the Raritan bank it would be folded into the National State system.

Even during the cooling off period both sides continued to line up stockholders who were willing to sell their shares. When the cooling off period ended, it was back to suit - countersuit and purchasing of shares. In addition to my office in Highland Park I had a desk in Chandler's office from which I ran the fight for control. Chandler periodically got tired of the whole process and went to Florida or Las Vegas for extended periods of time. He left me with a checkbook full of signed checks and three million in the bank, with which to buy shares in the Raritan bank. Our adversaries were also buying shares but I could not figure out where they were getting their money. To find out, I had our attorneys (we had a larger Newark firm by then) ask some pointed questions in a deposition at the bank's main office.

Under court supervised questioning it was disclosed that the Board members were using the bank's depositors' money to buy stock: a clearly illegal act.

When we presented this information to the Court, the Board members were made to replace the money that they had literally stolen and they were reprimanded, but nothing more.

I was dumbfounded until I discovered that the judge handling the case had been the senior partner in the very law firm that was handling the case for the Raritan Board members.

If Chandler or I had done anything like what the Raritan board did we would have been remanded to free accommodations in jail. Unfair, would be the mildest word I could put to the Court's action. The legal system was fixed and I was fit to be tied. I decided that this was "war," and soon my opportunity presented itself.

When both sides were permitted to send tender offers to the remaining stockholders, our adversaries were required to disclose their illegal actions, and their reprimand, in their purchase offer. Their lawyers, being experienced hired guns, not to mention being well connected, contrived to bury the disclosure information in the small print near the end of their offering document. Each side was required to show a copy of their tender offer to the other side prior to sending it but, by Court order, the contents were not to be disclosed to anyone else.

When I got our adversaries' tender offer, I dissected it with a fine tooth comb and discovered the neatly covered up damaging information. I made copies of the offending tender letter, underlined the information concerning the Board's illegal acts, and sent the tender offer to all of the New Jersey newspapers and The New York Times under the guise of a press release. Then the shit really hit the fan.

The New York Times sent a reporter to investigate, checked it out, found that the information I had sent was correct, and filed a quarter page report on the front page of the second section under the heading: "Illegal Acts of New Jersey Bank Directors Disclosed." The reputation of the Raritan bank directors was ruined and they started pointing fingers at each other.

The judge, friendly to the Raritan people, however, had

other ideas. He ordered a hearing to determine who had sent the bogus press release, which act was in direct violation of his order. A full hearing was then held in Trenton but none of the bank's directors, or Chandler or I, admitted to the deed.

By this time, Bill Langille, the then 80 year old chairman of the Raritan bank was disgusted by the bickering of his Board members and told the Court that he had not sent out the press release, but should have, and he was glad that it was out. The Board was clearly demoralized and the next day they fired their president, an aggressive young man, who had taken my place. The hearing was inconclusive, but the beginning of the end was in sight.

> In *State Bank of Raritan Valley vs. Chandler*, the court found that a press release by one of two competing offerors that disparaged the target (and which the court found to be manipulative in that it would depress the target's stock) violated Section 14(e) and warranted an absolute injunction against going forward with the offer for a period of eighteen months. The court rejected the argument that Section 14(e) violations are not significant when there are competing offers because the shareholders will tender to the higher offer no matter what has been said about the target.
>
> *Direct quote from 1978 Business and Economics magazine*

Our original lawyer, Milton Diamond, a sole practitioner, had been an assistant prosecutor with Warren Wilentz, of the politically connected, Wilentz, Goldman and Spitzer law firm in Woodbridge, New Jersey. David Wilentz, the senior partner, then 96, still came to the office several times a week. He had been the prosecutor in the Lindbergh kidnapping case in 1932 and became a political power in New Jersey. To avoid being buried in paperwork again, Diamond introduced us to Wilentz who quickly brought the battle for control of the bank to a conclusion.

Apparently, a politically powerful law firm can be very persuasive. Chandler was allowed to buy all the stock he wanted and the Board members were allowed to submit their shares and get the same price as the public. The long battle was over. We had won and I experienced some of the happiest moments of my career. Chandler signed 200 checks, gave me the checkbook, with the needed $3,000,000 and said: "George, go ahead and buy as many shares as we need, I'm going to my place in Florida."

It was truly a triumph of motherhood, apple pie and justice over the forces of evil and insufficient capital. (Please note that winners write history and tell jokes while losers say "deal the cards".)

Edward Chandler wound up with 91% of the shares in the Raritan bank and I moved rapidly to take the resignations of the old Board and put a new Board of Chandler's choosing, in place. The new Board members were mostly local businessmen and Chandler's gambling buddies. They were a rubber stamp Board but they were *OUR* Board. Almost as soon as he gained control of the bank, Chandler started to lose interest.

He allowed me the pleasure of going to the bank, meeting with the old Chairman and accepting the prepared resignation letters of the entire old Board. Then Chandler told me that he was going to Las Vegas for a few days and that I should take care of the procedural details.

Which I did; almost gleefully.

I convened the new Board and had Chandler named Chairman and myself named Vice Chairman, president and CEO. The old Chairman, Bill Langille, having been a senior officer of a large corporation, experienced in corporate bloodletting, saved his directors from the ignominy of facing me and had gathered their resignation letters and handed them to me together with his keys. Then, without a word, he turned around and marched out. I could not help admiring his composure. He knew when he was licked and walked out with his head held high.

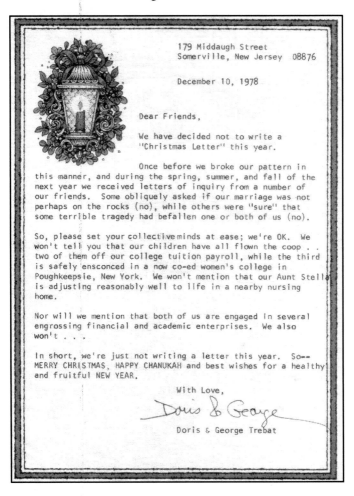

This is the first of the Christmas Letters that I decided to include in this memoir. Of course if you read it carefully, you may come to the conclusion that it is more a spirit of the season letter, than a document packed with personal details.

Details and a Reprise of Retribution Monday

It was almost opening time at the State Bank of Raritan Valley, a small commercial bank in central New Jersey. Outside the bank an attorney impatiently stood with a newly minted widow and her immediate family, waiting for the guard to open the door so that they could get to the unpleasant formalities of opening the safe deposit box of the deceased to see the will. Inside the bank the staff and tellers were getting ready for another busy Monday morning.

In a stone country squire's mini-mansion several miles away, a different kind of formality was being prepared for. At the bank's Board Chairman's house in the horsey section of rural New Jersey, a half hour's drive west, Bill Langille was getting dressed in his usual dark blue suit, white shirt and striped tie. He was getting ready for a ten o'clock meeting at the bank with George Trebat, the bank president he had fired almost four years ago.

Langille, and he always introduced himself as "Langille," and not Bill, was by then an unusually vigorous 80 and was on the back end of a long and distinguished career as the retired president of the Diehl Manufacturing Company.

In better days, in his almost daily lunches with me at the Raritan Valley Country Club, he enjoyed retelling his experiences during the War during which he was awarded large government contracts in rapid order by manipulating the bureaucrats at the War Production Board and other enabling agencies in Washington.

As noted, the Board at the bank was a clubby affair headed by a local lawyer named Allgair, and functioned pretty much as a small savings bank whose primary business was the accumulation of savings accounts and making of mortgage loans to the local community. "Judge" Allgair's law firm, of course, handled all the mortgage closings for the bank, earning a nice income as well as a stipend as bank counsel. The bank, however, was not growing enough to adequately service its assigned area in central New Jersey that was rapidly becoming a New York suburb, because no other local lawyer was permitted to refer mortgages to the bank and therefore referred their commercial business elsewhere. In other words, the bank was a club of "good ole boys".

In time, Langille, who had time on his hands, was appointed president of the bank and came in for a couple of hours every day despite not having any actual financial experience. This suited Judge Allgair just fine because Langille recognized his appointment as a friendly sinecure and was not about to rock the boat.

Now, several years later, Langille was getting ready to meet me in the Board room of the bank at 10 am, to hand in his resignation as Chairman, as well as the resignations of the other eleven Board members.

At about the same time that Monday morning, I was at home in Somerville, a five minute drive from the bank, also getting ready for the ten o'clock meeting. I was in no hurry because the meeting with Langille was an anti-climax. I was fifty one, had a bachelor's and master's degree in banking from New York University and had been a commercial loan officer at several large banks before coming to the Raritan bank where I hoped to remain for the rest of my working days.

But, to paraphrase the poet, Robert Burns who said it much more eloquently, life does not always work according to plan. After being fired in 1975, I got together with Edward Chandler, the largest individual shareholder, and a director, at the bank and then headed a bitter proxy fight, financed by Chandler, who was a wealthy industrialist. This particular Monday morning was not important because Ed Chandler now owned 90% of the voting stock of the bank and it was just a routine matter to accept the resignations and name a new Board. I then became president once again and received the added title of Vice Chairman. Chandler was named Chairman in a reorganization meeting held later that afternoon and a Board, composed mostly of his business and gambling friends, was duly elected.

Ed Chandler, a tall, lanky pencil-thin multi-millionaire, did not bother to attend the ten o'clock meeting with Langille. When we met the Friday before, to prepare for the turnover, Chandler told me, "You go ahead and handle it; after all, Monday is your day." After that, Chandler got bored with the bank and didn't attend Board meetings very much. He let me run the show and spent his time with his 55 building, 100-acre industrial park; that in his words "made real money".

Assuming that the Raritan bank would soon be merged with National State Bank, in rapid order I aligned the bank's computer services with those of National State Bank but the merger was not to be. Emlen Roosevelt got interested in acquiring a much bigger bank in north Jersey and asked Chandler and me to put our arrangement on hold for a couple of months. The couple of months became a year, because Roosevelt was having trouble getting regulatory approval to acquire his big fish, and Chandler was getting restless. He did not like having debt and he owed National State $5,000,000, most of which he had used to buy the Raritan bank, and was anxious to pay off the loan by selling the Raritan bank to National State. In the end, National State did not buy the large bank it was after and lost the Raritan Bank too because Chandler lost patience. He had proven his point and wanted out. He urged me to find another buyer and soon the bank was sold. And, I had worked myself out of a job. But this time it didn't matter, or so I thought, because I would soon have the promised income from Chandler's building and could devote myself to other interests.

The Raritan Bank was sold shortly thereafter, to an entirely different and larger bank. The new owners of the Raritan bank relieved me of my duties and gave me six months' salary and good wishes for my future career. This was okay with me since I had an arrangement with my great and good friend Ed Chandler, whose word, as he never tired of telling me, was his bond. Chandler, however, was by then 74 and a sick man. He started spending, first one day, and then two days, a week on the dialysis machine. He also started spending more and more time at his Florida home in Redington Beach, just south of St. Petersburg. Doris and I visited him and his wife, Jackie, whom he married sometime after divorcing his "old" wife, the mother of his two grown children. While Chandler and I had little in common now that our bank project was over, I kept in close touch with him, waiting for him to formalize his pledge to sell me the industrial building which would give Doris and me financial independence. He kept referring to the building in question as my building but I could never quite pin him down as to exactly "when". A few months passed but I couldn't push him because of his delicate health. Finally, however, the word came from Florida that Chandler had died. Several weeks after his death according to his wishes, his family held a big memorial dinner at the Redwood Inn in Bernardsville, inviting about fifteen hundred friends, acquaintances and employees. Recognizing my closeness to Chandler, the family asked me to act as unofficial host and to be one of several speakers, praising Chandler for his good deeds, of which there were some, and relating anecdotes of interest.

Did I get "my building"? – well, not exactly. But that's another whole story to be covered elsewhere in my memoir.

Investment Management

In my capacity as a registered investment advisor, I formally launched Cambridge Investment Management of Somerville and Highland Park in February 1978.

My interest in securities began in earnest and not just as a class project when I exercised a stock transaction to finance my master's studies and the start of my marriage. Over the years and while remaining a full time banker, I continued my interest in securities and built my personal portfolio into the six figure range. I was the unofficial investment advisor to many of our family members and close personal friends.

When I became president of the State Bank of Raritan Valley in the early 1970s, I applied my investment skills to sharply increase its earnings and I was particularly proud to have acquired high quality bonds for the bank's portfolio at low prices that subsequently increased substantially. This investment strategy enabled the bank to show excellent profits even after I was forced to resign my position in 1975 during the shakeup that eventually led to his control of the bank.

Since moving on from the Raritan bank, I continued my interest in it and I still remained a major bank shareholder, although my financial interest broadened into other areas. I became an active real estate investor and convinced my investment management clients to participate with me in real estate ventures.

Investment counseling is a very personal business and really became my first love.

Accordingly, I spent a lot of time getting to know the investment philosophy of my clients; their financial goals; the kind of profit expectations they had, as well as the amount of risk they wished to assume.

Believe it or not, I turned away more clients than I accepted because some people wanted me to guarantee a doubling of their money on an annual basis. Others wanted to make money but didn't have the patience or emotional makeup for it.

After all, I insisted, there's a direct relationship between the reward one seeks and the level of risk one's willing to accept. When I met a potential client who really shouldn't be in the stock market, I recommended that he or she buy bonds.

Investment counseling has been an exciting and rewarding business but it was also a lot of hard work. I did my own research and read constantly while maintaining connections with several major New York investment firms who serviced my clients. I did not earn commissions on stocks bought and sold, but I earned an investment advisory fee based on the total value of the portfolio put under someone's management. That way I was independent of any broker, since his primary interest is in the growth of his client's portfolio. A broker may mean well, but he put bread on the table only when his customer bought and sold. That was the reason why a broker's financial interest was not always coincident with that of his customer.

My greatest single advantage in investment management was a sense of accomplishment in moving toward a future goal.

Most people who had some money in a checking account, a savings account, or some bonds began to feel antsy. Over time they started to feel that is was not growing enough and it worried them. Or they had some stocks which were not acting very well. This worried them also.

I felt that once people took a part of their money and retained someone trained to manage it they began to feel better. They usually would say, "Now I can go about my business of being a doctor, lawyer or candlestick maker and making money by the work I am trained to do. I have hired a competent money manager who is trained to manage money. He will make my money work harder for me."

That's why being an investment adviser was a job I loved.

This was, of course, "Plan B" which I did not execute.

1980 – A Year of Celebration

May 31st must surely be recorded as a high point of 1980. It was the date of Alan's wedding to the former Janice Bolton. Attended by friends and family, the event lived up to all expectations. The young Trebats, as they are now called, live in Boston where Alan is now in his first law school year.

Alan, Julie, Doris, Jan, Betsy, George
The Happy Trebats – Christmas 1980

Julie, a Vassar junior, spent the summer working as a juvenile detention center supervisor in New Jersey, is doing other interesting things while also concentrating on her studies.

Betsy, whom we last saw at the wedding in May, is in Benton Harbor, Michigan. working and forging the beginnings of a social work career.

Final Directions

Cleaning up the Carteret Bank

I don't remember the exact timing, but while waiting for Ed Chandler to make good on his promise of a building, my friend, Roger Wagner, the Banking Commissioner, put me in touch with a small bank in Carteret, New Jersey, urgently in need of a president. The former president had been fired because of loan irregularities and my job was to dig out all of the problems, put the bank on a sound footing, and then sell it to a larger institution.

I ran the Carteret Bank and Trust for about two years and after solving all of the loan, operating and personnel problems, I tried to convince the Board members not to sell the bank. The bank had an excellent franchise in an industrial area and was earning 25% per year on its capital. One doesn't have to be an expert in banking to realize that an annual capital return of 25% is nothing short of outstanding. The Board members however were demoralized and old and wanted to sell their shares and go somewhere to live happily ever after. The best that I could do for myself was to buy as many shares as became available and let the bank go into the hands of another organization. Along with the Board members and other stockholders, some of whom had held their shares for many years, I sold my shares and made a modest profit.

Having done a good job in cleaning up the Carteret bank, Roger Wagner wanted me to take over another bank, this one at some distance in Ocean County. He wanted me to be the New Jersey Banking Department's trouble shooter, but, by this time, I had had enough. Being a trouble shooter was tough work.

Being president of Carteret Bank and Trust had been a stressful and unpleasant experience since it included putting two people in jail for fraud and trying, unsuccessfully, to educate a Board of Directors who were tolerant of slipshod ethics. In addition, my executive vice president, a holdover from the prior administration, also had larceny in his heart, and was later to spend a year in jail as a result of a process that I started while still at the bank.

Sending Christmas Letters

I considered our Christmas letters to be so "fascinating" that a few deserved to be included in this memoir for your enjoyment; not all of them of course, but just a few.

Many of the nuances in the Christmas letters are indirect, such as the 1981 letter, below. As you will more easily see, later on, we enjoyed visiting relatives.

I can't remember how it came about but in 1966 Doris and I decided to give up sending Christmas cards and started to send an annual Christmas letter to our relatives and close friends. Over the years we've received a lot of feedback concerning our Christmas messages. The reviews were mixed. My advice to people who didn't like our newsy chronicles was – throw them out. Doris and I enjoyed the job of reviewing our year.

I have selected a few our Christmas letters to include intact. These and excerpts from the remainder should give you a feel for how we lived and tell you something about our lives. Our letters from 1978 and 1981 have previously been displayed. I hope you will enjoy reading or in some cases, re-reading the complete Christmas letters for 1986,

The Immigrants' Son, An American Story

1992 (2 pages), 1995, 1998, 1999, and 2006 included in the following pages.

Some letters have been lost to the ravages of time, but many remain that are still meaningful to us. We will pause frequently to share significant memories and comments in fleshing out the details, and provide insight into our thoughts.

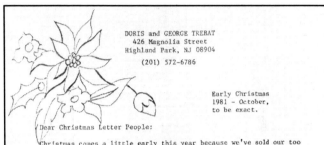

DORIS and GEORGE TREBAT
426 Magnolia Street
Highland Park, NJ 08904

(201) 572-6786

Early Christmas
1981 - October,
to be exact.

Dear Christmas Letter People:

Christmas comes a little early this year because we've sold our too big house in Somerville and have moved into rented quarters (a small house) in Highland Park. Please note the new address in pencil because it is our intention to acquire a house in Highland Park suitable for a couple whose grown children come only for periodic visits and vacations.

1981 was not a vacation year because George was involved in negotiating the sale of his bank to a larger institution, and Doris, his loyal wife, could not bear to go off somewhere without him.

As we review the year, we must admit that we have not augmented the knowledge of the world by improving upon the theory of relativity - in fact, we barely made some feeble efforts to understand it. On the other hand, we made some pretty good progress in our effort to stamp out poverty (ours mostly).

Please be assured, also, that we continue to be in favor of motherhood and against sin. One of us is teaching at the elementary school in Highland Park while the other is still presiding at the bank in Raritan and mucking around in real estate and other financial matters. To be sure, we're not strangers to the cultural advantages of New York City, and we try to lead an active social life in our area. Our children are, respectively, working at a cable TV company in Madison (and studying); finishing up at college in Poughkeepsie, and law schooling in Boston.

Since we already know the names of most of you who will receive this letter, we hope that, should you care to respond by way of a Christmas card, you will also include a message telling us what's happening in your life and how you feel about it. After all, we do care about you - that's really why we go through this annual letter writing exercise.

Your friends,

Doris & George

A Smaller House

In 1980 Doris and I decided to move back to Highland Park. Doris was still teaching there and it was where we had lived for some years before a move to Somerville.

We liked Highland Park, had made a lot of friends there and now that the Raritan bank was sold, we were free to move back to Highland Park. Since our three children had, by then, gone their separate ways, never to return to our house, except for visits, we decided that we should seek a smaller ranch type house. We wanted three bedrooms so that our children could visit whenever they chose and we wanted the house to be all on one floor because we figured that, by the time we were 90 or so, we might not want to climb stairs.

We looked all over Highland Park but found no houses that fit our profile. Then, one day in the spring of 1982 we were attending a Democratic spaghetti dinner at the Highland Park VFW Hall, where an acquaintance told us of a house just over the border in the Twin Brooks section of Edison that seemed to fit the description of what we were looking for. The Twin Brooks section of Edison is at the very southern border of Edison which, in itself is a very large township extending some twenty miles north, west and east of Highland Park in Middlesex County. Thus, Twin Brooks (an unofficial name), a development built around 1953, is sort of tucked into the back of Highland Park, and for all practical purposes, except for postal address, is part of Highland Park and not really a part of Edison.

We bought the house at Eight Olden Road in Edison in the spring of 1982 and we moved into the three bedroom house in June 1982 and we stayed there for 21 years. While we were living there, Doris took early retirement from the Highland Park School System and I retired from banking a little before my time after yet another merger.

The Immigrants' Son, An American Story

For all practical purposes, we really lived in Highland Park. Our house was just five or ten minutes, by car, away from the center of New Brunswick, which is the county seat and is best known for being the world headquarters of Johnson and Johnson, the large pharmaceutical company. Very often the same symphony orchestras that play in New York on Friday are to be found in New Brunswick either one day later or one day before. All of this, together with our network of friends, dating from around 1966, and its proximity to New York made the ambiance of Central New Jersey quite pleasant. We would not have minded spending the next thirty years right there.

As we settled in, we got to know our neighbors. Mostly secular Jewish business people and professionals, they were all friendly in varying degrees and, as we lived on Olden Road longer we got to exchange neighborly visits and enjoyed back yard small talk in season. Most of our neighbors were our age, that is, they were then in their post child rearing years so they had a certain amount of time to socialize and enjoy life. Some, like Bernie and Pearl Mirinov, just behind us, were retired from the operation of their family run chain of convenience stores but still kept up a lively interest in the business. Next door, Betty and Dan Schulman had sold their New Brunswick dress shop but Dan was deeply involved in developing a chain of retail home furnishing stores being run by his son and daughter-in-law.

Filling out the picture of our immediate neighbors were Viga and Doctor Morgenstern. Dr. Morgenstern was, at 75, still active as a well-known local physician. When I first met him over our side yard fence, being the younger person I hastened to put out my hand and introduce myself as George Trebat. Morgenstern smiled wanly and said that his name was Doctor Morgenstern. I had known, from other sources that he was a physician, but I came home and told

Doris that I had met the man next door and his first name is "Doctor." Doris assured me that I must be mistaken and that his first name can't be Doctor but that he actually is a doctor. Nevertheless, for a long time thereafter I persisted in my little joke. Actually, Dr. Morgenstern, whose first name, I later learned, was "Mates," was a gentleman of the old school, somewhat formal, but unfailingly friendly and sincere.

Notes from 1982 and 1983 Christmas Letters

Because there were a host of business, family and social activities, getting me to agree to vacation in England and Wales in 1982 had not been easy. As I was wont to say *"The Queen kept calling our hotel in London inviting us to tea; but really, we didn't have time for sitting around since we had to put about a thousand miles on a rented car, seeing all those interesting places they write about in the National Geographic and the New York Times travel section. For the record we also visited New York, New Brunswick, Princeton, Boston, Newark, Tampa and Atlantic City this year. With luck, next year we hope to hit Long Island, Piscataway (local joke!) and maybe even Philadelphia, PA."*

At the bottom of a full page also bursting with good news about the family, the letter continued with: *"As you can see, our days are eventful and our activities, as those of our children, are a measure of the good health we all enjoy. We find Christmas to be both the happiest and saddest time of the year - - happy because of our own good fortune and the religious mysticism that touches all of us; but sad because we're deeply conscious of the greed, manipulation, injustice and self-seeking that is part of the world we live in."*

In late 1983, for several months, our house was in a shambles because we put in a new kitchen, a sliding glass door to the deck, knocked down an interior wall and other things too numerous to mention. We were fortunate to be back in business by the first of the year.

We did make a trip to Scotland that summer. Like the English, the Scots drive on the wrong side of the road but they were otherwise very hospitable and their whiskey was not too hard to take.

Expanding Commercial Lending

At about the time my tenure in Carteret was ended, banking laws in New Jersey were changed to permit savings banks to get into commercial lending and operate the same as commercial banks.

I decided to find a large savings bank that wanted to start a commercial banking division. Before I left the Carteret bank I got in touch with the Provident Savings Bank, a venerable old line bank in Jersey City with two billion dollars in deposits and branches in the northern part of the State.

I enjoyed starting their commercial lending department but became distinctly unhappy with fighting an hour, or more, of rush hour traffic up and back on the New Jersey Turnpike daily. The ride on the turnpike wasn't so bad but once I got to Exit 15E, I ran into ten minutes worth of big trucks before getting through the pay booth and then another twenty minutes in snarled city traffic before getting to the bank's parking lot. At night, getting out of Jersey City was just as bad, if not worse. During the day, if I wanted to go out and call on a customer or prospect, I had to walk the three blocks to the bank's parking lot, unlock the chain that was strung across the entrance, drive the car out, then pick up the chain and relock it. Not a pleasant job in the rain, snow, or slush of winter... and, I was tired.

One day, after nine months at the Provident Savings Bank, I mentioned my commutation travails to Ralph Voorhees, my long time stock broker, neighbor and friend. Ralph was also a Board member at the New Brunswick Savings Bank, a one billion dollar, fourteen-branch bank in central New Jersey with headquarters in New Brunswick, a five minute ride, or fifteen minute walk, from our house. I liked and got along well with the people at Provident Savings, but I decided to "this time, take care of George" and, before long I was sitting at a quiet lunch with Bill Kuhlthau, a long-time acquaintance, who was president of New Brunswick Savings.

Although Bill chiseled me down on salary, I gladly gave up my company car and joined New Brunswick to start up their commercial banking division. My friends in Jersey City were a little miffed at my sudden departure, but, in the end they were gracious; understanding that I was by then 57, had most of my business contacts in central New Jersey and would probably add a couple years to my life by avoiding the stressful daily commute to Jersey City.

I was still working and the bank barely survived, when Doris and I chose to take a month to visit "exotic, stimulating, interesting" China, during the Year of the Tiger.

1986 – Year of the Tiger

Coincidentally, our visit to China occurred during the year of the Fire Tiger, which occupies the 3rd position on the Chinese Zodiac. Many of the Tiger's characteristics fit my life, although I was born in the Year of the Rabbit, but then I was conceived the previous year, which is also a Fire Tiger year.

The Immigrants' Son, An American Story

DORIS AND GEORGE TREBAT
8 Olden Road
Edison, New Jersey 08817

Christmas 1986

Dear Friends,

This was a momentous year because the good things happened on cue and the bad things we read about were pushed yet another year into the future.

The good things were that, although not of ripe age, Doris decided to retire from teaching and is spending more time on recreational activities. She is still weighing the options available to her now that she has shrugged off the yolk of the classroom. Another good thing was our trip to China in September-October which, you might say, was by way of celebration.

Being familiar with London, Paris and places like that, you might expect us to take China in stride, but the truth is that we found it to be exotic, stimulating, interesting and it's an experience we would recommend to anyone who can cope with a few indignities and a physically strenuous trip. When we got back, George found out that his bank was able to get along without him for a month (but just barely).

Two of our children are now in their fourth decade, and our youngest made it to 26 on December 1st. At present, only Alan is married (he, and his wife Jan, live in the Boston area), while Betsy, in Wisconsin, and Julie, in New York are busily pursuing their careers.

To avoid the bad things of life, we're paying more attention to maintenance: like eating low cholesterol everything, exercising and thinking good thoughts while having the dentist work us over and over and over.

That's not the whole story, of course, but you get the general idea......

Merry Christmas,

Doris & George

Fire Tigers love to be challenged and will accept any challenge if it means protecting a loved one or protecting their honor. They don't worry about the outcome because they know they'll always land on their feet. Don't let their calm appearance fool you though; Tigers will pounce when they feel it's necessary.

Tigers can be stubborn if they realize they're not in

charge. They have a slight tendency to be selfish but overall, Tigers are extremely generous. They're very intelligent and they're always on alert. Tigers are very charming and are well-liked by others.

Tigers have a continual need to be challenged which may explain why they jump from job to job. This isn't necessarily a problem because they're smart and able to quickly master new subjects. The best jobs for Tigers are those that will lead them towards positions of leadership.

Tigers will never bore their partners. They're expressive, polite and trustworthy, but watch out. Tigers tend to dominate their relationships. This tendency is instinctive and when monitored closely, such behavior can be kept under control. Partners need to be equally active to keep up with the Tiger's sense of adventure.

Expressive, vibrant and a bit eccentric, Fire Tigers are always looking at the positive side of every situation. Because they're able to generate excitement in others, they're considered excellent leaders. When Fire Tigers speak, others listen – and do what they're told!

The Folly of a Verbal Contract

During the time in Carteret, Jersey City and then at New Brunswick Savings I kept in touch with Edward Chandler's family, waiting for some word about the building that he had promised to sell to me. His grown children, Marguerite and Eddie, took over running of the industrial park of which they became joint owners. Finally, I realized that Chandler did not leave anything in writing as to my "inheritance" and his children were not about to do anything for me.

Although it is very hard to sue a dead man on account of a verbal contract, somewhere around 1986 I hired an attorney and brought suit against Chandler's estate. The daughter denied knowledge of any arrangement between her father and me, but Eddie admitted, under oath that there had been some talk about Chandler selling me a certain building under favorable terms. After a five day trial, the jury found in my favor but could not decide on the method of transfer or who was to manage the building which was an integral part of the Central Jersey Industrial Park. It could not be split off. The judge told the jury to go back and think some more. After a couple hours the tired jury members came out and recommended that I be awarded $50,000. That was a far cry for the $600,000 I was seeking. I won the lawsuit. It was a Pyrrhic victory. I took the money, terminated relations with the Chandlers and went on with my life. I had other fish to fry.

My Final Bank

Not by coincidence, I had a friend on the board of New Brunswick Savings bank and they wanted to get into commercial banking. Working at New Brunswick Savings was like a breath of fresh air to me, both because of the physical convenience and because I knew the territory like the back of my hand.

The Board approved a $1,000,000 personal lending authority for me, and I set up the accounting and paper trail aspects of running a commercial lending operation, hired a secretary, and started to look around for new business. The first thing I did was to write a letter to all of the accountants and lawyers in Middlesex County, many of whom I knew, telling them that I was open for business.

In a matter of months, I increased the loan portfolio to the point where it became necessary to computerize the department. For this I hired a young man, who went by the tongue twister name of Charlie Luszcz (pronounced: Lutz). He was computer literate, had been a branch manager and became my primary assistant. In about three years' time, the commercial lending division was a major income producer for the bank and I was named Senior Vice President. By then, I had about eight people in my division and had time to sit on several policy making committees.

In 1989, after five years at the New Brunswick Savings Bank I had created a portfolio of $110 million in loans (still a lot of money in 1989) and was producing about one third of all the income of the bank.

More Historical Perspective

In the 1980s the harsh repression that followed the Prague Spring of 1968 finally began to find a voice within the "normalized" population.

A Charter 77 manifesto was initiated in January 1977 by 242 signatories, which represented various occupations, political viewpoints, and religions. It criticized the government for failing to implement human rights provisions of documents it had signed, including the state's own constitution. Official response was harsh, but it could not silence what had become a public forum. Dissent and independent activity had been limited in Czechoslovakia to a fairly small segment of the populace. Many Czechs and Slovaks emigrated to the West; other began to find a voice.

Doris retired from teaching in 1986 and she began spending her time as a literacy volunteer, taking French at Rutgers, singing in a community chorus, going to book club meetings and thoroughly enjoying early retirement from the teaching profession.

The Immigrants' Son, An American Story

National Theatre in Prague at night

This period of continued Communist control no longer dampened our spirits so in 1987 we made another trip to Czechoslovakia. In a month's time spread over May and June we spent one week at the Prague spring music festival and then on to a lot of gemütlichkeit with my cousins and their issue. Doris' lack of linguistic perspicacity was alleviated somewhat by teenage nephews, Tomas and Martin, who were happy to try out their book-learned English on a genuine American. The trip reconfirmed our feeling that Prague is our favorite city and Czechoslovakia, with its mountains, lakes and streams, our second favorite country.

As we left we carried a growing conviction that the days of the Communist regime were getting shorter. It was only a matter of time, whether the Soviet Union would collapse and implode, or whether it would go out in nuclear holocaust of unprecedented destruction.

Early in 1988, the anti-Communist protests accelerated. An unauthorized gathering of perhaps 10,000 Roman Catholics held the Candle demonstration in Bratislava (the Slovak capital) on March 25th. A demonstration was held in Prague on August 21; the anniversary of the Soviet intervention in 1968. Prague also held a demonstration on October 28th, which was the anniversary of the establishment of Czechoslovakia in 1918. These were merely forerunners to the anti-Communist revolution.

The Final Word on 1988

Doris joined a local literacy volunteer's group wherein she tutored two adult ladies recently arrived from Taiwan and Turkey respectively. Being Doris, she didn't let it go at that but also taught the volunteers who have signed up to tutor. She traveled to a local hospital twice a week, where for a modest remuneration; she taught their non-Hispanic employees the rudiments of English. She joined a community chorus and a local book discussion group; plus she subscribed us to concert, orchestra and two different playhouse series.

In October I failed my medical stress test. This required a balloon angioplasty procedure in November to ream out a plaque-plugged coronary artery, so I became fine now with my medications. Details of this adventure can be found later in the summary of "My Medical Adventures".

In our "together time", which is most of the time, we spent a week in January with friends in Los Angeles and Santa Fe, and another couple of weeks in France in April visiting the WWII invasion beaches in Normandy as well as the coast of Brittany, Chartres, Versailles, Paris and a lovely regional capital named Rennes where we were hosted by close friends.

The summer was devoted to Tomas and Martin, two teenaged sons of my Czech cousin. They spoke halting English when they arrived in June for their eight week stay.

After Boston, New York, Philadelphia, Washington, Canada and a few other places, their English was much improved and they left for home with a bag full of memories that wouldn't be soon forgotten. Immediately on their return, Tomas started medical school; which began a tough six-year grind. Martin, a little younger, had a hard time trying to convince his British-trained English teacher that the World trade Centre is known as the World Trade Center in the U.S.A. Being a budding politician, he decided to spell it her way.

Also enclosed are some tidings of encouragement from our 1988 Christmas Letter, as follow:

"Although we were once active Presbyterians we no longer belong to any organized religious group, but certainly, our spiritual heritage helps us appreciate the wonder and mystery of Christmas. Being unshackled, as it were, we are also free to appreciate the Hebrew heritage of our Orthodox Jewish neighbors, who walk past our house to the local synagogue each Friday night and Saturday morning, as well as that of our other Jewish friends. We don't know many people of other religious persuasions; however, having been in the Orient, we know that there are a lot of them out there. Somehow, we can't help but believe that God has a place in His heart for all of us. For our part, we're glad to know people from many places and cultures. Sometimes we've been invited to share their religious and cultural ceremonies, just as we welcome them to our house to share our Christmas tree."

Another Day, my Final Merger

But, good things never seem to last. New Brunswick Savings was a mutual savings bank having been started in the middle 1800s, but by 1989 it became fashionable, and legal, for mutual savings banks to convert to publicly owned shareholder institutions. This procedure was usually profitable for all concerned, as shares had to be offered to all depositors at a discount from market value and insiders could profit by picking up as many shares as possible. In this case, the Board members got greedy because they entered into an agreement to merge the bank into National State Bank (Emlen Roosevelt had, by then, retired) immediately after "going public." The end result that they envisioned was that they would profit substantially by stock options, and other benefits offered to the Board members, and senior management, would become part of a much larger sophisticated commercial bank with branches almost all over the state.

Along with five or six other senior officers, I received options on several thousand shares. The senior managers were very much against the merger with National State as it would make them "junior partners" in a much larger bank. Bill Kuhlthau, the president and chairman, was against the merger to start but was bought off with a handsome retirement package. As preparation for the merger, it was decided that my commercial banking department would be consolidated into National State's much larger lending operation.

Since I was 62 years old by then and was fully vested in the pension plan, Bill Kuhlthau suggested that I would do well to apply for early retirement. I was not inclined to retire and asked what would happen if I didn't retire. He said: "Well, George, National State wants you to retire and our Board goes along with them. If you don't go along, things might get a little sticky." It did not escape my attention that my good friend and stock broker Ralph Voorhees was conveniently absent when the Board voted to force me to retire.

At first, I resented being forced to retire, but in retrospect I realized that I was lucky because I got my stock options and pension, whereas, the others were simply fired. Bill Kuhlthau had spent his entire career at New Brunswick Savings and I would not be doing him an injustice to say that he was a patient fellow, with deep family roots in Middlesex County who rose to the top because he was a loyal company man. I'm sure he never dreamed that central New Jersey would become one of the fastest growth areas in the United States.

In prior years I had started a small investment advisory business, as Plan "B", and thought about expanding it from my client base of four or five to one hundred or two hundred clients. It then struck me that, to do it right, such a move would involve my putting in 10 hour days, doing computer modeling and even possibly hiring some numbers crunchers. After a few days' thought I dropped that idea and restricted myself to handling my own stock portfolio and that of a few friends.

The New Brunswick Savings saga did not end with its sale and my retirement because soon after the merger it was disclosed that National State was in poor financial shape. Their loan portfolio was full of bad loans and they were severely undercapitalized. The $67 million in capital that they added to their coffers when they acquired New Brunswick Savings gave them a couple of years of breathing space before they, themselves, had to sell out to a much larger bank.

I must admit to a little gloating upon this disclosure of National State's troubles. The former New Brunswick directors never made the expected "killing" on their stock options and, in retrospect looked very foolish. Within another two years, and the bank was forced into a merger with Corestates Financial, a $43 billion Philadelphia based bank holding company. Another couple of years later and Corestates, whose capital base was none too strong was merged into First Union, a $100 billion east coast holding company and the sixth largest bank in the United States, then on to become Wachovia and, in 2009, Wells Fargo.

As for me, I followed all these changes with interest as my bank sponsored medical plan fell into stronger and stronger hands and my modest pension check became more secure. With only a small fudge factor, I can now say that I retired as Senior Vice President of one of the largest banks in the country.

THE STAGE CHANGES

All the world's a stage, And all the men and women merely players; They have their exits and their entrances; And one man in his time plays many parts,
>-William Shakespeare's As You Like It,
>spoken by the melancholy Jaques, Act II Scene VII.

Years of Abundant Changes

The end of the decade (1989) saw the end of my banking career. Hardly had we returned from three weeks in Ireland, Wales and London in July.

Doris maintained a stable, but very active influence by teaching as board president and ESL (*English as a Second Language?*) tutor for the Literacy Volunteers of Middlesex County, and as an English teacher for 16 Hispanic employees at a local hospital. Between phone calls Doris helped run, and sang in, a community chorus, went to exercise classes, and was a member of a reading group.

We had now arrived at the stage where we could look back on a happy life while still looking forward to many years of new experiences. I was slowly beginning to appreciate the free time that my somewhat unplanned early retirement provided; while keeping one foot in the world of business by tending to several personal investment, and renting myself out as a financial consultant now and then.

Being of sound body, if not always of mind, we burned some rubber on an Elderhostel trip to North Carolina in the spring of 1990, and of course several round trips to Boston. We also contributed mightily to the welfare of the airline industry, with trips to Wisconsin and Salt Lake City, as well as a big trip to Europe to celebrate the Czech velvet revolution with our Czech cousins. The last was a not-to-be-forgotten, wonderful trip of joy and some rumblings of anxiety as the Czechs tried to erase forty years of economic neglect to join us in what is called a market economy.

The Velvet Revolution

The demonstrations continued into 1989, again in Bratislava and some other towns in remembrance of the death of Jan Palach on January 16, 1969.

In 1989, the Czechs were busy peacefully protesting against their pro-communist government. The protests finally achieved the desired effect. The anti-Communist revolution broke out on November 16, 1989 in Bratislava, with a demonstration by Slovak university students for democracy. It continued with the well-known similar peaceful pro-democracy demonstration of Czech students in Prague on November 17. This time the communist police violently broke up a demonstration and brutally beat many student participants.

Faced with an overwhelming popular repudiation, the Communist Party all but collapsed, a coalition government was formed, and Václav Havel was elected President of Czechoslovakia on 29 December. The Federal Assembly abolished the Communists' constitutional hold on power. In took only a matter of days the Soviets to dismantle the barbed wire barricades along the West German and Austrian borders, but it was several years before all of the Soviet troops were removed from Czech soil.

The first free elections in Czechoslovakia since 1946 took place in June 1990 without incident and with more than 95% of the population voting. As anticipated, 'Civic Forum' and 'Public against Violence' won landslide victories in their respective republics and gained a comfortable majority in the federal parliament. The parliament undertook substantial steps toward securing the democratic evolution of Czechoslovakia.

The pressure was mounting by the Slovaks to have their own independent country. Most of the former satellite countries were achieving independence and self-rule. In the latter years of Czechoslovakia's subservience to Moscow, the Slovaks had made great economic gains while the Czechs had been dormant. The Slovaks made the best of their servile state, and they resented the political dominance by the Czech majority. In each district the politicians acted for their local constituents rather than the nation as a whole. Despite the closeness in language, the media in each area was also polarized with separate publication goals. So much for goings on in 1989 Europe.

The 'Cousins' Visit

April 1991 saw us in Seattle, visiting the Betty-Bob's (a.k.a. Doris' sister and her husband). Bob, a 1940s music aficionado, taped his best Dorsey-Goodman-Miller records for me and I wallowed in nostalgia from then on. We took a week of courses through Elderhostel at Central Washington

U. in Ellensburg: "Writing Your Family History" – spring 1998, "Great Moments in Archaeology" and "Western Artists".

We usually tried to do one big overseas trip each year, but this year we were busy with a week-long Trebat reunion in August, plus a seven-week visit from my Czech cousins, Hana and Miroslav Vane. The August group convened to officially welcome our newest clan-member, Sarah, who weathered the attentions of Martin Vane, her 16-year old Czech cousin, and of her local cousins … (We refer to them all as cousins, even though some are second cousins once removed.)

We enjoyed hosting the Vanes, who had graciously entertained us in their home in Czechoslovakia several times. During their visit we touched down in Boston, Washington, D.C., and of course, New York, New York. To enable them to get a feel for our country, we drove out to Wisconsin to see Betsy and Terry's new house in Waunakee, just outside Madison. Back around Chicago, up through Michigan to Port Huron, and east across Canada brought us to Kingston, where we left our visitors with Hana's brother, Vaclav, and family, while we drove back to our digs in New Jersey.

When they returned, we got them onto the floor of the N.Y. Stock Exchange, a somewhat confusing experience for someone brought up in a totalitarian atmosphere. ("What do all those little numbers mean?") More in touch with their experience was a visit to our local medical center, where Miroslav got to compare Gyn/Ob techniques (his specialty).

When they returned to Europe, it was to a Republic of Czechoslovakia that would be split within another year. All the momentum for separation was with the Slovak leaders. I

THE IMMIGRANTS' SON, AN AMERICAN STORY

had no known relatives left in Slovakia, so my loyalties and interests were with the Czechs.

...

In case anyone is confused, I began my 1992 letter with a dream situation, but who wouldn't like to imagine themselves in conversation with a head of state.

Season's Greetings
Christmas 1992

Dear Friends, Relatives, Children and Grandchildren:

I was sitting on an elegant chair in Vaclav Havel's office in Prague Castle discussing the political situation and having a drink when suddenly I was jarred into wakefulness by the alarm clock. What? Seven o'clock already? Doris jumped up and hit the shower while I was still trying to figure out what day it was.

At seven thirty I grabbed a string bag and unlocked the apartment door, ran down the three flights to struggle with the ponderous double-locked front door, which reluctantly creaked open after I finally found the right keys. Then it was about two blocks and up a little hill to the tiny grocery store for the morning's supply of fresh baked rolls, some good beer for later, a couple of tins of tuna and a round of rye bread still warm from the baker's oven.

Back at the apartment, the aroma of freshly brewed coffee filled the kitchen and the breakfast table was set. Doris told me the phone had rung while I was out but when she answered, speaking only English, the caller hung up. It was a little past nine as we made sure the door was securely locked and passed nameplates marked Tvrdy, Bobek and Vytlacil on our way out. We were in the old Jewish quarter and strode out onto Dusni Street (they call it Dusni Ulice) and made our way up the stone steps, across a small square and through winding cobblestoned streets to the magnificent Old Town Square. After a stop to inspect a bookstore window displaying a new reprint of an old Kafka novel, we joined the hundred and fifty tourists who gather each hour to stare up at the Old Town clock as it strikes while a bevy of saints rotate past two windows in the clock tower. The drama ends with the crowing of a cock as the crowd disburses.

It was another one of those beautiful days that eloquent writers rhapsodize about, and already the tourists were arriving--mostly well dressed middle aged gawkers with guidebooks in hand. A few eighteen to twentyfive types from all over were dressed in nondescript worn clothing--a sort of uniform by which they, no doubt, recognize each other. The visitors with their Nike sneakers and straight teeth were trying to blend in with the native young people who were setting up stands displaying costume jewelry, tee shirts, dolls, posters and bric-a-brac. Amidst all this early morning activity, we strolled over to a newsstand where a budding Robert Maxwell tried to slip me yesterday's International Herald Tribune, but I reached below the first two papers in his pile to get the fresh issue. At one end of the Old Town Square workmen were erecting a wooden stage on

> which sat big loudspeakers attached to a maze of spaghetti-like wires leading back into a five hundred year old Gothic church.
>
> As a group of musicians started tuning up their violins, basses and banjos, a white haired guy in a checkered shirt, tight jeans and cowboy boots tested the audio system. In another few minutes the Square had filled up with what seemed like a thousand couples dressed in colorful "Oklahoma" costumes. The band struck up a typical American midwest square dance tune, and there was a sudden burst of color as a thousand skirts swirled and the caller belted out the familiar "swing your partner and do-se-do your corner". We had happened upon an international square dance convention. This, and many days before and after in Prague, Pilsen, Pisek, Vienna and Salzberg, in June 1992, were filled with many images like those we've just described.
>
> While not made up of unalloyed joy, 1992 has to go into the books as another good year, as we hosted a family reunion to welcome a new granddaughter, skipped around the United States on various pleasurable missions, did some charitable and some moneymaking work, went to Elderhostels in Austria and Connecticut, entertained some medical students from Czechoslovakia, read some good books, enjoyed the company of a few good friends, and did some thinking about our future.
>
> Please don't consider us too arrogant as we impose a slice of our life on your consciousness. We sincerely wish you a Merry Christmas and Happy New Year and hope to learn what was important in your life in 1992.
>
> With Love,
>
> *Doris George*
>
> Doris and George

The Velvet Divorce

The **Astronomical Clock**

Even while we enjoyed the atmosphere of the Old Town Square and attended the hourly drama conducted at the Old Town Clock, time was running out for the nation of Czechoslovakia.

In June Czech voters backed the center right while their Slovak neighbors supported Slovak separatists and left wing parties. The two prime ministers agreed to the separation of Slovakia from the Czech Lands, despite the objections of President Havel and a general lack of popular enthusiasm. Havel resigned only to become the first president of the Czech Republic (1993–2003).

January 1, 1993 saw the dissolution of Czechoslovakia. It was an event that saw the self-determined separation of the federal state of Czechoslovakia. The Czech Republic and Slovakia, entities which had arisen in 1969 within the framework of Czechoslovak federalization, became two independent countries. It is sometimes known as the Velvet Divorce, a reference to the bloodless velvet revolution of 1989 that led to the end of the rule of the Communist Party of Czechoslovakia and the formation of a democratic government.

Consulting Jobs

After I officially retired from New Brunswick Savings on December 31, 1989, I continued my long established investment management practice and kept active with my real estate partnerships. Being still of sound mind and body, I decided on a new career. Being an Executor was socially fulfilling and useful but still did not take much of my time so I decided to offer myself to the legal fraternity as an expert witness in banking matters.

Back when I was president at State Bank of Raritan Valley I had done a couple of stints as an expert witness in banking matters, and my retirement gave me time to pursue that vocation. I put an advertisement in the New Jersey Law Journal and pretty soon was getting one or two expert witness jobs a month. My expertise was in the area of lender liability (when a borrower sues a bank) but I also took on simple check fraud and similar cases. Sometimes I would be hired by the lawyers for banks; sometimes by insurance company lawyers and at other times by lawyers representing unhappy borrowers.

On my very first expert witness job, my client, a lawyer, used my written opinion to settle the case but was not anxious to pay my fee. This taught me to require that they send a check, as the saying goes - up front.

From then on being an expert witness worked out well with about one case a month coming in. Occasionally, when a case was not settled I had to appear in court and I found this quite empowering. On one occasion that I remember clearly, the judge told both lawyers to sit down because he wanted to talk to the expert to find out what the legal issue was about and what actual banking practice was.

One day I came home from court and found my blood pressure to be on the high side, so I stopped advertising my availability in the legal newspaper. In a year or so the cases ramped down.

This sideline paid rather well and I had a lot of fun doing it for about three years, but, as time went on, I found court appearances getting enervating. And the inevitable delays sometimes cut into Doris' and my travel schedules. As I got older and after my bypass operation in 1998, I started turning down consulting opportunities and really retired.

I had never really fit the image of a New York banker. After my first five years and training in New York I started an eight-bank job-hopping trek, during which I accrued little money but many titles topping out as president of a couple of small banks in New Jersey.

It has occurred to me that Doris was a saint to put up with my restlessness as with each new bank there would be a new and different house and more work for her. She was always supportive and never complained.

I may have mentioned it in another context, but just about the time of my retirement, I got four executorships which involved little actual work since the legal and accounting formalities (over a period of months) were attended to by an excellent trust attorney and a CPA, both of whom I hired for the jobs. This kind of profitable work is usually snagged by lawyers but the two businessmen – and subsequently their wives named me as executor in their wills - were former bank customers of mine.

A number of years before, a customer who evolved into being a friend and neighbor asked me if I would be willing to be named as his Executor. Maurice Aaron, a plumbing wholesaler with several locations, had three children but went over their heads and hired me as executor, very wisely noting that he wants his children to remain friends after he dies. And so it was, I took the heat of carrying out his financial wishes and his children remained on speaking terms. After some twenty years of being his designated Executor, the will, as the expression goes, "matured." In addition to performing a necessary service for the Aaron family, I discovered that being an Executor paid very well and the work was well within my capacity.

A year after Maurice died I had the sad duty of performing Executor services for his wife, Vivian. One of Maurice's two sons, Jeffrey, showed some resentment at his father's having named an outsider to be Executor. He never knew, however, that I made a lot more money for him and his siblings, by applying my financial expertise to the Estate's several million dollar bond portfolio, than what it cost in Executor's fees.

Later, I became an Executor for my good friend, and sometimes real estate partner, Roger Varney and eventually managed his, and his wife's, estates of some eight or ten million dollars (also big money in those days). Roger Varney had no children but left more than 5 million to his college and also named me the trustee of several trusts.

I mention the Aaron and Varney estates because the pay was on a par with my banking salaries with an input of only 5% of my time. The actual legal and tax work was performed by a lawyer and Certified Public Accountant experienced in such matters. Into my 80s one of the resulting trusts was still yielding me a small income.

Enjoying Great Britain

We had made several annual forays involving the lives of my kinsfolk, but in 1993 we had other bells to ring. The reunion of the 20-30 Club was a momentous event, after which we relaxed.

After the activities of spring and summer, we slipped off to Great Britain for a 3 week Elderhostel program, sleeping in college dormitories, listening to lectures on the life and struggles of the ancient Celts, Romans, Vikings, and Druids. We traveled by bus and spent a week in London, another in Wales and the third in and around Cornwall and the Moors.

Two highlights of this trip were a dramatic Druid sacrifice ceremony which I wrote and directed, and an afternoon tramping across Dartmoor examining ancient religious stones.

My Philosophy – The Fiddler Poem

Around 1993 or 1994 Doris and I attended an Elderhostel study program in Sligo, Ireland, the subject of which was the life and works of the poet, W.B. Yeats. Among his writings I found a little poem which, I feel, exemplifies my personal philosophy. It's not particularly profound but it speaks to me in a way I can't put into words that are any better than the poem itself. His poem is entitled The Fiddler of Dooney. So, here it is, with apologies to Mr. Yeats for the few changes I have made to fit my own lifestyle.

The Immigrants' Son, An American Story

The Fiddler of Moravian Village	*The Fiddler of Dooney*
When I play my fiddle in the Village, Folk dance like a wave of the sea; My cousin's a doctor in Prague, My brother's an engineer here.	WHEN I play on my fiddle in Dooney, Folk dance like a wave of the sea; My cousin is priest in Kilvarnet, My brother in Moharabuiee.
I passed my brother and cousin: They read in their technical books; I read in my book of songs I bought at the Bethlehem fair.	I passed my brother and cousin: They read in their books of prayer; I read in my book of songs I bought at the Sligo fair
When we come to the end of time To Peter sitting in state, He will smile on the three old codgers, But call me first through the gate:	When we come at the end of time, To Peter sitting in state, He will smile on the three old spirits, But call me first through the gate;
For the good are always the merry, Save by an evil chance, And the merry love the fiddle, And the merry love to dance:	For the good are always the merry, Save by an evil chance, And the merry love the fiddle And the merry love to dance:
And when the folk there spy me, They will all come up to me, With 'Here's the fiddler of the Village!' And dance like the wave of the sea.	And when the folk there spy me, They will all come up to me, With 'Here is the fiddler of Dooney!' And dance like a wave of the sea.
George Trebat	William Butler Yeats

1994 was a "Mix"

My word "Mix" alludes to the 'pretty bad' of times and the 'better' of times. It was not as Charles Dickens wrote in a Tale of Two Cities, *"It was the best of times, it was the worst of times,"* but it certainly had variety.

After our Great Britain excursion we got busy with a couple of Family holiday trips – Bethlehem (Thanksgiving), Boston (Christmas) and Waunakee (New Year's). Wisconsin is always cold in the winter, but in January of 1994 we hit some super freezing weather.

The water pipes froze at the small industrial park where my partner, Karl, and I are managing partners of a five member group. There was a lot of running around and not a little panic before repairs were made and the 12 tenants were happy again. ... We have our fingers crossed that the old industrial boiler will give us another season.

Doris and George 11/28/1994 Edison, New Jersey

In May we went down to Ocean City, Md. For an Elderhostel program where we learned about blue crabs, famous Atlantic coast shipwrecks and marine biology.

June was back to Wisconsin with Betsy, Terry and Danny. This time the weather was much more to my liking.

The *pièce de résistance* was our summer trip to the Czech Republic and Slovakia. The Elderhostel program in Slovakia was run by a group from Slippery Rock U. in PA. Because of the favorable exchange rates, our trip was filled with festive dinners, dancing and Gypsy music. Some interesting lectures focused on the breakup of the former Czechoslovakia and the economic and political consequences. We spent some quality time with relatives and friends in southern Bohemia and Prague before KLMing back home.

We both enjoyed Rutgers University extension courses and we were continually in a whirl of social, community and family activities.

Doris was very active as president and tutor of two students for the Middlesex County Literacy Volunteers, both of us were going to Lifetime Learning lectures. She had her Tuesday book group; her community chorus, and our satisfying social life with a few close friends.

In November we were in San Diego at the Literacy Volunteers convention (I was the 'spouse'), then a wonderful Elderhostel at the San Diego Zoo and wild animal park, and a visit with friends in the area.

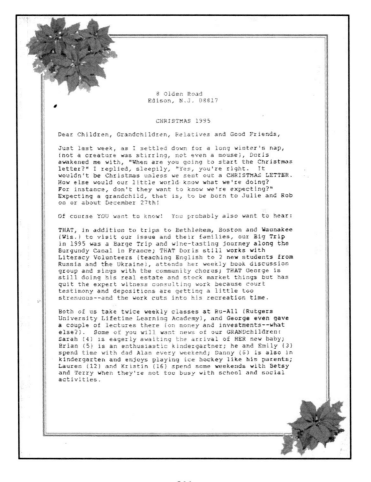

8 Olden Road
Edison, N.J. 08617

CHRISTMAS 1995

Dear Children, Grandchildren, Relatives and Good Friends,

Just last week, as I settled down for a long winter's nap, (not a creature was stirring, not even a mouse), Doris awakened me with, "When are you going to start the Christmas letter?" I replied, sleepily, "Yes, you're right. It wouldn't be Christmas unless we sent out a CHRISTMAS LETTER. How else would our little world know what we're doing? For instance, don't they want to know we're expecting?" Expecting a grandchild, that is, to be born to Julie and Rob on or about December 27th!

Of course YOU want to know! You probably also want to hear:

THAT, in addition to trips to Bethlehem, Boston and Waunakee (Wis.) to visit our issue and their families, our Big Trip in 1995 was a Barge Trip and wine-tasting journey along the Burgundy Canal in France; THAT Doris still works with Literacy Volunteers (teaching English to 2 new students from Russia and the Ukraine), attends her weekly book discussion group and sings with the community chorus; THAT George is still doing his real estate and stock market things but has quit the expert witness consulting work because court testimony and depositions are getting a little too strenuous--and the work cuts into his recreation time.

Both of us take twice weekly classes at Ru-All (Rutgers University Lifetime Learning Academy), and George even gave a couple of lectures there (on money and investments--what else?). Some of you will want news of our GRANDchildren: Sarah (4) is eagerly awaiting the arrival of HER new baby; Brian (5) is an enthusiastic kindergartner; he and Emily (3) spend time with dad Alan every weekend; Danny (5) is also in kindergarten and enjoys playing ice hockey like his parents; Lauren (12) and Kristin (16) spend some weekends with Betsy and Terry when they're not too busy with school and social activities.

One of Many French Trips – August 1995

In one of many trips we happened upon a barge trip along the Burgundy Canal in France. The barge had "L'Escargot" painted on the front and it held 22 passengers and seven crew. Actually, we were

> **Escargot** is a dish of cooked land snails, usually served as an appetizer in France and in French restaurants. The word is also sometimes applied to the living snails of those species which are commonly eaten in this way.

in France two weeks but our stay on the barge was only a week. Stretching my knowledge of French to the limit, I figured that L'Escargot meant snail and, true to its name, the barge slithered along at about three miles an hour, giving us plenty of time to enjoy the scenery or walk along the towpath.

One of our fellow passengers was a short, baldheaded retired Lincoln-Mercury dealer from Visalia, California. He came to my attention almost as soon as we boarded the barge because; about twice a day he would swallow ant-acid pills.

That night, just before nodding off to sleep in our cute little stateroom (complete with shower and toilet), I asked Doris if she too had heard this guy calling out for Rolaids. "No", she heard no such thing and "maybe you've been hearing things". So, the next morning, I purposely steered Doris to the same breakfast table as Bill (that's his name I soon found out) and Trudy. Breakfast was cold cereal, fruit, a croissant, and some very average coffee (they call it, café), he did it again. I think croissants contain about 110% fat.

The barge had a sort of open veranda at the front which you enter from the bar area where all kinds of drinks are available for something like double what they would cost in the US of A. After finishing breakfast we found a comfortable seat in the shade and watched the crew put the barge through one of the many canal locks. A fellow tourist kept saying "Lazy lay barn tops Rolaids", so I asked Doris if she had heard what he said. "Sure", she said, "that was his idea of French and he said, 'Let the Good Times Roll'." At last, the mystery was solved. Then I tried to update his fractured French and came up with 'Laisez le bon temps rulé.

> **Laissez les bons temps rouler** (French pronunciation: [lɛse le bɔ̃ tɑ̃ ʁule]) is a (Louisiana) Cajun French phrase literally translated from the English expression "Let the good times roll."

Before we ever got on the barge we spent several days in'Lyon and Dijon having come south by bus from Paris. In Paris we were met by an Elderhostel guide named Carole. Carole, it turned out was a marine documentary photographer filling in some time between assignments. She wore long skirts which were curiously hung from her hips so as to reveal more than one would expect. Doris didn't think that her costume was sufficiently decorous but I had no complaints. At one point, Carole lit up a cigarette and when I commented on her smoking, she asked why none of the 22 Elderhostel group smoked. In my most stentorian voice I told her that smokers usually don't live long enough to get to the age to qualify as Elder hostellers. Of course, being immortal, she was not impressed.

We were treated to tours, by local guides, of Lyon, Dijon and, to cap our trip, of Paris. In between there were about a dozen small towns that we explored when the barge tied up for the day---usually about four o'clock. The trip was billed as a wine country barge trip, so you can imagine the several Burgandian wineries where we were obliged to taste the local wines. The wine tasting was quite a drag, but we had to be polite so we tasted the proffered liquid and cleared our pallets between vintages with good French bread. After winetasting it was back to the barge by bus for dinner and more wine. Some of the folks did seem to overindulge just a bit, but Doris and I were constrained by the fact that the bar on the barge was not "open", that is, you had to buy your own if you wanted more than what was served. Before I leave the subject of the barge, I hasten to mention that the crew included three rather high spirited young ladies who doubled as waitresses, chambermaids, barmaids and 'ou knows what? The head waitress, who was English, would read the lunch and dinner menu in French and then explain the finer points of Burgundian cuisine in her native tongue. The chef, whom we saw only once or twice, spoke no English and when, toward the end of the trip, he was called out and lavishly complimented on the delicacy and high style of his presentations, just smiled and said something which sounded like "eyes, Kimo sabe".

We arrived at the Trianon Rive Gauche at Rue de Vaugirard and Rue Monsieur le Prince right off Boulevard Saint-Michel which, in case you are not familiar with Paris, is just a few blocks from the Seine in one direction and another short distance from the Jardins du Luxembourg in the other The temperature was something like 37 degrees Celsius which translates to about 95 Fahrenheit and it soon became appropriate to carry one of those store bought plastic bottles of water. Needless to say Paris was in the midst of one of its usual very unusual heat waves. The local Parisian guide somewhat condescendingly informed us that all of those people on the streets were tourists since no-one who is anyone is fool enough to stay in Paris in August. In addition to the usual touristy things one is supposed to do in Paris, we were treated (if that's the right word) to a little excitement because just three days before we arrived a bomb was exploded inside the Cluny metro station which was uncomfortably near our hotel. I think it was set by some Algerian terrorist group wanting to get the attention of the authorities.

Before jumping onto the KLM plane for home, we

had what they call a "free" day, which means that there were no museums or lectures scheduled. So, along with Bill and his wife, Trudy (who wore big rings on ALL her fingers except the thumbs), we took a train to Giverny, an altogether soon to be forgotten town, except for the fact that it was the hometown of Claude Monet, an impressionist painter. There we found copious memorabilia in his former house, now a museum (twenty francs, 's'il vous plait'). There were extensive gardens that were reminiscent of some of his paintings and another museum, also twenty francs, called Maison Americaine, where they served a very respectable lunch washed down with another local wine.

When we got home, they told us we were lucky because we were out of the country during a severe heat wave.

> This description is of just one of the many delightful trips Doris and I went on in the summers between 1974 and 2003. For health reasons (hers and mine), we stopped travelling in 2003 and found it best to stay close to home. More about the reasons for this are to be found elsewhere in the book.

Some Family Visits

At our ages, medical problems seemed to occur more frequently. In the spring we had to cancel a planned Elderhostel trip to Italy because Doris needed an operation on her big toe and I had some drug interaction problems with my cardiac medications (no, not life threatening). Be patient, some of my medical situations are reviewed in "My Medical Adventures".

We did, however, enjoy a six week visit from George's cousin, Miroslav Vane, in the spring. At the end of last year, Miroslav retired from the hospital in his home town of Pisek in the Czech Republic. He now had time for a relaxed visit but alas, his wife, Hana, had to stay at home and keep her nose to the grindstone. Of course, Miroslav's main focus was New York City and it was interesting seeing the Big Apple through his eyes. His prior trips to New York had been the usual whirlwind of museums and it was a real pleasure to show him some of the less frequented neighborhoods. Naturally, his visit with us included a trip to Bethlehem, Pennsylvania to see Julie, her husband Rob, and their daughters Sarah and Rebecca. … We also visited Alan and his children, Emily and Brian, in Dover, Massachusetts. Miroslav didn't speak much English, but quickly developed a rapport with the children who, having a little trouble with his name, dubbed him "Uncle M". While we were in New England we went up to Maine for lobster.

In the summer we made a visit to see Betsy, Terry, and Danny in their new lakeside house in McFarland, a suburb of Madison, Wisconsin. While there we made a side trip to Spillville, Iowa, which is a town of 500 inhabitants. Their only claim to fame is that Antonin Dvorak spent the summer there in 1893 and worked on several of his renowned symphonies while visiting a Czech relative. Spillville was settled by Czech farmers around 1860 and their descendants still proclaim their Czech ancestry although only a few of them can actually speak the language. We also visited Cedar Rapids, which is home to the National Czech and Slovak Museum and Library.....we were surprised to learn that one out every four people in Cedar Rapids claims Czech ancestry.

In addition to our regular teaching, social and cultural actives, we attended classes at RU-ALL (Rutgers University Academy for Lifetime Learning). I was into the history of chemistry and environmental studies while Doris heard lectures on the plays of G. B. Shaw and took a class on writing

THE IMMIGRANTS' SON, AN AMERICAN STORY

her history. She still rejected my numerous subtle hints to start writing about her past. I of course, have been working diligently – sort of – since 1992 on my autobiography.

Doris questioned me as to why we did not just go to our Elderhostel in Williamsburg in December and send them all a modest Christmas card....one that did not disclose our religious preference and with our names printed on it so that we wouldn't have to bother to sign them?

August 10, 1998

Dear Family, Friends and Enemies (short list only) :

We didn't want to wait until Christmas to bore you with our usual litany of activities and events because we know that you're very busy at that time and can't always focus on our very interesting missive. But, that's OK, like the companies that send periodic updates on the rise and fall of our stock holdings, we just want you to reelect us so that we can continue drawing our pay.

This year we really didn't do anything, what with George still being a little cautious after his quite successful bypass operation in January and Doris' not entirely satisfactory big toe realignment. At the end of May we rented a six bedroom house (aka cabin) in Dennisport on Cape Cod and hosted a whole slew of our grandchildren, together with their parents. I t was sort of cool, but warm enough for the kids to swim every day and for the fisherman son-in law to catch enough fish for two gigantic fish frys. At one time, there were fourteen people in the house, not counting a few ants that joined us from the neighborhood.

We usually try to get out of the country for a few weeks in the summer, but this year, except for a slight foray into a corner of nearby Canada, we pretty much stayed in the United States. Toward the middle of July we flew into Seattle and after spending a few days with Doris' sister and our jont brother-in law, we took a train to Vancouver where we boarded a ship, called Universe Explorer, together with some 750 assorted vacationers. We were with an Elderhostel group consisting of forty eight hardy souls and had our own program although we were pretty much had to rub shoulders with the riff raff who came only for the glaciers, salmon fishing, kyaking, white water rafting and sumptuous food, not to mention the crass night time entertainment and Lester Lanin band.

We sailed north from Vancouver along the inland waterway and stopped in cities, really towns, with such quaint names as Ketchikan, Wrangell, Sitka, Valdez and Juneau. Then there was Seward, with it's multi-million dollar new Alaska Sea Life Center, Glacier Bay, the train excursion on the famous White Pass Rail in Skagway............and lots of other things, too numerous to mention. However, we should mention that all of Alaska seems to specialize in selling tee shirts to the tourists; yes, we saw millions and millions of tee shirts and not a few eskimo dolls and sweat shirts with the obligatory embroidery, or whatever they call the imprinting.

The Elderhostel group had an authentic Tlinget Indian (er, Native American) attached who told us a lot about the native culture and history and a lot, lot more. All things being equal, we may zip into the Czech Republic in the fall where our relatives just happen to have an extra apartment in their house near Prague. But we'll save that and ensuing events for Christmas letter, which, we realize, you'll be anxiously awaiting.

The Two Trebats
Eight Olden Road
Edison, N.J. 08817

Doris & George

GEORGE TREBAT

Season's Greetings

Christmas 1999

Dear Friends:

About a month ago I wrote a turgid essay spelling out my lifelong quest for the answer to the mystery of life. It was my idea that this essay would be my contribution to our annual Christmas Letter and that Doris would write a separate page telling you what you really want to know. Well, the essay got longer and longer and I got all tangled up with my ideas about religion, science, astronomy, philosophy, mysticism, genetics, gravity, electromagnetics, the big bang, superstring theory, theology, mythology ....and a few more. After letting the essay sit for a month, or so, I said to myself; "No, I can't impose all of this on my friends. I'll have to cut it down and just share the essence, if that's possible".

So, what was I trying to say? To start with I made it clear that I was raised without any religious training whatsoever and I look upon this as a big plus because I entered my quest for the meaning of life (or God, if you like) without any ritualistic preconceptions. This led me to the study of various religions and ways of thinking.

Now, if you think that I'm some kind of agnostic or anarchist, you're dead wrong. Science has convinced me that the world is round, (no matter what the pope says), and that there are billions and billions of stars out there. Next, none of the scientists really know what came before the so-called big bang. My personal insight is that we're in an evolving universe and that the mind of mankind has yet to evolve to the point of being able to understand what it's all about. Many of the more sophisticated thinkers throughout history have tried to rationalize their belief in God by saying that it really boils down to a matter of faith. That is, when you don't know, and you know that you don't know, you make a mystical leap and say, "I believe, because I must". Well, I just can't make that leap.

My instinct tells me that there is some kind of creative force out there and I'm quite willing to call it God. You can call it what you like.....or call it nothing. My hope is that maybe, in a few thousand, or a few million years (if we're still here), God will see fit to reveal herself in a way that our minds can understand.

Until then, stay tuned, and have a Merry Christmas and Happy Chanukah.

The Immigrants' Son, An American Story

> "WHAT YOU REALLY WANT TO KNOW" (as told by Doris)
>
> To begin on a happy note, the biggest event of 1999 for Trebats big and small, was THE WEDDING, on January 9th, of Alan and Leslie (Lee) Guertin, on January 9th. Our clan and assorted others gathered in Boston on that snowy weekend to share in the celebration. The wedding ceremony took place in an historic Unitarian church near the Boston Commons; our grandkids (Sarah and Emily, Brian and Danny) were thrilled to be included in the wedding party as junior bridesmaids and ushers. We're very happy to have Lee as a member of our Trebat family.
>
> This year has brought sadness, too, with the deaths of Lee's mother and of three other long-time beloved friends. We will miss all of them, and have been reminded that we should treasure every day of life and live it to the fullest.
>
> George is doing very well, having recovered fully after last year's bypass; he is fortunate to have good doctors, and is conscientious with his diet and exercise. He keeps busy, what with picking up new skills on the computer (with the help of our son-in-law, Rob), and keeping close tabs on the stock-market. Courses at Ru-All (adult lifelong learning institute) offer him plenty of opportunity for mental activity, along with the great quantities of material that he reads in financial publications, science tomes, and an occasional novel.
>
> Keeping up with the reading for my book group's weekly discussion in the library provides a challenge for me. Recommended best reads: "Poisonwood Bible" by Barbara Kingsolver, and "Voyage of the Narwhal" by Andrea Barrett. On Tuesday nights I enjoy being part of a teaching team that leads a Conversation Group in the library for people from a wide variety of countries who need help in speaking English. A bi-weekly swimming class at the Y is less interesting, but helps me to keep the joints oiled so that I can keep up with George when we go traveling.
>
> Speaking of travel: We spent two enjoyable weeks in late May visiting George's cousins in the Czech Republic. In August we relaxed with Betsy, Terry and Danny at their lakeside home near Madison, Wisconsin. You haven't tasted really GOOD fish until you've eaten the ones that Terry catches, and cooks! In late October we cruised with Elderhostel, up the Columbia and Snake Rivers, mostly in Oregon, but also briefly in Washington and Idaho. It was a wonderful experience, both on the ship and on many field excursions, to learn about the Oregon Trail and the geology of the region. On this same trip we had a memorable reunion with my closest childhood friend, Lee; we grew up together in John Day, a small town in eastern Oregon, and hadn't seen each other for 50 years or so. Our husbands got acquainted while Lee and I reminisced, especially about the many hours we'd spent playing piano duets as kids, and shared pictures of our children and grandchildren.
>
> We've just had a busy Thanksgiving weekend with Alan's family --Lee, Brian (9), and Emily (7), from Boston, and Julie's family--Rob, Sarah (8), and Rebecca (3), from Bethlehem, Pa. Our co-grandparents, Bernice and Larry Leder, came to join us for the feast. Now we're looking forward to Christmas, when Betsy, Terry, and Danny (10) will be here to visit, and Julie and her family will join us for Christmas Eve and Christmas Day. The older kids will be locked in deep trading sessions with their Pokemon cards while waiting for the presents to be opened. Rebecca will be excited--it will be a big week for her, with lots of presents, since she will celebrate her 4th birthday on December 29th.
>
> Our best wishes for a happy and healthy New Year, and on into the Millenium.
>
> *Doris*

As you may have surmised from our sampling of Christmas letters, we are secular Christians (*I like to tell people I'm a Druid*), but we align our lives with the Judeo-Christian ethic. Many of our friends have been secular Jews and/or Christians ... which means that they come from, and adhere to, their particular cultural and religious background, but go light on the formal part of the religious practice. Luckily none of our children or friends professed any fundamentalist faith so we were pretty much free to think about the mysteries of life and its origin within a larger context of Peace on Earth and Goodwill to all Men (also women). ...

You can glean many more details of some of our other traipses by reading the entire 1988 Interim letter. Perhaps the most telling contribution from the regular 1998 Christmas letter (which we didn't include) would have been the dialogue in the cartoon at the end. A man is speaking to his wife and reporting, "Mail is running three to one against our Christmas newsletter." That's an interesting observation, or is it?

My portion of the previous 1999 Christmas letter dealt at length with religion in the context of the mystery of life. Doris followed up by contributing some less esoteric writings.

IN THE CZECH REPUBLIC

My Czech Connection

As I've noted before, my connection with my second favorite country, Czechoslovakia, with its language and its people are a permanent part of my psyche.

That part of the world represents my roots, even when the names Bohemia, Moravia and Slovakia keep getting mixed together; then separated; then rejoined. At the center of its culture, if not geographically, is the golden city: Prague. To the south, in South Bohemia, are the homes of my Czech cousins.

Nowadays, referring to 1999, this is a picture of life in the Czech Republic, but it wasn't always that way.

To briefly recap: it's almost ten years since the so-called velvet revolution, which overthrew the Czechoslovakian Communist government. Václav Havel, the dissident playwright, imprisoned by the Communist Czech government because of his "disruptive activities and subversive plays," was elected president of a new, western style, democratic government. In 1992 or 1993 the Slovaks, led by an unreconstructed Communist, and listening to the siren song of nationalism, decided that they wanted their "own" government and, in a peaceful manner, the country was split into the ten million population of the Czech Republic and the five million population nation of Slovakia. Since the split-up, the Czechs, which have most of the industry, have prospered and the Slovaks have done well too.

I was particularly sad to see Czechoslovakia break up; first, because I thought it was not a good move for the Slovaks, and second, because I've always considered myself to be a true Czechoslovak - my father being a Slovak and my mother being a Czech. The two languages, in fact, are so similar that they are practically interchangeable, with the main difference being a matter of accent. For instance, when my father married my mother, he, being the more verbal, simply changed his accent and spoke Czech at home. The only time I heard him speak Slovak was when he was in the company of some of his Slovak drinking buddies.

As in many things, the difference between communism and capitalism is not a matter of black and white. What I'm trying to say is that I don't think that the communists have it all wrong and that capitalism is an unalloyed good. The Communist ideology has some good features, for instance, under the Communist government, everyone was employed and everyone was basically paid the same. While this ideology sounds good, history has shown that when everyone is paid the same there is no incentive to excel, and the quality of manufactured goods goes down and services are delivered in a surly manner. All of this contributed to a downward economic spiral, which in due course, caused the downfall of the Soviet empire. If you want to know more about Communist ideology and why capitalism works better, you'll have to go to the library or the internet and look these subjects up since there are thousands of good sources that explain the economics of totalitarianism and capitalism a lot better than I can.

What I noticed on my several trips to Czechoslovakia during the Communist era was that very lack of incentive to work hard. People became very self-centered in the sense that they did what work they had to and lived for the weekends when they could escape to their country cottages. Retail clerks, waiters, teachers, and even doctors all performed their duties in an apathetic manner - how could it be otherwise, when everyone was paid almost the same?

During my 1999 visit, I quizzed my cousin Miroslav on this subject and he told me that while there were differing income levels in the Communist era the spread was quite narrow. For instance, as an experienced physician, he got paid about twice as much as an unskilled laborer and just one third more than a nurse or office clerk.

In 1999 I made my eighth visit to my ethnic roots in the Czech Republic (I had also been to Slovakia twice, but since I have no contacts, and don't know of any relatives there, most of my comments relate to my Czech side). My first trip had been in 1930 when, as a three year old, I stayed the summer, with my mother, at my grandmother's house in the tiny village of Vitence. In my archives I have photos of my three first cousins and I gathered around my grandmother, who was then a 76 year old widow. (One of those photos has been reproduced on page 26.) My second visit was as an American soldier in 1946, just as the war was ending. After that I didn't see my relatives again until 1974 when Doris and I flew to Prague with our two daughters, then 13 and 18 (Alan, then 16, was on a trip to Germany with his high school class). After that Doris and I were in Europe, and particularly, the Czech Republic, on many more occasions, and somewhere there are more photo albums to prove it.

By 1999, after ten years of sometimes halting steps toward full democracy, the Czech Republic had clearly made amazing economic progress. Albeit with compact cars, by then they had excellent roads crowded with traffic; supermarkets were the preferred shopping venue, town squares had been reconstructed, and stores were full of imported and domestic merchandise.

On the down side, the beautiful Prague metro system became rife with pickpockets who preyed on unwary tourists. During the Communist era, there were no pickpockets because the punishment was very severe and did not fit the crime. During the 1990 – 2000 era, the enthusiastic democratic government encouraged free enterprise by distributing shares in previously government owned enterprises. Since then, teams of American lawyers and government officials helped the Czechs put in place a Securities and Exchange Commission and other institutions needed for a free functioning market economy (more or less). During the 45 years of foreign domination such democratic institutions, as there were in 1938, had long since eroded and the bureaucrats had to be retrained (the Communist functionaries, like opportunists everywhere, disappeared when the government changed - they resurfaced as government servants who said they had been "forced to" work for the Communists).

During my visit in late May 1999, Doris and I spent two enjoyable weeks in the Czech Republic. Every time we visited, Doris and I made the rounds, visiting my three first cousins; children of my mother's oldest brother, Jan, who did not immigrate to America but stayed to take over Grandpa's job as forester for a large estate. As in the past, my most prosperous cousin, Miroslav Vane, a retired physician who lives in the town of Pisek, was our host and guide.

The time had come for him to return the favor after his six week visit to the United States two years before. Pisek is a beautiful regional capital in southern Bohemia and Miroslav put us up in what amounts to an apartment in his hillside house overlooking the city. His wife, Hana, also a physician, is ten years younger than Mirek and was not much to be seen because she was still working during many of our trips. We saw sons Tomas and Martin, but most of our time was spent with Mirek who drove us all over the country in his new four door Mitsubishi sedan.

On the particular day I'm going to describe, we set out for Plzeň (Pilsen, of Pilsner beer fame), an industrial city of 200,000 an hour northwest of Pisek, to make our traditional visit to see Mirek's older brother Jiři, another of my first cousins.

Visiting Jiři in Plzeň

The street on which Jiři lives looks exactly the same as it did five years ago, ten years ago or even fifteen years ago. Jiři lives in a once nice, spacious apartment, in a run-down apartment house that had not seen repairs in over fifty years. Jiři's second floor apartment still had that look of having seen better days and Jiri's sixteen year old cat still looked upon us with suspicion.

The doors on his dingy, run-down apartment house looked ready to fall apart and the gray-brown stucco on the building was peeling. The only change was the number of cars; there were about five times as many, both in traffic and parked on both sides of Borska Ulice.

Jiři, five years older than I, was an engineering technician at the Skoda munitions plant in Pilsen. He is a widower who lives with his unemployed 43 year old bachelor son, also called Jiři. Jiři, the younger, hardly says a word and seems to be more than a little retarded.

Jiři, who had lived in the same apartment house for some fifty years, lives on a small government pension which he supplements by collecting rents and making minor repairs for the absentee building owner. Jiři, Sr. is a five foot tall hunchback who was dealt a bad hand in the game of life.

First, he had rickets as a child, which caused the problem with his back; and then, he grew to maturity during the four year Nazi occupation of his country. In those days, the Germans planned to make their Slavic subjects into a servant class for the 1000 year Reich. Thus they closed the universities and limited the educational possibilities of their brighter subjects to technical schools. Jiři, at least as smart as his younger brother, Miroslav, never had a chance, and had to spend his working life as a draftsman.

Back to our trip to Pilsen.

After recounting the state of health of our respective children and grandchildren we got down to the business of "the showing of pictures", as I call the obligatory review of the photos that Doris carries in her purse. I wondered what was going through Jiri's mind as he glanced at the wedding pictures of our son, Alan. The pictures were taken the prior January in an opulent looking private club in the Back Bay section of Boston. Jiři did not comment when I explained that Alan had divorced three years ago and that the flower girl and usher in some of the photos were the children from his first marriage. When the conversation started to run out of steam, Mirek noted that it was almost one o'clock and suggested that we find a good restaurant for lunch. Just down the street from the apartment, there was a small hotel with a restaurant where the food was quite good. Not being a Czech, Doris stuck to her usual glass of wine instead of joining the rest of us in the Czech custom of quaffing a tall glass of Pilsner beer. (They engage in this ceremony at the least provocation.)

Jiři has another son, Jan, who is tall, strong, and gainfully employed at the Pilsen Skoda Works, where everything from turbines to tanks and aircraft are manufactured. I think he's some sort of technical administrator.

In contrast to his brother; Jan has been happily married

for many years and has fathered six boys. The oldest, maybe 37 (as of 1999), went to college and the youngest, about 17 is just finishing high school. On some visits we go to see Jan and his super-efficient and pleasant wife, Mariska, who manages to keep a four room apartment (replete with double beds) looking spotless.

We strolled around the now beautiful town square in Pilsen and then back to Jiri's apartment. After coffee and cake it was time to head back to Pisek. Before leaving, Doris gave Jiri a token gift and some toys for the grandchildren; privately, and under protest from him, I gave Jiři an envelope with some money to be used for the children.

The Forester's Cottage

While in Pilsen, we talked about the forester's cottage in Tisov. Strangely, Mirek, (who does not seem to have a strong sense of family history, but who lives only fifteen minutes from Tisov) had never been there and had never seen the Tisov cottage. My mother, the last of the thirteen, was born there when her mother was 49 and in 1922 said goodbye, possibly forever, to the house in Tisov.

The next day, with a little urging from me, we set out to find the house. The village was so small that it did not show up on any of the maps we had, but Mirek had an idea as to where it might be. We found it pretty easily. On the edge of town, Mirek asked an elderly resident where the old forester's cottage might be found, explaining that "these Americans are looking for their roots". The old man had no problem in directing us to the old cottage, which he said was empty and in disrepair.

After a few wrong turns, we found it on a bend in the one lane road. From the front door I could see the open field, where my mother tended geese as a girl, and to the right were the three large trees that my grandfather planted more than ninety years ago. As my grandfather was the forester employed by the local landowning baron, he never owned the house, but was allowed to live in it as part of his job. The baron lived in a castle at Lnáře, and owned a large tract of forest and ponds where fish were raised for the market, but more about that in another chapter.

Later that night, Mirek telephoned his high school classmate, Mrs. Zralá, the present day owner of both the Lnáře Castle and the surrounding forests. She also still owns the forester's cottage which she plans to fix up as a weekend cottage. When asked about it, she said, "Oh yes, I know the cottage well, that's the place where your grandparents lived in the early part of the century. At that time a baron owned the Lnáře Castle and the cottage was part of his property."

To the present owner, it's just an old house in need of repair, but to me it's a font of nostalgic memories. I can't guess at how many times, my mother told me about her life in Tisov; when she was a goose girl; when she was saved from drowning in the pond by her older sister; and when she and three girls from nearby villages left for the train to Hamburg and unknown adventures across the sea.

The Baron's Tenants

Around 1880, give or take a few years, Jan Vane, my grandfather, an itinerant bricklayer came to a town with the tongue-twister name of Lnáře near Kasejovice in South Bohemia. Bohemia was then a part of the mighty Austro-Hungarian Empire and now forms with Moravia, the Czech Republic.

We don't know where my grandfather moved from, but family legend has it that he was hired to build a brick wall in the front of the chateau belonging to a Baron Ludwig who owned the surrounding forests, lakes and a large number of villages.

Baron Ludwig inherited the chateau from ancestors who were granted it and the surrounding lands for services to the crown in the Hussite Wars. The lands remained under the control of the family through the dissolution of the Austro-Hungarian Empire after 1918.

Baron Ludwig spent the winter and social season in Vienna. In spring and summer he came to the 200 window chateau in Lnáře. The surrounding forests were rich with wildlife and were used for hunting parties for Baron Ludwig's guests. Sumptuous feasts were served in the castle, as the chateau was then known.

The local peasants were the Baron's tenants, but to support his lifestyle the Baron had to make the property income producing. He developed a fishing industry by seeding the local ponds and streams with carp. The peasants harvested them for markets in Prague, Vienna and Budapest.

Apparently being satisfied with my grandfather's industriousness, Baron Ludwig asked him if he would consider coming into the chateau's employ and taking on the job of forester. Grandpa, then in his early 30s, jumped at the opportunity. His primary job was to keep the streams oxygenated in the winter by chopping holes in the ice and to watch over the forests and fields which were part of the Baron's estate.

Grandpa was quite handy, and in time became a self-taught veterinarian taking care of the sick animals for the estate and for local farm tenants.

In due time grandpa settled in, was given a small cottage on the estate and married a local girl named Marie Klima. Over some twenty-five years he and grandma had thirteen children, of which seven grew to maturity. In those days there was no family planning, everything was left to God's will. My mother, Albina, youngest of the thirteen came to the United States in 1922, following her oldest sister, Marie as well as two other sisters and one brother.

The two oldest brothers, my uncles, stayed in Bohemia. My oldest uncle, Jan, inherited grandpa's job as forester for the Baron's estates after my grandfather's death around 1912. The second oldest uncle, Anton, became an apprentice tailor in Vienna for five years. After the term of apprenticeship was completed he returned to Bohemia and opened a tailor shop in a neighboring town of Hvožďany.

The Chateau at Lnáře

Now fast forward to 1999. It was springtime and my wife Doris and I were on our sixth visit to what was then, the Czech Republic. On these visits our "headquarters" had usually been my cousin Miroslav's house in Pisek, in southern Bohemia, a beautiful town of some 30,000 souls, the centerpiece of which is the oldest stone bridge in the Czech Republic.

Miroslav, Uncle Jan's youngest son, had recently retired as the head of the Ob-Gyn department. Miroslav asked what I wanted to do or see. Having been to Prague many times, I said I would like to concentrate on the villages and towns of particular relevance to our family.

One of the first places we stopped was the chateau at Lnáře. The present day owner was sixty something lady named Anna Zralá; a retired chemical engineer. Mrs. Zralá, it turned out, was a high school chum of my cousin Miroslav. Before going out to the chateau, a half hour from Pisek, Miroslav phoned her and she invited us "for coffee". Together with Miroslav's 29 year old son Tomas, then a resident in neurology at the Pisek regional hospital, we drove out to Lnáře where Mrs. Zralá met us at the chateau's main entrance. I didn't know it at the time, but Miroslav later told me that Mrs. Zralá is the granddaughter of the lawyer who bought the property in 1918.

For forty years during what they called "the Communist time" the chateau and surrounding estate had been taken over by the government. For many years the chateau was left to decay but in the late 70s the government decided to renovate the chateau and gardens. As one would expect of a totalitarian government, they used prison labor to plant the gardens and repair the stone walls. They conscripted artists and artisans from Prague to renovate the historic murals that covered the walls and ceilings of the large ballrooms, sitting rooms and dining areas. Parquet floors were restored and the 200 some odd windows and slate roofs were repaired. The communists, we were told, planned to use the chateau, which included many bedrooms, as a meeting place for party functionaries.

In 1989, following the velvet revolution, former owners started to petition the democratic government for the return of properties confiscated by the Communists. Mrs. Zralá and the other members of her family regained possession of the chateau at Lnáře and certain surrounding forests and fields. She and her brother split the property and she wound up with the chateau itself and its several acres of gardens.

She met us at the chateau entrance, where there were also several other adults and a number of children. There were mumbled introductions all around and we discovered that Mrs. Zralá was hosting a birthday party for a six year old grandchild. We tried to excuse ourselves but she insisted that we join "the party". She led us to an enormous dining room on the second floor of the chateau which we reached by way of a six person elevator. A T-shaped table with exquisite dinnerware was set as if for a banquet. Luckily, there was no banquet but a lovely low key birthday party with ice cream, cake and toys for the birthday child. After they devoured the cake and had their fill of soda, the five children almost disappeared with the toys to the far side of the dining hall. After urging upon us several rounds of coffee and irresistible cakes, Mrs. Zralá took us on a tour of the chateau.

She explained that since the house and grounds are very expensive to maintain, she had to develop a source of income. Thus, the sign outside the chateau advertising rooms for rent and proclaiming a conference center fell into context. After we looked at what seemed like hundreds of restored frescoes, our hostess led us outside to a still winter-logged Olympic sized swimming pool and tennis courts also in need of much tender loving care. Mrs. Zralá, in her relaxed way, noted that her architect has improvement plans for the entire property but that progress depends on cash flow – a very capitalistic concept and something with which the Communist government never concerned itself.

A Walk in the Woods

One day Doris and I decided to take a walk in the woods behind Miroslav's house in Pisek. He lives half way up a hill at the foot of the forest in a house that it took him five years to build, during the communist era. In those days, it was hard to get building materials, and worse than that, construction people were almost impossible to come by. All of the electricians, plumbers and masons worked for the government during the week and did private jobs on the weekends. And, they had to be catered to with free lunch and beer and, in Miroslav and Hana's case, free medical care.

The forest starts a short but steep walk up the hill from the house and has a very pleasant walking path that leads to a large pond. When we got to the pond, we sat at a picnic table to enjoy the view. There were four or five children splashing around in the shallow part of the pond and now and then one could see hikers trudging up the hill. As we sat there, an older red Skoda automobile drove up to the edge of the pond and a gray haired man got out and proceeded to take off his pants, shoes and shirt. The disrobing revealed emerald blue swim shorts and a well-tanned body. The man, who looked to be in his seventies, must have been familiar with the pond because, without testing the water, he briskly walked up to a concrete footing and dove in head first. He disappeared for about a minute and surfaced some fifty feet out, then swam back, climbed the embankment, shook off the excess water and ran his fingers through his still abundant hair.

The man noticed that Doris and I were watching him and waved to us, saying (in Czech), "Nice day, isn't it?" We walked over to where he was toweling off and, in the course of exchanging pleasantries we learned that his name was Dr. Kolar.

When he realized that we were obviously Americans, he told us that he had been all over the United States some years ago on a lecture tour, mentioning New York, Chicago, Los Angeles and several other cities.

Getting interested, I asked, "And what was your subject?"

He replied that he had been head of surgery at the Pisek regional hospital and was giving talks in hospitals on certain aspects of surgery. Still speaking in Czech, and translating for Doris between sentences, I said, "Oh, then you must know my cousin, Miroslav Vane, whom we're visiting and who is retired from the same hospital."

He laughed, saying, "....of course, everyone in Pisek knows Mirek."

Later in the conversation I asked Dr. Kolar if he was now in private practice since the change in governments in 1989 had permitted physicians to set up independent offices. "No," he replied, "It would be too expensive to set up in practice at my age so I'm not practicing as a doctor anymore." And then, for me came the shocker.

He continued, "I now have a job as a night watchman at a factory." With lots of questions running through my head, but not wanting to pry any further, I turned the conversation back to my relatives who live just down the hill and, as we parted he asked me to make sure to give his regards to Mirek.

On the way back to our host's house, I told Doris how shocked I was that a clearly eminent surgeon, who undoubtedly held the lives of thousands of people in his hands in his forty, or more, years of practice, would have to spend his retirement years working as a night watchman. When we got back to the house I immediately told Miroslav that we had bumped into one of his medical colleagues and how disappointed I was to learn that he would be working at a menial job at the age of 72. Miroslav didn't seem at all surprised and explained that Dr. Kolar could no longer practice because the medical insurance companies would no longer "accept" him and that his pension was so small that it was not unusual that he would be supplementing it with a menial job. I pressed on, "But, really, Mirku, this man was the head of surgery. Is a meager pittance of a pension all that he's entitled to after a lifetime in a highly responsible job?

"Yes," Miroslav replied, "although we're now a democracy and living conditions have greatly improved since the days under Communism, there are still a lot of inequities in the system. One of them, as you have discovered, is the pension system." He went on to explain that under the Communist system the pension would have been reasonably adequate because the general wage and price levels were strictly controlled. But now, there is inflation and people are earning much higher incomes. The pensioners, however, are stuck between a rock and a hard place because no funds were set aside for their retirement and the government has no choice but to pay them under the old system.

Miroslav himself, as a retired physician, gets the same pittance of a pension but is better off because his wife, Hana, ten years younger and now, a neurologist in private practice has a much higher income than she did under Communism. Miroslav supplements his pension by teaching in a nursing school one day a week and also by filling in one afternoon a week for a fellow obstetrician/gynecologist, in private practice. He said that he is "sort of moonlighting under his friend's license, and just doing check-ups, because, like Dr. Kolar, he is no longer able to practice his profession because of insurance company restrictions,

If they were retired physicians in the United States, both Miroslav and Dr. Kolar would be living in nice houses, driving Jaguars and, either still working, or spending their time chasing little white balls on a golf course. As you may remember, my original observation was that although the Czech Republic is no longer run by a Communist government, their citizens' living conditions are immeasurably improved. Well, not exactly.

Some Czech Geography
Some Proper Names and Locations in the Czech Republic

Praha or **Prague** *Praha* [pronounced 'praɦa] is the capital and largest city of the Czech Republic in the NW of the country on the Vltava river, the city is home to about 1.3

million people, while its metropolitan area is estimated to have a population of nearly 2.0 million. [50-04N, 14 -26E]

Plzeň, or **Pilsen** is a city about 90 km west of Prague . [49-45N, 13 -23E]

Poděbrady is a historical spa town 50km east of Prague . [50-08N, 15 -08E]

Kolín is a town some 55 km (34 mi) east from Prague. . [50-01N, 15 -12E]

Kutná Hora is a city in Czech Republic in the Central Bohemian Region. [49-47N, 15 -16E]

České Budějovice is the largest city in the South Bohemian Region . [48-59N, 14 -29E]

Třeboň is a historical town in South Bohemian Region of Czech ***Republic***. [49-00N, 14 - 46E]

Modrava is a village and municipality Klatovy District in the Plzeň Region [Cannot locate]

Vimperk (Pronounced: [vɪmpɛrk] ;) is a town in the South Bohemian Region. [49-03N, 13 -47E]

Strakonice (Pronounced: [ˈstrakoɲɪtsɛ]) is a town of 24,000 in the South Bohemian Region. [49-15N, 13 -55E]

Sedlice may refer to several places in Czech Republic and Slovakia

Blatná (Czech pronunciation: [ˈblatnaː]) is a small town in the South Bohemian Region. [49-26N, 13 -53E]

The Immigrants' Son, An American Story

Kocelovice. 177 people 24km N of Strakonice, 81 km SW of Prague. [49 -28 N, 13 – 50 E]

Kasejovice is a town of 1300 in the Czech Republic in the Plzeň-south District. [49 -27 N, 13 – 44E]

Lnáře (English *Lnar*) a small municipality of 700 in the Czech Republic 35km NW of Pisek or 50km SE of Pilsen. [49 -28 N, 13 – 48 E]

Hvožďany a small municipality 70km SW of Prague [Cannot locate]

Hejnice (Czech pronunciation: ['ɦɛjɲɪtsɛ]) is a small town of about 2,600 in the Liberec District in Liberec Region. . [50-25N, 15 -11E]

Vitence where grandmother lived. Where I spent summer in 1930.

Nepomuk (Czech pronunciation: ['nɛpomuk]) is a town in the Pilsen Region 30 km to the S-SW from Pilsen.

Tisov a little village, not on the big map, where my grandfather died in 1920 and from which my mother emigrated (while he was still alive).

Radonice (Pronunciation: ['radoɲɪtsɛ]) is a village of 1000+ situated in NW Czech Republic 10 km S of Kadaň,. Its name is derived from a personal name Radoň – *the village of Radoň's people.* [Cannot locate]

Písek (Czech pronunciation: ['piːsɛk]) is a town in the South Bohemian Region of the Czech Republic. It has a population of 30,000 [49-19N, 14-10E]

Pisek Festival Five to six hundred performers take part in the Písek festival every year.

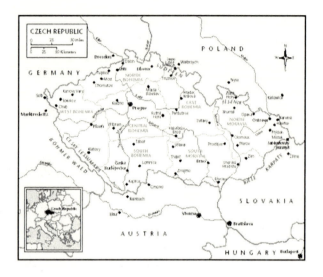

The Millennium and Beyond

Entering the Millennium

When we reached the year 2000 alive and well, we were still traveling and still learning.

As those of you who read beyond the first paragraph of our 1999 Christmas letter may remember, I was trying to figure out "what it's all about". You'll be relieved that I still don't know, although I may be getting a little closer. The following year I buckled down and read some more books on theoretical physics and astronomy. I hasten to admit that my science background is very limited (I can't do the equations) but it literally blew my mind to discover that we are all made of stardust. Every atom of every element in our bodies, except hydrogen, was manufactured inside stars scattered across the universe and recycled to become part of us. (Did you remember to take your calcium, zinc, magnesium, chromium, potassium and all the others today?)

Our travels in 2000 included a wonderful barge trip in January and February on the Mississippi from New Orleans to Memphis, then in June we were in Galway, Ireland. Locally we finished our third year at RU-ALL (Rutgers University – Adult Lifetime Learning) in their medical school's Mini Medical School, looking forward toward getting our mini-medical degrees in 2001 (or whatever you can get without homework or exams … and it was only once a week for five weeks).

I was still writing my autobiography, sporadically. Doris suspected that I kept stalling because I thought that if I kept my story "in process"; I'd be able to hold off the grim reaper for years, and years, and years.

In the 2002 Christmas letter, I wrote in some detail about our moving to Pennsylvania. "It seems like only yesterday that I was a ten year old risking his life jumping from roof to roof and hitching in my Yorkville (NYC) tenement neighborhood. Well, anyway, now I'm looking forward to May or June 2003 when we are scheduled to move into a retirement 'cottage' as they term it, being built for us, and for 250 others, in Bethlehem, Pennsylvania. It's called Moravian Village and the structures are going up even as I write this message. While I love our Edison house where we've been for the past twenty years, there are a few things I won't miss, such as mowing grass, clearing snow, cleaning gutters, and on and on. Houses for sale here are scarce and the time to sell seems ripe.

"Besides which, our neighborhood had become more and more upscale with people making large additions and even buying houses and knocking them down to make way for new, so called, trophy houses. Not only that, but I'm about the only guy on our block who does not hire a lawn service. (translation: cheap) When neighbors look questioningly on while I hand wash our cars I tell them that this is my way of saving money and getting 'free' exercise in the bargain."

Doris added more real perspective by noting some basic motives. We would now be close to Julie and her family; we could enjoy numerous cultural activities in the Lehigh Valley, and we would have more of what we wanted in a retirement community.

We expressed our sadness in having to leave good friends and neighbors in central New Jersey, but we hoped, and expected, lots of visits back and forth since it's a quick 75 minute drive on Route 78.

Our Neighborhood Changed

As time passed, the neighborhood had started to change. Those moving in were professionals who were drawn by the proximity of several synagogues and an excellent Jewish elementary school.

First, the widow across the street and her teenaged daughter moved out just after her son got married. In their place came a young Jewish lawyer and his family. I knew all about him, including his salary and financial status, before he moved in because, at that time, I sat on the committee at the New Brunswick Savings Bank that approved mortgage loans. I never mentioned that I had this information to my new neighbor, and when I went over to meet him I asked him questions to which I already knew the answers.

Next, Dr. Morgenstern had a stroke which ended his tenure as a medical practitioner and he and his wife moved back to New York City to be near a son and where Viga Morgenstern, a non-driver, would feel more comfortable. To take their place came Sandy Milgraum, a dermatologist, his wife Sima, and their growing brood of babies, six to be exact. For the first couple of years, Sima seemed always to be pregnant. They moved about a block away to a much bigger house after about two years when his practice went into orbit, because, while still at New Brunswick Savings I urged him to buy a $250,000 laser machine that enabled him – as the local expert in zapping out – to zap out purple grape marks (aggregations of blood cells) that disfigured some faces.

Since he was one of the first dermatologists to own the laser he had patients coming from all over the world and was featured in the media. Of course, I had financed his purchase of the equipment. There they finally seemed to end their orgy of reproduction at seven. Apparently, as in most fundamentalist religious groups, the Orthodox Jews are encouraged to be prolific, but, at some point, most of them seem to call a halt. Maybe they got a special dispensation from their rabbi. When the Milgraums moved the ten houses to Hedges Road, they were replaced by another Orthodox couple. Herb Engel, an accountant, who commuted to New York daily, has a wife, named Cindy, and two children. He left his office early on Friday nights and I sometimes picked him up walking from the New Brunswick railroad station.

But then the neighborhood really started to change as several large orthodox Jewish temples, and a school, were built nearby. By 2003 the neighborhood had become almost completely "observant," as our Jewish neighbors termed it, and people started knocking on our door asking if the house might possibly be for sale.

We sold our Edison house for more than it was worth.

On August 4th 2003 we were among the first "settlers" when we moved into our cottage at 596 Riverwoods Way, and we quickly became involved in our new community. Moravian Village is a continuing care retirement community (CCRC) in Bethlehem, Pennsylvania. We moved into an independent living "cottage" with the option to move into an apartment and get various services in later years.

When you get older it's nice to be near your children. With Betsy having settled in Madison, Wisconsin (where it tends to be very cold in winter) and Alan being unsettled in the Boston Massachusetts area, Julie became the proximate cause that pointed us toward moving to Bethlehem,

Pennsylvania. (Our younger daughter Julie and her husband, Rob Leder, are raising two daughters in Bethlehem.)

THE FAMOUS TREBAT CHRISTMAS LETTER 2006

596 Riverwoods Way
Bethlehem, Pa. 18018
geebat@hotmail.com

Dear friends, near and far:

We've been sending a Christmas Letter for more than 50 years and we're not going to stop now so, please grin and bear it.

The truth is, that we're doing quite well health wise and otherwise. We're into our 4th year in Moravian Village and we're both happy here, and grateful for the many new friends we've made. We'd sure like to see our long-term friends more often but we're always pleased to hear from them by e-mail, snail mail, by phone, and better yet, in person.

Together, in March, we'll be 164 years old. Life here in the Village has many advantages, such as the fine concerts, musical events and plays we enjoy at Lehigh University and other local colleges; bus trips to Pennsylvania hot spots and even to Philadelphia and the Big Apple. On our agenda we still have three daily newspapers, plenty of books, many laps to swim and sights to see.

We're glad that about 35 years ago we decided to take overseas trips annually, as now the urge is still there, but standing in long airport lines or dealing with flight cancellations or missed connections seems a bit daunting. We still get around the country to visit our children, grandchildren and relatives. This year we drove to two Elderhostels in the Northeast, flew to Wisconsin and Doris ventured as far as Seattle to visit her sister.

Before we moved to Bethlehem we had the idea that it would be a quiet backwater where the pace of life would be slower than in commuter-centered New Jersey. Not so. The population explosion here and the rate of new house construction is something fierce. It seems that New Yorkers and Jerseyites have discovered the Lehigh Valley.

Sadly, the happy hunting ground is increasingly claiming some of our friends, neighbors and relatives. We know that we're sitting on the same slippery slope and have accepted the inevitability of our eventual demise (5 years, 10 years, more?) as something better to be accepted than denied.

We wish for you good health, laughter, and a pleasant holiday season.

Doris and George

Doris' Accomplishments

Doris is a lady with many positive attributes, but one she lacked was the willingness to share her thoughts about her life on paper. She didn't put many of her memories to pen, but those few thoughts have been included in the section titled "Early Career". In addition, we worked together to prepare our annual missives. Doris allowed me to execute my flights of fancy, while she edited the pages into more acceptable reading. Some of her many activities and contributions have been captured in those letters, and I will share them now with you.

Doris rose from very simple beginnings, displaying her natural talents for music and teaching throughout her career and beyond. Doris did very well in the field of academe. Doris was born in Chicago, Illinois on April 3, 1923, but she spent most of her youth in Oregon. Part of her C.V. includes her graduation from the University of Oregon in Eugene in 1944. Once she became acclimated to the hustle and bustle of New York, she quickly expanded her academic horizons. In 1945 she received her Master of Arts degree from the Union Theological Seminary of Columbia University; followed in 1951 by another degree from Teachers College of Columbia University.

Outside the halls of learning Doris began as a church worker at First Presbyterian from 1945 to 1947, after which she advanced to be the Director of Religious Education at Mineola on Long Island until 1950. She returned to the Madison Avenue Presbyterian to teach (nursery school) until after we were married. All of this training was of much help to us in later years and she developed great satisfaction in helping others both inside and outside the classroom.

I can't remember how it came about but in 1966 Doris and I decided to give up sending Christmas cards and started to send an annual Christmas letter to our relatives and close friends. Over the years we received a lot of feedback concerning our Christmas messages. Some people liked them; some people hated them and some just keep sending their annual Christmas card with their names printed on the bottom.

Doris and I enjoyed the opportunity of reviewing and providing a brief summary of each year. I felt sure that those who wrote those interminable chronicles firmly believed that 90% of the ones they received were a crashing bore. Ours, of course, were utterly fascinating. I looked through our Christmas letters and selected a few to include intact in this book. These may possibly give you a feeling for how we lived and tell you something about our lives. In addition to those Christmas letters that were printed in full, inserts from the other letters contributed still more about the years we spent together.

Our first letter, in 1966, chronicled our return from California to Highland Park, New Jersey. While I drove east to my new position in May, Doris closed up the house and three months later was confronted with an airline strike. Being both resourceful and adventuresome she made the most of the primarily rail trip east. First she gathered the children and detoured to Seattle to visit her sister and family and then on to several points in Oregon. From there the group continued east to Deer Creek, Indiana, where they spent a week with her father and stepmother.

In August we moved into a multi-level (five levels in all) house at 418 S. Fourth Avenue in Highland Park, NJ. The LA house was empty and un-sold for a while making us the proud owners of a house on each coast. It was sold soon by a competent real estate agent, without complications.

We considered being only 50 miles from NYC and just across the Raritan River from New Brunswick and Rutgers University as a real bonus. The University was a magnet for a rich variety of social and cultural activity in which we looked forward to participating. But for a night out we still considered Manhattan was the place to go. Making new friends and getting reacquainted with many old friends in NY and NJ was a genuine pleasure. When not otherwise occupied, Doris was also a relaxed but highly capable hostess for our social endeavors.

While I concentrated on my business responsibilities, Doris tended to the proper rearing of our small brood, as the children quickly absorbed the middle-class standards while Doris carried on her love for music, both instrumental and choral.

Within a year after moving to Highland Park, Doris began donning many more hats, which led to expanding and using her knowledge in highly useful ways. She became involved in all manner of good works, took courses at the local university, and worked part-time as a reading instructor in a local elementary school. Later, Doris began teaching remedial reading three hours a day, still taking courses, and putting in time with the PTA, church, and League of Women Voters.

In the summer of 1969 Doris and I got vacation time separate from our brood. With Betsy (14) and Julie (9) at church camp and Alan (13) loaned to friends for a week, we flew to Florida. We visited Doris' brother Don and his family in Miami then drove up to see my mother and other relatives in the Tampa area. From then on, for almost thirty-five years we vacationed together from Europe to China, and across much of the United States. Our Elderhostel catalogs became dog-eared as we chose our next destinations and the courses that interested us the most.

After I changed jobs in 1972, we moved to a small-town colonial abode in Somerville, New Jersey. This meant that Doris now had a 13 mile commute to Highland Park where she ran a training center in an elementary school. By contrast, I had a quick five-minute drive to the neighboring town of Raritan, where I became president of a small community bank.

We made our first trip to Czechoslovakia together in 1974, with the two girls. We left Alan with a summer job and the rest of us flew off for a wonderful visit. My command of Czech was adequate enough to enable all of us to jump the communications gap. A passport gaffe took a little more un-doing.

Doris' earnings were what sustained us in 1977. Her elementary school learning center and part-time Rutgers instructor's stipends provided the tuitions for Betsy at the University of Wisconsin and Alan at Connecticut College. I was busy with lawyers and my moneyed partner, Ed Chandler, trying to gain control of a bank whose directors had deposed me as president.

In August of 1979, our finances and honor restored, we squeezed in a little sail-boating (once) and art show hopping in Laguna Beach. We also visited friends and relatives in Los Angeles, San Francisco and environs, and then saw the forests, the coast, and Doris' hometown and college campus in Oregon.

1980 was a year of family highs and lows. In January we lost my Aunt Stella, 84, and in the fall Doris' brother, Don, incapacitated by a severe stroke four years ago, passed away in Florida.

As noted earlier, May 31st was the high point of the year. It was the date of Alan's wedding to the former Janice Bolton. Attended by friends and family, the event lived up to all expectations. The picture shown in this memoir in "Life in New Jersey" included Jan, who was a mainstay in our family for many years.

The 1984 Christmas Letter included an excellent conversation, as follows:

Just as we were sitting down to dinner at our

favorite Chinese restaurant a week or so ago, Doris suddenly announced, "This is it!" (If you know Doris, you know she practically never makes such startling pronouncements.) This one caught me short, so that I almost spilled my egg drop soup as my life flashed before me.

After I regained a dollop of composure, I hesitantly asked, "What do you mean, this is it? What is what?"- So she explained, "You may not have noticed, but Christmas is approaching, along with the end of our thirty-first year of connubial bliss; we've fulfilled our biological purpose and our careers have topped out....-"

Getting the drift of her thoughts, I interrupted: "Wait just a minute, maybe your teaching career has topped-out, but I recently started a new department at a not insignificant bank." Reasonable, as always, Doris pointed out that, in her opinion, I don't have a Czech's chance of becoming president of chase Manhattan or even chairman of the Federal Reserve. Her logic was irrefutable, so I dug into my Ling-Tung-Ting Shrimp and attempted to change the subject, with "I'll bet there aren't too many couples as compatible as we are.".

A long silence gathered momentum until, apparently reconciled to her fate, Doris observed, "It's getting a little colder. Don't you think it's time to order some firewood, take down the screens, and get our cars serviced?"

Always one to know when to leave well enough alone, I murmured, "Sure, sure, I'll get to it this weekend."

1986 was the year that Doris, although not of ripe age, decided to retire from teaching and to spend more time on recreational activities, such as a trip to China.

In 1987, during a month in Czechoslovakia, Doris extended her linguistic challenges to my teenage nephews,

Tomas and Martin, who were happy to try out their book-learned English on a genuine American.

Doris spent the rest of the year as a literacy volunteer: plus taking French at Rutgers; singing in a community chorus; going to book club meetings and enjoying early retirement from the teaching profession.

Almost every year we happily noted Doris' expanded workload in tutoring. By 1988 Doris had been an active member of the Literacy Volunteers of Middlesex for five years. She now included tutoring two adult ladies recently arrived from Taiwan and Turkey respectively. Being Doris, she didn't let it go at that but also taught the volunteers who have signed up to tutor. She traveled to a local hospital twice a week, where for a modest remuneration; she taught their Hispanic employees the rudiments of English. She belonged to a community chorus and a local book discussion group; plus she subscribed to concert, orchestra and several playhouse series.

The summer of 1988 was devoted to a visit from Tomas and Martin. They spoke halting English when they arrived in June for their eight week stay. After Boston, New York, Philadelphia, Washington, Canada and a few other places, their English was much improved and they left for home with a bag full of memories that won't be soon forgotten.

Additional annual Christmas letters continued to underscore the prodigious efforts of Doris' literacy and social efforts. Further along in this section are a picture and a copy of a well-deserved lifetime achievement award from the Literacy Volunteers of Middlesex.

Their Mission Statement is:

Literacy Volunteers of Middlesex County is an organization of trained volunteers that provides free tutoring services to adults with limited literacy skills, enabling them to achieve their personal goals and to enhance their contributions to the community.

(1989 Letter) "Doris is teaching as board president and ESL (*English as a Second Language*) tutor for the Literacy Volunteers of Middlesex County, and as an English teacher for sixteen Hispanic employees at a local hospital. Between phone calls she helps run, and sings in a community chorus, goes to exercise classes, and is a member of a reading group. She cooks delicious meals now and then, and provides George with T.L.C."

Doris getting Literacy Award at dinner in recognition of 20 years post-retirement service

(1991 Letter) The year included many trips and visits, including my Czech cousins for seven weeks. "Between all of these family visits, Doris kept more than active as board president and ESL tutor (her present student is from Costa Rica), with the Middlesex County Literacy Volunteers; a weekly book discussion club, and a community chorus."

(1994 Letter) Doris was very active as president and tutor of two students for the Middlesex County Literacy Volunteers. In November we attended the Literacy Volunteers convention, where they let me as Doris' 'spouse'.

For several years we both attended Lifetime Learning lectures at Rutgers, and maintained a satisfactory social life with a few close friends. Singing and reading were also essentials to her.

In Doris' writing in 1999, she reminisced about a

memorable reunion with her closest childhood friend, Lee; especially after they'd spent many hours playing piano duets as kids.

After she returned to New Jersey she mentioned again playing duets for several years, this time with a lady named Shirley as tutor and president of Literary Volunteers of Middlesex County, NJ. 2003

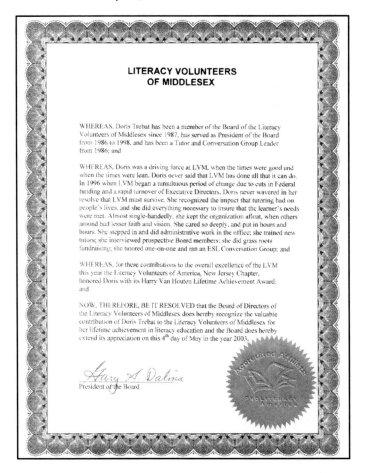

My Medical Adventures

In 1990, I wrote a "Memo" to my children giving them some historical background about their "Genetic Inheritances". I updated the "Memo" in 2012 and also added a section on "Alzheimer's disease", with which their mother was diagnosed in 2009.

As of this writing Doris has been my wife, lover, companion and mother of my children for almost 60 years. I can imagine life without her but I don't want to.

As you will see in the details on the Alzheimer's section, as of 2012, we pretty much have a handle on Doris' ultimate destiny but since I'm sitting up and writing my best guess that, at 85, I may be among the living for another ten years, or less. A longer time frame, although possible, does not seem reasonable.

Genetic Inheritances

The Memo
(Date Written: April 13, 1990)

An article I read indicates that genetic flaws in the blood of some of your ancestors which seemed to predispose them to early heart attack or stroke. The article also describes the experiences being developed since the 1960s with statin drugs, which have proven to control and even reverse coronary artery disease. Both your mother and father have been taking statin drugs for many years with excellent results. The article and its implications are particularly important to you because:

(1) Your maternal grandmother (Doris' mother) died at 47 around 1940 long before medical science was into cholesterol. Little is known

of her medical profile except that she died of stroke and had high blood pressure.

(2) She apparently passed her genetic makeup on to her oldest child, Doris & Betty's brother, Don. Don had a heart attack at 38 and a catastrophic stroke at 52 after which he lived in a vegetative state for another four years. He apparently had a very high cholesterol count which caused the coronary artery disease. In addition, he refused to stop smoking or change his eating habits or life style despite the fact that the medical profession was starting to zero in on these risk factors by the middle 1970s.

(3) Your mother has somewhat elevated blood pressure and moderately high cholesterol both of which are being controlled by medication. Your maternal grandfather lived to 86 and presumably passed on some good genetic material.

(4) Your paternal grandfather (George's father) died of a stroke at 56 after having suffered numerous small heart attacks. He had rheumatic fever as a child and had damaged heart valves. He died in 1945 and we don't know anything about his blood lipid profile. However, as he was overweight during his 40s and 50s and loved fatty food, we can make a good guess.

(5) George's coronary artery disease was discovered at 60 during a routine stress test. An angiogram disclosed a 90% blockage in one artery which was successfully opened by way of a balloon angioplasty procedure. Later, a new stress test revealed some insufficiency under heavy exercise

but, absence of any symptoms, further medical intervention is not required.

The above history tells you several important things. One, you are apparently not predisposed to cancer or any other organic or exotic disease. Coronary artery disease which is evident on both sides of your family is being controlled, and in some cases reversed, both by drug, lifestyle change and by angioplasty and by-pass procedures. Because of the above, as family medical histories go, you can't be oblivious of the risk factors we live with but you can take steps to reduce your exposure as more medical knowledge and experience is accumulated. As you live longer and develop a longer range outlook you can consider that this knowledge, and your acting on it, can inure to the benefit of those dependent upon you.

Alzheimer's disease

This book is primarily my personal memoir, but I believe that it is relevant to include this update on Doris' medical condition.

In February of 2012 Doris was admitted to the skilled nursing facility of Moravian Village because she was entering the advanced stage of Alzheimer's disease, and I was encountering increased difficulty in taking care of her in our cottage at the Village.

As of 2012 in the fullness of hindsight I can recall that almost fifteen years ago Doris started to show some very early signs that something was going on. First, she decided to retire early from her job as a teacher in the Highland Park New Jersey school system. I thought it was a little strange that she decided to retire after only nineteen years. Her explanation was that she was having problems with a deceitful fellow teacher and that the atmosphere at the school was changing. Doris retired and seemed content to take up a career as a full time volunteer in the Literacy Volunteers organization. In this role she was a tutor, organizer and eventually President of the Literacy Volunteers of Middlesex County for ten years. Along with our happy home life and extensive travels she seemed quite fulfilled. At the same time it often occurred to me to wonder why she hesitated to put her personal feelings into words. (Only in later years did I learn that she was present in an upstairs bedroom when her own mother had her fatal stroke.) Since I was always more verbal than Doris I wrote off her increasing hesitations to "more of the same".

Around 2010 her doctor noticed profound changes in how Doris responded, and gave her the standard written test for early Alzheimer's. Doris failed; and as legally proscribed, she soon got a letter from the state motor vehicle bureau to turn in her driver's license. Doris complied almost willingly as she knew that there was something wrong. Thereafter, in rather rapid fashion she started to see me as three different Georges and I increasingly took over cooking, shopping and other domestic duties.

During most of 2011 Doris' dementia progressed. Her doctor prescribed state of the art medications and gave me the bad news. From the doctor's and my own extensive reading on the subject I found out that there is no cure available for and there's nothing that her children or I, or indeed anybody, can do except to keep her comfortable. The serious stage of the disease may last for months or years. As I write she has just passed her 89th birthday and is in good overall health although she often does not know me or anyone else.

My best option is to make regular contributions to Alzheimer's research in the hope that someday medical science will find a cure.

More Recollections

I don't know of anyone who likes to think about death. I certainly don't. At the same time we all have to face that most dreaded event. I say this despite the fact that I know that most people under twenty or twenty five seem to think they are immortal; that's why it's so easy to get young men to put on a uniform and go to war.

I have already recounted being at a cemetery when I was only five or six for the funeral of a man with a heart attack at only 37. There are other stories noted in this section on the family genes.

I've read that more than 600,000 Coronary Artery Bypass Grafts are performed worldwide every year. Also, it is my understanding that maybe, in as little as ten years , bypasses will be a thing of the past and that physicians will be able to "instruct" arteries to grow and/or clear themselves out by way of genetic manipulation of cells. In 1945, when my father died of coronary artery disease and bad heart valves (he had rheumatic fever as a child), bypasses were probably only in the imaginations of a few medical scientists. He was only 56 and there wasn't much they could do for him.

Somewhere around 1955, when my mother was 53, and living in Florida, she came up to visit us in Bellmore, Long Island and made a mysterious visit to her former doctor in Manhattan. She felt an irregular heart beat and was worried but did not want to talk about it. She did note however, that her father had the same problem around 1915 and consulted a cardiologist in Prague. A few years later, after walking two hours to take care of a neighbor's calf he came home, sat down at the kitchen table, and keeled over. He was 62. My mother had a severe stroke when she was 56 and lived ten years longer, only partially recovered, before succumbing to a stroke at 66. While most of my relatives were quite healthy, living into their eighties, as a rule, there seems to be a thread of atrial fibrillation running through the family and traceable to my maternal grandfather.

In this generation, the only people in my family afflicted with chronic atrial fibrillation (not a life threatening condition, if treated) are my cousin Miroslav who lives in the Czech Republic, and me. Even today, it is not quite clear what causes atrial fibrillation, AFib, but it's a glitch in the electrical system and is most likely an indicator of some degree of underlying heart disease. There are three million people in the United States living with atrial fibrillation and the cardiologists look on it as "no big deal". My first indication of AFib was when my heart would not settle down, as it was supposed to, after a routine stress test: They hospitalized me and put me on standard medication which seemed to do the trick.

1998 Bypass Surgery

In January 1988 Doris and I were planning a trip to Santa Fe New Mexico, but, before going, I decided to check with my cardiologist. According to my health plan, the way to do this is first to get a referral from my primary care doctor. When I went in to see my primary care physician, she took an EKG and saw some disturbing changes from tracings done only a few months before. This talented diagnostician minced no words; she pointed me to the cardiologist in no uncertain terms. This was a Friday and I immediately made an appointment to see the cardiologist the next Monday.

I never got to the Monday appointment because about 5 am Monday I was awakened by a steady pain in my neck and jaw; my pulse was racing and my blood pressure was hitting the ceiling. I was sure that I was having a heart attack! I called 911 and the emergency people came in less than ten minutes and their instruments confirmed my diagnosis. So into the ambulance and to the Emergency Room at RWJ University Hospital I went. At the hospital they slowed down my heart and lowered my blood pressure with drugs and called my cardiologist who told me that I did not have a heart attack but had an attack of unstable angina. That was the first time that I had felt any angina pain without exercising.

From then on things moved fast. The cardiologist scheduled an angiogram to find out exactly what was going on. A couple of hours after the angiogram, when he reviewed the film, my cardiologist gave me the news. He said that substantial new blockages were developing and that my choice was to continue treating my angina with drugs and expect a heart attack in the near- to mid-future or have the arteries involved bypassed and live without heart disease. In my mind there was no choice and I told him to go for it.

My cardiologist, a professor at the medical school to which the Robert Wood Johnson University Hospital is attached, said that he could arrange to have the bypass done the very next day. The next person to visit me was the vascular surgeon who heads one of the bypass teams at the hospital. He seemed to want to assure himself that I really wanted the operation and I signed the consent form telling him that I had no doubt whatsoever. From there on I didn't remember too much because I think they started to sedate me with valium so that I would be relaxed. The operation was scheduled for 2 pm on Wednesday the 14th of January.

It was 2:30 am when I regained consciousness in the recovery room. I was lying there with a bunch of tubes and lines sticking out of me. When I recalled where I was the first words that came to my mind were "I'm alive!" In the next succeeding few minutes an immense feeling of gratitude and thankfulness overcame me. I still had a breathing tube down throat and couldn't talk to anyone, but my thoughts were all positive. I was, indeed, glad to be alive. Doris told me that she came to see me in the recovery room about 7 pm but I was still dead to the world. She was assured that I was OK and she was sent home. The next morning, still in the recovery room, it was the greatest pleasure in the world to see the smiling faces of my wife and three children. First the breathing tube and then the other lines and wires were taken out of me over the next few days while Doris, Betsy, Alan and Julie gave me wonderful moral support. Without doubt, when they crack open your chest, stop your heart and sew new arteries into place, it's a major operation. This was not the time or place for the handing out of awards, but I found the skill and compassion of the bypass team and the recovery nurses and doctors almost unbelievable.

I initially wrote this story on January 26th, when I was at home for the fourth day, and getting better by the minute. My chest still felt as if an 800 pound gorilla had stomped on me but the gorilla was gone and I was glad to be living in a world where I could now expect ten to fifteen more years of quality life. And, with new medical advances being announced almost daily, who knows? (I re-edited this section when I reached 85.)

Unexpected Surgery – 2005

By 2005, when I was 78, I thought that I had pretty much had all the medical procedures and illnesses that I was going to have. To recount; starting with a broken leg and adjustment of two misplaced glands having to do with my reproductive system and then catching, and throwing off a bad cold, which turned out to have been an undisguised touch of polio in my teens; I lived a pretty normal childhood.

The polio left me with a slightly weaker right leg. I can remember that I was once chastised for not lifting my feet while walking home from a gym to which I belonged. I actually thought that somehow my character was deficient because I had an uneven gait and my mother was annoyed because I wore out the tips of my shoes unevenly. The polio consequence was really a constant presence but, in the long run was unimportant and didn't keep me out of the Army in WWII. So, assuming that I had the polio bug when I was about 14 the next 50 years or so were health-wise uneventful.

Then around the age of 60 I had what is known as a silent heart attack which was discovered while doing a routine stress test. A medical technician putting me through my paces looked at the tape asked when I had my heart attack. I answered, "What heart attack?"

I never got the answer as to when, but my cardiologist Abel Moreyra at Robert Wood Johnson hospital in New Brunswick said it didn't matter, but the important thing was that the EKG showed that somewhere in the past there was one.

The above is all by way of background leading up to my latest unexpected medical procedure which, technically, is called a total colon resection.

On a morning in January 2005, a morning much like any other in Moravian Village, I woke up to find that I was hemorrhaging – from the bottom, to put it politely. Having had a clean colonoscopy a few years earlier, I was not too worried, thinking that maybe my warfarin was wacky or that I had a bleeding polyp. After some blood work eliminated the former, and with the bleeding continuing, my primary care physician calmly suggested I go to the Emergency Room at St. Luke's Hospital in Bethlehem.

I signed in at Emergency still not worried, thinking that a bleeding polyp could easily be cauterized. A few hours later, after a lot of poking and testing nothing had been resolved and I was still bleeding. Then they gave me a transfusion and decided to do a colonoscopy. Still, I was not very worried. After the first colonoscopy, Terry Reilly, a gastroenterologist kept me in the hospital. I was still bleeding and they gave me more blood.

In the next day or two he did two more colonoscopies, but I was feeling no pain because I was, by then, well doped up. While Doris and the children were worried and consulting with the doctors, I was busy joking with the nurses and doctors.

Finally, after three days of testing, Reilly's senior partner, Camille Eyvazzadeh, who had apparently been in on the deliberations from the start, came to my bed and calmly said something like: "George, we don't know what's going on so we'll have to open you up and look around. We'll operate tomorrow morning."

Still doped up, I took the news calmly and said, "OK, you're the doctor." Doris, Julie and Rob (and I think Betsy and Alan by phone) were very concerned.

Hours and hours later in the recovery room with the anesthesia wearing off I started to feel a lot of pain. Eyvazzadeh, who did the operation assisted by Reilly, came to me and said that all had gone well but he decided to take out the whole colon because otherwise he could not be certain they had stopped all the bleeding. He somewhat calmly added that he did not want to open me up again in case there would have been more hemorrhaging.

A day or so after the operation Dr. Eyvazzadeh came to see me, checked me out and apparently decided that his job was done and we spent ten minutes talking about jazz and classical music.

The post-operative pain was substantial and the nursing care was not too good, maybe because they parked me in a room on the cardiac floor so that my chronic heart condition could be monitored. I don't know how I would have gotten through those first few days if not for the fact that my daughter Betsy (a registered nurse in Madison, Wisconsin) came and set up a cot for herself in my room. She gave me the best possible nursing care for a couple of nights. I was most pleased by her professionalism as she came in, evaluated the situation, went out to the nurse's station, chatted up the nurses, asked them where the supply cabinet was and took over my care. The nurses, overworked as usual, were more than happy to have one less patient to care for.

From that point on I had a routine recovery and was on my way home in eight days. Of course, the doctor's happy talk about my being able to live comfortably without a colon was only partially true. The final diagnosis was that I had chronic diverticulitis, diverticulosis and hemorrhage.

In actuality the colon is a necessary part of the digestive system and although the small intestine expanded to take over some of the colon's functions, my life was in for a substantial change.

There's a list of about 100 things I can't digest: roughage, fats, chocolate, vegetables … and it goes on and on. Often in a restaurant I'm blindsided by a delicious but indigestible sauce and this makes travel and casual eating (such as a hotdog at the ball game - - no, **no**, No!) I sometimes get a bad case of flatulence but otherwise life is, as the doctor said, quite tolerable.

Seneca[13] – A Serious Comment

And my final thought on this subject, cribbed from a favorite philosopher.

---

[13] Lucius Annaeus Seneca (ca. 4 BC – 65 AD), a Roman Stoic, philosopher, statesman, dramatist, and in one work humorist, of the Silver Age of Latin literature. Nero forced him to commit suicide.

Death is the release of all pain and complete cessation, beyond which our suffering will not extend. It will return us to that condition of tranquility, which we had enjoyed before we were born. Should anyone mourn the deceased, then he must also mourn the unborn.

Retirement and Recollections

In the late 1990s, Doris and I started thinking about where we might want to spend our senior years. We got interested in two continuing care retirement communities about to be built in New Jersey. One in Bridgewater was under Quaker auspices, and another in Princeton being developed by the Presbyterian Church.

We preferred Princeton. It was a favorite weekly destination of ours because of obvious cultural advantages and the several favorite restaurants where we felt comfortable.

Finally, after many meetings and a few lunches we put down a deposit on Stonebridge at Princeton. Alas, we were a little late and had to settle for a one bedroom apartment – being 18th on the list for a two bedroom upgrade.

While we were waiting for the Princeton accommodations to be available, our daughter Julie brought the proposed Moravian Village of Bethlehem to our attention. In 2002 we cancelled at Princeton and signed on in Bethlehem.

So it came to be that in August 2003, Doris and I moved into a newly built "cottage" at Moravian Village. We had a two-bedroom, two-bath, semi-attached house with a full downstairs playroom into which I soon installed a pool table, ping pong table and treadmill. Our physical environment was well taken care of.

Moravian Village, it should be noted, is what is termed

by law, a continuing care retirement community of which there are many throughout the United States. It is sponsored and operated by a religious organization, the Moravian Church, a small 250,000 member Protestant sect. The sect had its origin in Moravia, a section of the Czech republic, where more than 500 years ago the Protestant Reformation was led by people like: Jan Amos Komenský, (Latinized to John Amos Comenius); a teacher, educator and writer; and Jan Hus, a reformer burned at the stake in 1415.

Jan Hus' spiritual heirs were almost wiped out but they developed one of the first organized Protestant religions, Unitas Fratrum (or Moravian Church). The spirit of Jan Hus still touches my life, despite my lack of overt religious preference. As noted earlier, the Jan Hus Presbyterian Church and the Jan Hus Playhouse (in which I was sometimes active) are located in the area of my beginnings, Yorkville, New York City.

The history of the Moravian Church is very interesting, but I'm not going to detail it here. Anyone interested can find voluminous information by way of the internet and the several museums in and around Bethlehem, Pennsylvania.

Suffice it to say, that while the Moravian Church leaders planned, organized, and financed the enterprise under a charter from the Commonwealth of Pennsylvania, the Village is a non-sectarian organization and only in subtle ways promotes its particular brand of Christianity.

Doris and I were 'early adopters' at the Village, moving into the very first section of 16 cottages, while the rest of the 105 cottages were still a construction site. When we moved in, the main 152 unit apartment house and healthcare center (built in 2004 – 6) were still in the conceptual stage. We watched the main building (which I call "the big house'), dining room, library, chapel and totally inadequate lobby for entertainment and meeting purposes turned into a beautiful and useful retirement community.

As was the case in Princeton, where we came too late to the game, many of the residents moving into Moravian Village were drawn from the Bethlehem – Allentown – Easton community and came with their social support systems intact. We, on the other hand, were almost foreigners moving from far away Edison/Highland Park, New Jersey; about 60 miles east. Not knowing anyone when we moved in was almost a blessing because we were all but forced to meet new people as they moved in. I for one made it my mission to learn the names of all the new residents as each new cottage became tenanted.

In our first year of residence we made our final trip to the Czech Republic, and Doris soon found a Literacy Volunteers unit in Easton where she became active as a tutor.

I was elected to the first Cottage Council, chaired by Ed Bauer, but I resigned when the other council members voted me down, 6 to 1 when I proposed that the Village should merge its Cottage Council with the Apartment Council. In my estimation, the cottages and apartments should be looked upon as one unit possibly with two committees to represent the several separate interests of the cottages and apartment dwellers. In ensuing years the cottage and apartment residents did, for the most part, integrate. But this incident was just a bump in the road as the community grew and we got to know each other; even Jack Burke, longtime president of the Apartment Council became a close friend of mine.

As I was going through my colon adventure (and even before) Doris was very slowly showing signs of Alzheimer's disease, probably inherited from her grandmother and prior ancestors. Doris' sister Betty, a year younger, sank into Alzheimer's much sooner than Doris. Memorable is a visit by Doris, escorted by daughters Julie and Betsy to visit Betty, then living in a nursing home in Seattle and no longer recognizing even her own family. Betty died at 84 in 2009 and Doris was given over to the skilled nursing facility in Moravian Village in early 2012.

I became Doris' full time caregiver sometime in 2010 and it was an emotionally very difficult experience for me when I had to admit that I could no longer take care of her at home. Possibly even more heartbreaking was the look in Doris' eyes when she was already into Alzheimer's but still had periods of lucidity and fully realized what was happening to her. Her mental agony was palpable.

Airplane crashes, heart bypasses and colectomies can all be thrown to the wind, but watching Doris' once very active mind being stolen away from her has surely been the most terrible experience of my life. I can't even imagine how it must have devastated her when she was still "in and out" of the disease.

When we moved to Moravian Village in 2003 we took advantage of the many cultural activities of the Bethlehem area, but still kept in touch with our long time New Jersey friends.

For a number of years I was still a partner with my friend Harold "Hesh" Berman in a profitable three story office building across from the County Courthouse in New Brunswick. Originally a five partner venture, Hesh and I became the last men standing, as in a period of 25 years one partner after another dropped out; taken mostly by the grim reaper. After I moved to Bethlehem, Hesh continued to manage the building until 2010 when he engineered a very profitable sale. To Hesh, who recently died at 92, and to prior partners Murray Margolis and Roger Varney I owe a vast practical and emotional debt for their friendship and Doris' and my subsequent financial well-being. We engaged in a number of partnerships together and I remember them fondly as friends who entrusted me to administer their eventual estates.

Doris and I left behind many friends in New Jersey and in other parts of the United States. Rudy Cerny was my boyhood friend in the Yorkville section of New York. Rudy and I exchange Christmas cards and phone calls (once meeting for a temporary reunion in Prague). I still keep in touch with his widow Anne who lives in South Carolina. Keeping in touch being a sentimental addiction of mine, I still talk by phone to my onetime girlfriend, Blanche (Ledecky) Fiorenza – my only contact from the "old crowd" – who stayed in New York and became an art director. She lives on Central Park West with her husband Vito, also a retired art director.

About 10 years ago one of my closest boyhood friends, Bill Lev, died of cancer. At his funeral and subsequent reception at his and Vera's (also a Yorkville friend) house I had the opportunity to say goodbye to a number of my boyhood friends. When we kissed or shook hands, I knew I might never see this group, from several states, ever again - - and I have not.

Getting back to New Jersey, after moving to Moravian Village our good friends, with whom we shared many happy moments, began to depart this life. There was George Winnet, a Rutgers professor, who used to call me "Egroeg". He and Elaine were our Friday night dinner companions for many years. ("Egroeg" is George spelled backwards - - a joke between us, since he was also named George.)

And then Jack Shapiro died at 93. Jack and Shirley Shapiro, together with Ellen and Karl Rebarber and Cathy and Ed Fry were the people with whom we shared some of our best moments.

Jack was a dental technician who really wanted to be a philosopher.

Karl had a plastics company located in our jointly owned 100 year old factory building that I eventually sold my interest to Karl. When I was in a battle for my economic life Karl loaned me $100,000 when I really needed it, all without even an eye blink.

Ed Fry was another Rutgers professor and close friend and confidant. He and Cathy left a void in our lives when they moved to California to be with family around 1995. It was a good decision for them but not for us. We kept in touch until Ed, who doubled as a very successful author and publisher died in 2010.

Among our favorite people in the world were Ruth Samsel and her partner Barbara Living-stone who started as neighbors and became long-term buddies and, shall I say it? Soul mates.

As in most cases all of these gals and guys (except Egroeg) left loved ones – but it's not the same here without them.

Luckily, Doris and I made many new friends who are now aging in place in Moravian Village. I won't memorialize them in these pages because, as I write, they are still a work in progress.

The Futurist - A Meditation – "Looking at 2100"

You'll forgive me if I indulge myself in a little musing. It's time to look back and, more importantly, it's time to look ahead. Doris and I were born in the 1920s, a time when not everyone owned a radio, and television, not to mention computers, were just science fiction ideas in the minds of a few futurists. Jet airplanes were unheard of and most people traveling between the United States and Europe did so by steamship. A majority of the people in the United States lived on farms and a high school diploma was considered ample proof of readiness for entry level employment by most middle class people. When we were pre-teens, an ordinary person, say, a retailer, office manager, teacher or electrician was earning about $20 a week while a secretary or telephone operator would be earning about $10 a week. On the other hand, a glass of beer would be 10¢ and a man's haircut would cost 25¢. A nice house in the suburbs could be bought for about $5,000 and a high end apartment with a doorman in Manhattan could be rented for about $100 per month while tenement apartments on the east side of Manhattan, where I lived, cost $15 to $20 a month.

In the not too distant future my grandchildren will certainly be parents and probably grandparents. They will have paid several hundred thousand dollars to send each of their children to college, and graduate schools will be hard to get into and will be equally expensive. Of course, there will still be waitresses, delivery men, truck drivers, sales clerks, and laborers on the low end of the economic ladder but most "worthwhile occupations" will require technical knowledge of a high order. Run of the mill doctors and lawyers will routinely earn one to two million dollars a year, while super star professionals will earn ten million a year. And movie stars? The top stars got fifteen to twenty million a picture in 2000, so it's reasonable to expect that one hundred fifty to two hundred million per picture will not be unheard of in say, the 22nd century. As to the then eight foot tall basketball stars, well, that's anybody's guess! Minimum wage will be about $100 an hour and billionaires will be a dime a dozen (or, considering inflation, maybe $100 a dozen).

By the year 2100 there will be technological advances that are not even in the dream stage today. Physicists will learn how to control the use of atomic power and, instead of burning fossil fuels, houses, cars, machinery, factories and large office buildings will be run and warmed by tiny power packs. The great leaps in medicine that we saw in the second half of the twentieth century ... Coronary artery bypasses, heart transplants, cancer drugs and the advent of cloning will all seem as antiquated as crystal radios and buggy whips seem to us now. Body parts will be replaceable and chips will control our brains and maybe brains will be interchangeable. In America people live an average of 80 years (for men) and 84 (for women) and by 2100 I expect that another fifty years will be added to those numbers. I won't be surprised to see some very old senior citizens living upwards of 130 in good health - what with replacement body parts and other yet unimagined medical advances pushing longevity past 150.

Since I have more free time than when I was employed one of my abiding hobbies is reading everything I can find about how the sun, other stars, planets, galaxies, and the universe work (usually in a magazine called Scientific American). I have a little background since I studied physics and chemistry in high school and college so I focus my readings in the area of basic principles... The mathematics of science is far over my head and I still can't explain the theory of relativity... Although, once in a while I think I get the idea. The mere fact that there are billions and billions of stars and billions, billions of galaxies and billions and billions of universes boggles my mind. By the time 2100 comes around I'm sure that every school child will know about black holes, quarks, bosons and a hundred other celestial phenomena that are yet to be discovered. Certainly, by then humans will have colonized Mars and have spotted planets circling stars in other galaxies and other universes. I would like to live for two hundred years so that I could satisfy my curiosity about the advancements in the sciences that will be made in the years to come. Except for the technological end of it I expect that banking won't change too much by the year 2100 because the basic purpose of a bank; to make credit available to consumers and to the business community, will still be the same (a deal is a deal is a deal). Sure, more computer programs and microchips will be in use but the basics have been in place for 5,000 years and won't change too much in 100 or 500 years.

With all of the things that will be different, probably there will be a lot more things that will be the same. Religion, for instance won't be too much different. Since we still won't know how the universes were created, most people will still postulate an all-powerful creator - God. My personal theory of God is that most people can't live in a state of "not knowing" so they pray to a Father - God. They have faith that the god who created heaven and earth will also take care of them. I guess that's okay because I don't know the answer to the big question of what it's all about either. Probably I'm part of the minority who can live comfortably with simply not knowing. I imagine that in, perhaps, a million years, if humankind is still on earth, man's mind will have evolved to the point where people will actually know God instead of merely hoping that there's an all-knowing creator "up there." Do I believe in God? Well, my answer is yes. I say yes because I am just as ignorant as Einstein, Aristotle, Plato and every other scientist and philosopher that one could name, when it comes to the great question that has perplexed the world since man first sat by the fire in front of his cave and looked up wonderingly at the stars. In the year 2100, with all of the advances in knowledge that will surely occur, we still won't be much closer to knowing God.

One of the big problems in 2100 will be boredom. People will have a lot more time on their hands and won't know what to do with it. By 2100 technology will provide people with much more leisure time so, I imagine that theme parks, like Disneyland, will still be the typical vacation destination. There will be all kinds of moral questions to contend with such as: How do you keep people from killing each other? What do you do with orphans? How about the population explosion that will be triggered by advanced medical care? What do you do with the large numbers of old people who can no longer contribute to society but who are living longer and longer? How will we pay for it all? There will be lots of problems to solve and, luckily, there are a lot of bright minds still unborn, well able to deal with the problems of the future.

Acknowledgment

I first thought about writing an autobiography, which later turned in a memoir, about twenty years ago when I retired from the work-a-day world of banking and had some time to reflect on my life and experience. Around 1991 Doris and I attended a one week Elderhostel program teaching us the elements of putting one's life story into book form. For us, that was still the pre-computer era so I started out by writing incidents from my childhood and subsequent periods in my life.

This memoir was fashioned from those early writings and was done into fits and starts. I produced two or three copies written at different times in different places; my facts and my memory often were at variance with each other. So, over a period of time my memoir notes turned out to be a beehive of personal thoughts, evaluations of people sometimes important to my story and at other times worthy only of a place in my wastebasket. In pursuing my writing I nurtured the hope that my children and successor generations would someday be curious enough to use this memoir as a source book about my life in the 20th and 21st centuries. I was particularly motivated by this line of thinking because I had often wished that my parents, grandparents or even those further past had taken pen in hand to tell something of their lives, feelings and experiences going back to the World War I era or even further back into their lives in the Europe of 1850 or 1800.

Many people can trace their family histories back several hundred years, or even more, but my ancestry is an almost complete blank. Except for locations; before about 1850, I have only the approximate birth times of my grandparents. Would that my grandfather, a fairly literate peasant in Bohemia, had left a written record of his parents and grandparents! Then I could have found my grandparents' families (on both sides) to about 1780, or before. But no such luck.

I labored on my project singlehandedly off and on for a number of years, and then in 2012, by a stroke of good luck, I came across an autobiographical episode of a deceased neighbor that was edited and partially ghostwritten by Ron Littlefield, another neighbor. Ron is quite alive and he was willing to help me by editing, fact checking and organizing my undisciplined notes into a memoir that had continuity and was worthy enough to be printed in book form.

Ron called himself a tinkerer who promised to help me organize my notes, but over a period of several months of 2012 Ron's modest self-assessment turned out to be far short of reality. In addition to straightening out my syntax, Ron, an engineer by training, took on the task of fact checking my memoir and researching the episodes that I presented and digging out fascinating detail upon fascinating detail that filled out the story and actually brought my memoir to life. Ron Littlefield was, and is, much more computer literate than I am and converted my handwritten and typewriter written notes into computerese. He reached out to others[14] to scan documents and photographs into the text as he formed my story into a recognizable group of sections, and then chapters. In disentangling some of my overly complex sentences, Ron was always careful not to interject his own

---

[14] Ron's grandson, Matthew Reiss, and a fellow church choir member, Diana Severn, really put the "E" in Expert help.

interpretations into the text, but took special pains to retain my own wording exactly as I had fashioned it. We went through many drafts and reams of paper in coming up with exact meanings without losing any of the (I hope) spontaneity of my original text.

It is not an exaggeration to say that after several months of working together, Ron Littlefield came to know more about my life than I did. He was able to organize my story in a way that I could not have done without his insights, input, research, interest and, yes, grunt work. Time and time again he read my version of an incident or interaction with people important to my story and urged me to provide more information so that the reader would better understand my motivation and editorial involvement.

Most people who write memoirs list ten or more people who have read, corrected and collaborated on certain sections of their book. That is not so in my case, because Ron was my only muse and intellectual soulmate as I scratched out my sometimes faulty recollections. I hope my readers will engage with and enjoy this product of my inexperienced hand. The fault for any errors, omissions or clumsy expressions is, of course, all mine.

CPSIA information can be obtained at www.ICGtesting.com
Printed in the USA
BVOW042003261112

306512BV00001B/1/P